"Mark Ryan's *The Politics of Practical Reason* is a thoughtful, insightful, and timely book, patiently illuminating the importance of formation as a central yet overlooked aspect of ethical deliberation. Ryan highlights the virtues of Hauerwas's embodied, storied, and social approach to ethics by reading him as taking up Anscombe's challenge. By incisively articulating the limitations of Stout's and Taylor's alternatives, this book deepens the character of conversation regarding practical reason in religious ethics today."

—WILLIE YOUNG
Faculty of Liberal Studies
Endicott College

"In this wondrously clear and seamlessly constructed book, Mark Ryan makes a compelling case for the centrality of practical reason in any serious contemporary account of theological ethics. Further, he shows why this account must be rooted in a politics that knits us together around a shared conception of the good that is itself practical, a form of life that anchors a lived conception of the virtues, especially justice. This gives him firm footing for assessing the trajectories of key contemporary moral thinkers: Elizabeth Anscombe, Charles Taylor, Alasdair MacIntyre, Jeffrey Stout, and Stanley Hauerwas. His reading of Hauerwas is especially helpful for future work in theological ethics, as Ryan shows how Hauerwas can help us begin to discern together not only how we think but what we most love."

—CHARLES PINCHES
Chair of the Department of Theology and Religious Studies
University of Scranton

THE POLITICS OF PRACTICAL REASON

THEOPOLITICAL VISIONS

SERIES EDITORS:

Thomas Heilke
D. Stephen Long
and C. C. Pecknold

Theopolitical Visions seeks to open up new vistas on public life, hosting fresh conversations between theology and political theory. This series assembles writers who wish to revive theopolitical imagination for the sake of our common good.

Theopolitical Visions hopes to re-source modern imaginations with those ancient traditions in which political theorists were often also theologians. Whether it was Jeremiah's prophetic vision of exiles "seeking the peace of the city," Plato's illuminations on piety and the civic virtues in the Republic, St. Paul's call to "a common life worthy of the Gospel," St. Augustine's beatific vision of the City of God, or the gothic heights of medieval political theology, much of Western thought has found it necessary to think theologically about politics, and to think politically about theology. This series is founded in the hope that the renewal of such mutual illumination might make a genuine contribution to the peace of our cities.

FORTHCOMING VOLUMES:

Michael L. Budde
The Borders of Baptism: Identities, Allegiances, and the Church

Peter J. Leithart
Empire: A Biblical and Augustinian Analysis

The Politics of
PRACTICAL REASON

Why Theological Ethics

Must Change Your Life

MARK RYAN

CASCADE *Books* • Eugene, Oregon

THE POLITICS OF PRACTICAL REASON
Why Theological Ethics Must Change Your Life

Theopolitical Visions 10

Copyright © 2011 Mark Ryan. All rights reserved. Except for brief quotations in critical publications or reviews, no part of this book may be reproduced in any manner without prior written permission from the publisher. Write: Permissions, Wipf and Stock Publishers, 199 W. 8th Ave., Suite 3, Eugene, OR 97401.

Cascade Books
An Imprint of Wipf and Stock Publishers
199 W. 8th Ave., Suite 3
Eugene, OR 97401

www.wipfandstock.com

ISBN 13: 978-1-60899-466-3

Cataloging-in-Publication data:

Ryan, Mark.

The politics of practical reason : why theological ethics must change your life / Mark Ryan.

viii + 230 p. ; 23 cm. —Includes bibliographical references.

Theopolitical Visions 10

ISBN 13: 978-1-60899-466-3

1. Christian ethics. 2. Religion and politics. I. Title. II. Series.

BL65.P7 R87 2011

Manufactured in the U.S.A.

Contents

Acknowledgments vii

Introduction 1

1 Elizabeth Anscombe: Practical Reason as Political and Linguistic 15

2 Charles Taylor: Practical Reason as Becoming Articulate 51

3 Stanley Hauerwas: Practical Reason as Performance 99

4 Practical Reason, Justice, and Liberation 147

5 Alasdair MacIntyre and Jeffrey Stout: Practical Reason as Traditioned 193

Conclusion 219

Bibliography 225

Acknowledgments

Part of the task of theological ethics is to help us be truthful about the gifts that make our lives possible. I will attempt to exercise that skill by acknowledging some of those gifts in connection with this book.

I have many people to thank. I would like to thank Chad Pecknold and the acquisitions editors for inviting me to develop and publish my work through this series—a real gift! Charlie Collier and Kristen Bareman at Cascade have worked hard to prepare this book for publication. This book has roots in my education as a graduate student at the University of Virginia. Charles Mathewes introduced me to "philosophical psychology" as well as to the philosophical texts that became integral to my dissertation and now this book. Peter Ochs helped me see how the critique of modern moral philosophy was connected to theology. He helped me in those mentor-like ways that are difficult to make explicit, and also perhaps paved the way to my encounter with the work of Hauerwas, which is so crucial to this book. His Jewishness mysteriously allowed me to see being a Christian as an adventure. I would also like to thank Stanley himself for his generous and careful attention to my work. I thank him also for introducing me to friends and former students of his, like Joel Shuman and Charles Pinches. Charlie's book *Theology and Action* has helped me understand better what I was trying to say. I would also like to thank James Childress for his help in my progress through graduate school, not least through keeping me employed as a graduate assistant.

I would further like to thank the faculty and administrators at Georgian Court University where I have been gifted with students to teach and colleagues with whom to labor. I am particularly grateful to the Faculty Development Committee for their support of my scholarship through the award of a course release to work on this book in the fall semester of 2009. I am especially grateful to my students who are part of the Institute for Lay Ecclesial Ministry for teaching me about the hard work of being church and inspiring me to keep thinking about human goodness in the light of the gospel.

If the relationships named above provided the intellectual inspiration for the book, my family provides the condition for its possibility in just about every other way. My daughters Chloe and Meredith save me from the insufferable preoccupation that would otherwise dominate hours each day. They do so simply by virtue of their needs, and also their remarkable personalities. And I am aware of how our family is sustained by existing within the orbit of my wife's (large) family, my (small) one, and the church that makes ours and many of their lives possible. My father was an attentive reader and editor of these chapters when I desperately needed one. His editing, furthermore, deserves much of the credit for the readability of the text. Though we have theological differences, he has exercised generosity of imagination and sympathy in his help with this book. I dedicate the book to him, along with my wife, Jaimee. She has sacrificed a great deal these last four years—more than she could have calculated when she married a recently minted theologian and willingly moved to a foreign place called New Jersey—in order to make my life, and thus this book, possible. It has been a struggle for her to find the reward in this, and that is to say she is a person of faith and hope. She is a great gift for which I must learn to be more thankful.

Introduction

PRACTICAL REASON

This book is about practical reasoning in moral philosophy and theological ethics and it attempts both to describe and display practical reasoning. More particularly, I hope to discuss practical reason in moral philosophy in order to glean insight into theological ethics. What do I mean by practical reason? It is helpful to distinguish between two significant ways in which the term "practical reason" is frequently used. It is sometimes used by philosophers to talk about a component of a philosophical account of human agency, namely the deliberation that leads to decision and action. A paradigm of such use is Aristotle's naming of *phronesis*, or practical wisdom, as one of the virtues. Practical reason is not reasoning for its own sake, but is rather undertaken when we are called upon to act. Therefore, in this context, one often finds a contrast between practical reason and "theoretical reason." Theoretical reason, conversely, is reason not immediately directed to action.[1]

In recent times one also finds the term used in more general contexts, such as studies that seek to display a cultural outlook or social imaginary and perhaps compare them with others. Alasdair MacIntyre's *Whose Justice? Which Rationality?*, for instance, shows that conceptions of practical rationality, like those of justice, are contingent upon historically situated forms of life, such as the code of military honor manifest in Homeric poems. This enables him to write a history of rival conceptions of practical reason. Charles Taylor's *Sources of the Self* makes a

---

1. Imagine, for example, the difference between a desire to go on a trip in someone who is actively taking measures to plan and execute the trip versus in someone lounging by the hearth and thinking, "wouldn't be nice to go some place warm!"

similar assumption about the historical nature of practical rationality, and sets out to trace the transformations of practical rationality that lead to, and explain, the modern identity or the "self." Human agency, practical reason, conceptions of the good and social matrices that support it are all parts of a complex web.

In this study I use the term "practical reason" in the general way like MacIntyre and Taylor—as an interpretive window on a complex form of life—but I hope with special care for the more local way described above. But I will also be making an argument concerning how practical reason *should* be conceived, and that will involve moving back and forth between its local and general or comparative sense. I try to acknowledge that practical reason is both tied to historical communities and peculiar to the embodied and finite character of human actions. It is easy to lose sight of the local sense of practical reason. In fact I believe practical reason must be guarded against abstraction. Recognizing the historical character of practical reason allows us to use it as a kind of theme as we compare how distinct communities at distinct times have embodied a conception of the good—that is, to perform a kind of intellectual and cultural history. Yet this thematization of practical reason is also a danger, especially for people like us who have an affinity for abstraction and disembodiment. My treatment of Charles Taylor is in part meant to draw our attention to this danger.

One way of trying to keep practical reason from becoming overly abstract is to insist that practical reasoning be tied to politics, or a polis. In fact, I will here try to show that the very character or form of practical reasoning is "political" in a certain sense, as well as grounded in action.[2] But given how contested the term "politics" seems to be in contemporary American discourse, one wonders whether it would be wiser to choose a different term.

---

2. I should say that I am using the term "politics" here with the Aristotelian *polis* in mind. Since the term means something different in today's common parlance, if it even has a single meaning, I will ask for the reader's patience in allowing me to display in the following chapters the sense I am trying to claim for the term—the Aristotelian bias in the *Nichomachean Ethics* that locates the polis in relation to the place and common activities where virtue can be cultivated and lived. But, drawing on MacIntyre, I will also wish to call attention to the historical nature of politics, so that the concepts of narrative and tradition become necessary.

Why "Politics"?

In his recent and important study, *To Change the World*, James Davison Hunter cautions Christians against an overemphasis on politics as the primary means for helping transform the world. By stressing politics, he claims, Christians facilitate a drive toward fragmentation characteristic of contemporary social trends in America. To assess Hunter's claim, however, it is important to get clear on how he is using the term "politics" here.

Hunter argues that politics has become so dominant a concept for Christans that we now see all possibility for faithful action in the world through its lens. Politics has become a "social imaginary," he claims, borrowing a term of art from Charles Taylor. On a deeper reading, one finds that Hunter's real concern is that the brand of politics with which American Christians have become enthralled is the Nietzschean politics of interest-group conflict. In giving themselves to it, furthermore, Christians help constitute American politics as the ideology-driven power game it has become.

Hunter's warning cannot be easily shrugged off, since his arguments provide much insight into what "politics" has come to mean for contemporary Americans. His own orthodoxy defines politics primarily in terms of the state's procedures and other instruments for exercising coercive power, and this also explains in part his counsel to Christians that we leave the political social imaginary behind. By distinguishing politics in particular from the "public realm," which includes a broader range of activities and institutions, Hunter hopes to leave plenty of room for Christians to imagine their contribution to redeeming creation in other ways.

But my choice in this book has been not to avoid the term "politics" in light of its heavy baggage, but to dig deeper into its conceptual resources.[3] That is, I hope to recover the broader idea of politics found

---

3. Hunter himself admits that recovering a broader meaning of "politics" would accomplish many of the ends he seeks. Yet he expresses doubts regarding whether this could be achieved. "The [attempt to redefine politics] is certainly worthy of serious debate but as a sociologist who is attentive to the power of institutions, I am inclined to think that all such efforts will be swallowed up by the current ways in which politics is thought of and used. It is why I continue to think that it is important to separate the public from the political and to think of new ways of thinking and speaking and acting in public that are not merely political" (186).

in its ancient usage, an idea which comprehends some of the breadth Hunter seeks to capture with the term "public." Yet Hunter's implied criticisms make clear that such a conception of politics must also be recovered. My intention is that this book might contribute to the effort of recovering a non-reductive conception of politics.[4]

Ethics as Grammar: Why Ethics Should Change Your Life

Furthermore, I will try to show that recognizing the *political* character of practical reason helps us bring together in our understanding the relationship of practical reasoning to human agency and history. Practical reason, human agency, and politics are the concepts that provide the gravitational center of this book. How we conceive of any one of them implies some account of the others. To speak of practical reasoning, it turns out, always implies some assumptions about what human agency is like. And this, in turn, assumes some account of the meaning of belonging to a particular community amidst others.[5] To be able to perform practical reasoning, in other words, implies having been formed into agency and the locus of such formation is always a common life that embodies politics. These terms will, I hope, be elucidated together over its course. Yet because it is so important, I will make a first effort here, aided by the work of Brad Kallenberg.

Kallenberg displays the relations between agency, practical reason, and the political in his study of Wittgenstein and Hauerwas, *Ethics as Grammar*.[6] As contrasted with their self-conceptions as providing a neutral theory of morality, he shows how philosophical and theological ethics involve transforming human agents to reason about the good in

---

4. For an interesting account of the relation of the "theological politics" of the church advocated by Hauerwas and the politics to be shared between Christians and non-Christians working together to achieve commonly acknowledged goods, see Baxter, "The Church as Polis?," 132–50. While Baxter shares with Hunter the notion that Hauerwas has not adequately accounted for Christian engagement in politics outside the church, he importantly refuses to allow politics as such to be defined by its current associations in the nation-state.

5. One might say that the very fact that Aristotle begins the *Nichomachean Ethics* with references to human happiness and community shows that he assumed the connections among these three concepts.

6. Although I had not read Kallenberg's work when I wrote the foundation of this book as my dissertation, his work elucidates so well what I have wanted to say that I must make reference to him.

distinctive ways. He furthermore shows that such ethics ties reasoning to participation in a *lebensform* or form of life. In other words, he shows how theological ethics might be both transformative and political, or transformative because political.

As we will see in more detail in chapter 3, Kallenberg does this through two stages of his side-by-side readings of Wittgenstein and Hauerwas. In the first stage, which occurs in the first two chapters of his book, he traces the migration of the subject, or student, of philosophy from the periphery to the center of Wittgenstein's focus. This is why Kallenberg teaches us that it is best to see Wittgenstein's mature conception of philosophy as "therapy" for the mystification caused by distinctively modern ways of relating the mind to the world. The practice of philosophy became for him a kind of training in how to "go on" as a thinker. Wittgenstein's hope was that philosophers would no longer strive to found or join schools for the supposed advancement of philosophical knowledge but to become skillful in thinking. He hoped, in other words, that those who worked through his *Philosophical Investigations* would at the end be ready to let it go and move on. Kallenberg uses Wittgenstein's evolution to illumine Hauerwas's description of Christian ethics as an aesthetic task. What he himself learned from Wittgenstein allowed Hauerwas to view the job of the theological ethicist as facilitating Christians' ability to rightly see the world, as the Christian story configures the world.

The second stage of Kallenberg's study is equally important for this book. Here he traces the evolution of "form" as it used in the early Wittgenstein to its use in the later Wittgenstein. The early Wittgenstein saw form predominantly as a closed logical structure delimiting the space of the effable, so as to point beyond to the mystical. The later Wittgenstein began to place form within the hurly-burly of ordinary human life. This evolution means that those who follow Wittgenstein can no longer put credence in an Archimedean vantage point from which to see how language fits onto the world. Kallenberg observes that this focuses the political dimension of Hauerwas's Christian ethics, since Hauerwas's concern is how we learn to attend to the features of the world through the language we are given in community. We can no longer imagine that communication between communities can ignore the training that membership entails. Communication is political—that is, it requires formation in a polis.

Thus, Kallenberg helps us to see the connections among these three concepts. Human agency requires formation, or the cultivation of a "second nature." Our formation as reasoners implies our engagement in politics, as belonging to a community in the midst of others.

(Mis-)Reading Hauerwas and the Politics of Theological Ethics

This book attempts to display the connections of these concepts, highlighting the political character of practical reasoning, through its study of Anscombe, Taylor, and Hauerwas. More to the point, the comparison of Anscombe and Taylor on practical reason is meant to provide the backdrop against which Hauerwas can be properly understood and appreciated. My claim is that Hauerwas shows well how the wisdom gleaned from this largely philosophical discussion of practical reason can be taken up in theological ethics. What is going on in theological ethics and what is Hauerwas's role in it?

It is perhaps a tribute to Hauerwas's significance in the field to note that debates about his work will have an important impact on how the field of theological ethics goes on into the near future. At the same time, the results of these debates determine to some degree the way Hauerwas is taught and learned, or not learned. An assumption of this book is that we need to read Hauerwas well if we are to go on as we should in the field of theological ethics, particularly in a post-modern world. Hauerwas has something to teach those of us with the peculiar calling to do Christian ethics, and those of us who have learned from Hauerwas as students or otherwise have something to pass on. But Hauerwas's significance (for us) will itself depend on the practical reasoning embodied in our work. The relationship between writer and audience is a reciprocal one. In a sense, this book is an attempt to help make us the right audience for Hauerwas's work. Hauerwas will undoubtedly continue for some time to be part of the reading list in seminars studying Christians' obligations with respect to democracy or to politics in general. Underneath this will be questions regarding whether Christian convictions need be translated into a different idiom before being presented in public arguments, whether principles or virtues make the best ethical tools, and so forth. But to address the issue of how properly to read Hauerwas requires digging beneath these general debates that can easily mislead if we do not have more basic matters in order. To get at these, let us consider two kinds of common critique leveled at Hauerwas.

First, consider a certain kind of critic of the "Hauerwas position" not uncommon in the academy today, perhaps more among those purporting to do objective studies of religion than among moral theologians. This critic has been taught that Hauerwas and those who follow him have fallen prey to a particular kind of irrationalism whose mantra is to "obey the community," promoting a robot-like allegiance to the moral commitments of a particular historical community without inspecting it for entrenched injustices. We might label it for them "community-fideism." Such critics tend to believe that Hauerwas can easily be put aside in order to continue with the work of ethical inquiry in the current mode. Not only are his claims insufficiently rational, they seem to hearken back to a classical world, which moderns have surpassed. It was good of these folks to remind us that virtue says something important about our moral lives, but ethical reasoning must go beyond it just as modern societies have gone beyond pre-modern ones.

Admittedly, this is not an especially sophisticated kind of critique, but it represents a kind of thinking that unfortunately has been hard for us to shake. In this way, Hauerwas is put in his place so that his critics do not have to take Hauerwas's claims as seriously challenging their own. In cases like this, learning to understand Hauerwas rightly will involve learning that the account of rationality at work in his work cannot be easily dismissed. For Hauerwas's position can only pose the challenge it intends to religious ethics if we come to see why he believes that virtue names the reasoning proper to human actions.[7]

Second, to take the example of another kind of critic, in this case one influenced by the second half of Jeffrey Stout's *Democracy and Tradition*, the accusation is directed not so much to the integrity of Hauerwas's arguments but to his impact first on fellow Christians and then on the American democracy within which they have a part to

---

7. A "psychological" version of this critique is sometimes heard as well. The claim is that Hauerwas's emphasis on community is a way of responding to the cry for "absolutes" in a world where nothing seems certain. The church provides authority in a world suffering from the tyranny of choice. While one can understand the motivations of this critique, it too fails to grasp how rationality functions in Hauerwas, particularly in relation to authority. Moreover, those who hope to find "absolutes" in Hauerwas are bound to be disappointed.

play.[8] Hauerwas's rhetoric, they might claim, reinforces the walls between church and world. As a result, Christian citizens are less and less inspired to care about the condition of the society in which they live.

In this case, I suggest, a misunderstanding of Hauerwas arises from a failure to note a particular characteristic of his account of moral reasoning. Given the sophistication of his interlocutor, we ought to proceed carefully here. Stout pretends to provide an immanent criticism of Hauerwas, which is to say that he attempts to articulate, given Hauerwas's cognitive commitments, what Hauerwas ought himself to say. Yet Stout's whole perspective on Hauerwas in *Democracy and Tradition*—framed by his concern for Christian participation in or withdrawal from American politics—tends to underwrite the assumption that the church does not embody a politics of its own. Stout is primarily concerned with whether Hauerwas's work will make Christians better or worse American citizens. Put differently, Stout is trying to secure (political) peace through the practices of democracy. He has, in this sense, a political agenda. This means Stout is tempted to read Hauerwas through the lens of the particular politics Stout believes is necessary for peace—i.e., democracy. This in part explains his worries about Hauerwas's attempts to combine MacIntyre and Yoder in theological ethics for the church. But to Christian readers who are sympathetic to Hauerwas, I suggest, this way of going about things amounts to picking Hauerwas up by the wrong handle. They are more likely to see that the church must be the primary lens through which to interpret

---

8. In his article, "Hauerwas and Political Theology," Charles Pinches considers the question of Hauerwas's political "influence" by reflecting on recent contributions to political theology made by Hauerwas's students. He argues that their works "rightly and creatively seek to expand our political imagination beyond the narrowness of modern nation-state politics and its attending capitalist assumptions." His main point seems to be that the work of Hauerwas's students, at its best, stresses the political embodiment of Christian convictions spread out over our lives as participants in churches, families, and political economies. It thereby gives us resources to resist a Gnostic influence familiar to modern selves.

Whereas some might be unduly suspect of this way of evaluating the significance of Hauerwas, it is quite congenial to the perspective of this book. Insofar as learning is a kind of formation and proceeds in part by example, looking to those who studied with Hauerwas is a fine way to get insight into how Hauerwas does Christian ethics. To give a personal example, after reading my dissertation, which also has a pivotal chapter on him, Hauerwas gave me a recent book of his as a gift. He signed it, "To Mark—who knows me better than I know myself."

him. I try to show, I hope somewhat surprisingly, that this debate can be illuminated at the level of accounts of practical reasoning. I argue, especially in chapter 5, that Stout's account of practical reasoning does not go far enough in reclaiming tradition and politics as constitutive of practical reasoning. My hope is that doing so would change his reading of Hauerwas as harmful to American democracy.

Returning again to James Davison Hunter, we find a critique of Hauerwas, or the "Neo-Anabaptists"—a term for followers, at varying distances, of Yoder and Hauerwas—that bears significant resemblances to Stout's. Both, for instance, are concerned with the impact of Christians on America. Hunter criticizes the Neo-Anabaptists not for their talk of politics per se but because finally they do not offer an alternative politics and as a result unwittingly reinforce the status quo. In short, the emphasis they place on the church as distinct from the world does not as they claim produce an authentically gospel-centered political witness to Christ's lordship. Rather, for Hunter, it is another manifestation of the negation characteristic of contemporary culture wars.

On one hand, I believe Hunter fails to give due attention to one dimension of his work, namely the degree to which Hauerwas has begun to recover an ancient and non-reductive conception of politics through his use of the virtues. One might say that interest group politics has its own moral language—talk of "rights", for example—that embodies a logic distinct from that of the virtues.

But isolated from a social context, virtues and references to them inevitably become abstract. Therefore, answering Hunter's charge requires noting that Hauerwas must turn to a performative mode, doing ethics in a way that depends on the first-order language of Christians. This language, moreover, is rooted in distinctively Christian activities such as prayer and worship of God in Christ, and is carried out by the concrete community called church. Without this performance, Hauerwas and his followers would indeed be guilty of failing to offer hope of an alternative politics.

At the risk of oversimplifying, we can put the problem with this line critique in the following form. Hauerwas is often accused of negligence or apathy when it comes to moving from ethics to politics because the critic fails to see why he has always understood Christian ethics or practical reasoning to be political. One might say he refuses to go by several of the assumptions—about "ethics" and "politics"—that are made when the move from ethics to politics is considered to be an especially dramatic one.

I believe that insofar as both kinds of readings of Hauerwas just discussed gain widespread acceptance in the field we will be impoverished. Only when we can both see how Hauerwas's arguments are candidates for truth and appreciate the political nature of moral truth claims, can we embark on the challenge of considering them well. This will be a good in itself. Learning what Hauerwas is saying will be of help in every reader's learning to be more truthful about their own assumptions.

In short, if we learn to read Hauerwas rightly we will also learn a lot about the character of practical reason. We will unlearn common errors with regard to it.

The Book in Outline

But I do not begin with Hauerwas, but with G. E. M. Anscombe. Anscombe allows me to develop the essentially political accounts of practical reason and human agency that serve as the touchstone of this study, and she is thus basic to my reading not only of Hauerwas but of all the authors I consider. She is helpful especially because of the element of Wittgensteinian therapy that is inherent to her style. Anscombe helps us irremediable Cartesians (and Humeans) to see differently what reason in the service of action is. Practical reason, for Anscombe, is inextricably tied to human action. It must therefore be distinguished from the "observational knowledge" that shapes the outlook of modern epistemology. When we see it aright, we also learn to get beyond the antinomy between reason and desire, as well as that between fact and value, so typical of modern moral psychologies. Most importantly, Anscombe shows the tie between practical reason and the political, and begins to make clear the sense of political that I want to re-capture. For practical reason, according to its form, relies upon descriptions shaped and sustained by communities.

The second chapter considers the work on moral anthropology and practical reason in the philosopher Charles Taylor. If Anscombe lays down the essential framework for recovering a proper way of relating practical reason to human agency, Taylor here can be understood as the first to try and further this project. Taylor's work has contributed to such varied issues as the philosophy of language, the liberal–communitarian debate, the problems of behaviorist approaches to animal behavior, and the conditions of religious belief in the modern West.[9] Yet these broad contributions also have their roots in the issues of human agency and practical reason. He admits to being so obsessed with the theme of philosophical anthropology as to be a good example of Isaiah Berlin's hedgehog.[10] Taylor is widely considered a friend by theologically minded critics of modern moral theory and its conceptions of agency and reason. So it may come as something of a surprise that my chapter on him is in part a critical one. I will argue, in effect, that Taylor's account of the agent puts too much space between an ontology of human goodness and a concrete politics that sustains moral formation, and thus risks rendering the latter concern invisible. In different terms, Taylor's moral psychology relies on a "self" that is too general and abstract, and this is due to the fact that the social location whose narrative he writes in *Sources of the Self* is as broad and generalized as "the modern identity." I do not wish to deny the valuable insights we find in Taylor's work. I am using Taylor here, however, to help us see something of value in Hauerwas. That is, my criticism of Taylor for effectively dissociating practical reason from the political will help us to appreciate why and how Hauerwas succeeds in holding them together.[11]

My purpose in treating Hauerwas, who is the subject of chapter 3, is twofold. Hauerwas displays the connection between practical reasoning and politics that I indicate in the chapter on Anscombe. My choice of the word "display" in reference to Hauerwas's practical reason is not

---

9. The number and sources of responses to his recent book, *A Secular Age*, testify to Taylor's significance as a public intellectual. To take one instance, the lay Catholic magazine *Commonweal* ran two full-length articles. The first is by *New York Times* religion columnist Peter Steinfels ("Modernity & Belief," 14–21). The second, more a meditation in harmony with his ideas, is by the sociologist Robert Bellah ("Rules of Engagement," 15–21).

10. See the introduction to his *Philosophical Papers*.

11. I do realize that for some this "space," if you will, between Taylor's ontology of the self and the good, and political commitment, is Taylor's virtue. (See, for instance, White, *Sustaining Affirmation*.) Furthermore, in an unpublished paper given at the Society of Christian Ethics ("Transcendent Sources and the Dispossession of the Self"), Carlos Colorado (McMaster University), following White, connects the "weak ontology" of Taylor to both his "pluralism" and his theology of Christ's kenosis. The question of how to articulate the value of pluralism without drawing on clichéd forms of political liberalism ought to be raised.

accidental, but rather veils a claim. While my chapters on Anscombe and Taylor attempt to give a picture of practical reason in general, the same cannot be said for the Hauerwas chapter.[12] In the latter, I am attempting to follow along as Hauerwas performs a "theological ethics" by elucidating what the church says and does—most especially, the church's practice of the initiation of new members into a moral life understood as growing in the perfection of God as this is revealed in the stories of Israel, Jesus Christ, and the church.

The deeper claim involved in using Hauerwas this way is that the politics of practical reasoning cannot be directly described but must be shown or indicated. Put differently, the church is not merely an example of the politics of practical reason but the community that makes politics possible for Hauerwas. That is to say, the church's role is not only to enact politics but also to reveal that practical reason is political. Furthermore, as mentioned above, I wish to promote the value of Hauerwas's work in the field of theological ethics as a therapy to certain distortions to which we are prone when tempted to conceive practical reason apolitically.

To get at what causes these, consider the way R. R. Reno draws our attention to what is unique in Hauerwas's approach to the work of theological ethics in the *Blackwell Companion to Political Theology*. Reno exploits Hauerwas's own metaphor in comparing the work of Christian ethics to the laying of brick. "It was not surprising," he writes, "that in 1968 the students in Paris threw cobblestones and bricks, not books. Bricks hurt more. . . . Hauerwas knows that Christian truth is at least as dense and durable as are bricks." This is Reno's way of bringing life to Hauerwas's own claim that "the intelligibility and truthfulness of Christian convictions reside in their practical force."[13]

Reno provides an apt summary of the insight that animates this chapter on Hauerwas—especially the claim that the centrality of the church in Hauerwas equates to the affirmation that Christian truth claims are by nature political. Hauerwas's work depends upon a conception of rationality. This conception of reasoning is not thoroughly spelled out by Hauerwas, though he does at times show his indebtedness to philosophers who focus directly on these matters. Rather, it is

---

12. I say "more or less" direct because of the ghost of Wittgenstein that inhabits Anscombe's work.

13. Hauerwas, *Community of Character*, 1.

displayed, or performed, in the activity of doing Christian ethics—a Christian ethics that understands that it is made possible by the existence of the church, out of which it speaks. The church, at bottom, is the agent that carries out the activity of practical reasoning. Indeed it is likely that the conception of rationality underwriting things here cannot be fully explicated on its own—that is, without the sort of performance Hauerwas gives it.

The fourth chapter reflects my conviction that we can understand better Hauerwas's practical reasoning by examining the shortcomings of certain of his critics. The two I consider—Gloria Albrecht and Jeffrey Stout—both use justice as an angle from which to criticize Hauerwas's approach to theological ethics. What is unique in the conception of justice they employ, I claim, is its independence from any substantive understanding of the good.[14] In their use of it, there is lacking an account of how the application of justice will be formed by a shared vision of common goods. Such a vision, we might further say, can only be worked out through what I am calling politics.[15] Thus, the chapter at the same time begins to develop an alternative account of practical reason as political.

The fifth chapter also turns away from Hauerwas himself in order to shed more light on the rationality at work in him. Here I turn to Alasdair MacIntyre in order to continue philosophically to develop this account of practical reason rooted in Anscombe's challenge. The centrality of the concept of an "intelligible action" in MacIntyre's work makes it akin to the whole approach to intentions and practical reason in Anscombe's *Intention*. Furthermore, MacIntyre's re-constitution of Aristotle's account of practices and virtues might be viewed as the most significant attempt to respond to the problems and challenges Ancombe identified in modern moral philosophy. Hauerwas himself has argued that the virtues of Alasdair MacIntyre are found in the help he offers us in locating and naming the practices among us which serve the

---

14. For an impressive argument against separating practical rationality and justice, see MacIntyre's *Whose Justice? Which Rationality?*

15. For this reason, Albrecht's critique of Hauerwas can be charged with blindness to the historically contingent aspect of practical reason. Interestingly, this blindness is selective. For Albrecht does realize that to understand the claims of feminism requires narrating the movement's history. But for a politics of the church, on its own terms, she has little tolerance. I believe that Stout can and ought to be challenged along similar lines, although the critique will be subtler in his case.

development of virtue in pursuit of common goods; or, in my terms, the politics of practical reason.[16] I place him in conversation Jeffrey Stout, comparing and contrasting what practical reason amounts to in their work. Stout has criticized the politics displayed in both Hauerwas and MacIntyre, while maintaining that the virtues are key to how we deliberate, thus making him an interesting conversation partner.

Since Stout himself suggested the comparison between his way of speaking of the virtues and that of MacIntyre, particularly the MacIntyre of *After Virtue*, I look closely at the way each views the reasoning that constitutes human actions within social practices and within the moral life as a whole.[17] This allows me to tease out and focus upon Stout's conception of practical reason, so that I can consider some problems with it. In the conclusion of the chapter I outline the case for seeing these inadequacies as rooted in Stout's conception of politics.

---

16. Hauerwas, "Virtues of Alasdair MacIntyre."

17. It should be noted, of course, that the two may well have different and incommensurable conceptions of the moral life. For MacIntyre, this means a complete human life, or a human life seen as a narrative unity. One of the matters I am probing is whether Stout has, or can have, such a concept.

CHAPTER 1

Elizabeth Anscombe: Practical Reason as Political and Linguistic

The first business of this study is to establish clearly the aforementioned connection between three key concepts: moral anthropology or an account of human agency, practical reason, and politics. If this is, as I claim, the structure of an adequate account of practical reason, or one that avoids the distortions to which we are most susceptible, we must try to lay it out prior to considering its influence in theological ethics. Elizabeth Anscombe allows us to do just this.

In this chapter I will try to display the fundamental connection between the form of practical deliberation displayed in a moral theory and its requisite underlying account of human agency. Simply stated, theories of moral judgment are influenced by the way they conceive of practical deliberation, and accounts of practical deliberation, in turn, are both informed by and rest upon a conception of the psychology of agency. In order to articulate this basic conceptual connection between practical deliberation and its underlying anthropology, I will draw on Anscombe's influential essay "Modern Moral Philosophy"[1] and look as well to her book *Intention*. As we will see, Anscombe's biting critique of modern moral philosophy in terms of its inadequate psychology leads her to defend the distinctive character of practical reason as compared to theoretical reason.

Anscombe asserts that the right kind of psychology is something an account of which no current philosophers are capable of providing, herself included. Yet in her critique of the going theories, rooted in

---

1. Anscombe, *Ethics, Religion and Politics*, 26–42.

great modern figures such as Hume, as well as in her careful study of intentions, I believe that we begin to see an outline of such a psychology.

In "Modern Moral Philosophy," Anscombe shows that certain conundrums raised by modern moral theories and their views of the moral life lead naturally to the theme of anthropology, or what she calls "the philosophy of psychology"—i.e., accounts of human agency. These conundrums, she further implies, cannot be addressed any other way. She argues that the sense of "moral" associated with "overriding obligation" is a vestige from a worldview no longer prevalent, and therefore in seeking to explain this sense of "moral" current theories are chasing after a ghost.[2] Consequently, it is time to turn to more basic, psychological concepts such as those of human action and practical knowledge—i.e., philosophical psychology. In her book *Intention*, she gives an extended account of one component of a philosophical psychology—the intentions embodied in human actions—which informs how we understand practical reason itself.

In the first part of this chapter, I will examine the three theses Anscombe defends in "Modern Moral Philosophy." The examination of these theses will take us through some of her meditations on problems raised by Hume regarding reason, motivation, and human desire. It will ultimately arrive at Sidgwick's implicit account of "intention" and its relation to knowledge concerning the consequences of our actions. What I will highlight is that for Anscombe the relation between psychology and moral theories is best understood when we pay close attention to the "descriptions" embedded in our language and folkways.

In the next part, I will turn to *Intention*. Here Anscombe elucidates psychological concepts such as practical knowledge, practical reasoning, and, of course, intentions themselves. We will find that her treatment of these concepts, and in particular that of the form of description associated with intentional actions, provides a therapy for certain among the problems raised in her discussion of Hume and Sidgwick in "Modern Moral Philosophy." My treatment of *Intention* here will thus help to clarify psychological problems relevant to moral

---

2. "The moral sense of ought," together with its associated concepts of moral obligation and duty, are said to be, "survivals, or derivatives from survivals, from an earlier conception of ethics which no longer generally survives. . . ." (Anscombe, *Ethics, Religion, and Politics*, 26).

theory. Her treatment of these concepts also shows that practical reason is distinctive and how.

By all this I hope to, first, locate a principle that will be useful as we turn to assess other thinkers, and ultimately from moral philosophy to theological ethics. This is that all ethics must recognize that it relies on accounts of human agency, and that how a thinker accounts for this can be key to understanding and assessing her work. In modern moral philosophy, anthropology came to play a more and more inconspicuous role. Therefore, the anthropologies implicit in such work were largely unexamined.[3] Yet if we do not have a good enough account of practical reason in relation to moral psychology, our attempts to understand "morality" are bound to go astray. In the more polemical terms of Anscombe's first thesis in "Modern Moral Philosophy," moral theory should be "laid aside . . . until we have a more adequate philosophy of psychology . . . which we are conspicuously lacking."[4] I call this claim "Anscombe's challenge."

Second, and more important, I hope to begin to show that we can best recognize the distinctive form of practical reason by recognizing its connection to politics. Anscombe's analysis of modern moral theories, especially "consequentialism," shows that the notion of practical deliberation has been overtaken by abstraction and a theoretical model of reason. Her recovery of the "local" sense of practical reason is accomplished both by a more truthful moral psychology and by acknowledgement of the role of communal speech habits within practical reasoning. She thus helps provide the backdrop against which to read Hauerwas.

The Theses of "Modern Moral Philosophy"

In "Modern Moral Philosophy," Anscombe puts forward the following three theses: 1) "[I]t is not profitable at this time for us to do moral philosophy—that should be laid aside, at any rate, until we have an adequate philosophy of psychology"; 2) "[T]he concepts of 'obligation' and 'duty'—*moral* obligation and *moral* duty— . . . ought to be jettisoned if psychologically possible"; 3) "[T]he differences between the well-known English writers on moral philosophy from Sidgwick

---

3. See, e.g., Iris Murdoch's criticisms of Stuart Hampshire in her paper "Idea of Perfection," 1–45.

4. Anscombe, *Ethics, Religion, and Politics*, 26

[1838–1900] to the present day are of little importance"—i.e., are inconsequential in relation to their similarities. In interpreting these three theses, I will demonstrate how they all show that moral psychology is an unavoidable component of a moral theory and that practical reasoning is grounded in a form of life.

Thesis 2: The Use of "Moral" and the Lack of Intelligibility

I will begin with the second thesis, both because doing so follows the order in which Anscombe actually proceeds and because the thesis addresses what she sees as the current state of philosophy.

Anscombe suspects that the term "moral" as we are accustomed to using it in order to issue a summary verdict has a profound problem: it is without content. After quickly dismissing the abilities of Butler, Kant, and Mill to provide an intelligible account of our modern use of the term "moral," she offers an historical explanation. The sense of moral that implies a final judgment or verdict upon an action or policy is a survival from an earlier conception of the nature and origin of the world that we have since rejected. In particular, the reference to "obligation" and "duty" in our talk about what we ought to do is intelligible only in a context of general belief in God as a lawmaker—i.e., within such belief systems as Judaism, Stoicism, or Christianity. She finds that the failure to locate an equivalent of this sense of "moral" in Aristotle's influential ethical philosophy highlights its cultural particularity. It is natural, she goes on, for a Jew to understand what she or he ought to do as a matter of obeying God's law, but to bring the notion of being bound by law into Aristotelian language produces . . . a mouthful. In Anscombe's rendition: ". . . that is 'illicit' which, whether it is a thought or a consented to passion or an action or an omission in thought or action, is something contrary to one of the virtues the lack of which shows a man to be bad *qua* man."[5] The unavoidable clumsiness of translation shows that Aristotle's system had no need for such a concept.

Yet, even though our culture has largely left behind belief in a Divine law-giver, we have retained certain ways of talking deriving therefrom —such as the sense of the term "duty" as an overriding concern.

Anscombe's concern is partly with the efforts of theorists and partly also with a culture that has lost its traditional moorings. As

---

5. Ibid., 30.

regards the culture, Anscombe's concern is that a lack of correspondence between our worldview and our ways of talking implies a lack of intelligibility respecting the latter. This gap between what we say and our larger networks of beliefs—symbolized by the empty character of "moral"—then reveals a lack of linguistic resources for giving truthful descriptions of our actions. As regards the moral theorists, when they set out to give sense to the concept of a "moral ought" using the means provided by their theories themselves, Anscombe suggests they tend to exacerbate the cultural problem rather than giving an intelligible account of the relation between our moral terms and their relation to our beliefs.

This I believe sheds light on Anscombe's seemingly radical recommendations that the concept of a "moral ought" should be "jettisoned from the language . . . if psychologically possible." One cannot strictly separate the beliefs that help us make sense of our actions and the actions themselves. Insofar as the adjective "moral" used to pronounce judgment on an action or policy lacks a conceptual home, it signifies a problem for our culture. Moral theories that at this point go on while neglecting this problem do so at their peril, and ours.

Thesis 1: Hume on the Logic of Moving from "Is" to "Ought" or "The Naturalistic Fallacy"

Examining the objections Hume raised to moving from "is" to "ought" allows Anscombe to treat the problem posed by the concept of a moral ought in terms of its basic conceptual components. She particularly focuses on the relation between these components and how more complex concepts, or "descriptions," depend upon other, comparatively fundamental ones. The nature of descriptions will become clearer as we move on.[6]

---

6. It may seem loaded to use the word "description" for concepts. Anscombe's participation in a philosophy after the "linguistic turn" is in evidence here. By "description" she means basic "forms" of speaking and acting that emerge out of the background of a form of life. They also imply "facts," but the factual quality of a fact is defined in terms of its role in supporting a more "complex" description of what is the case that depends upon it. The connection of descriptions, in her sense, with forms of life is illuminated by her use of the phrase "under a description" in discussing intentional actions. "Descriptions," as used here in relation to her essay, "On Brute Facts," is related, but not to be confounded with "under a description," as it appears in the book *Intention*. Here, the emphasis is on descriptions as forms embedded in language, and

Hume's objections allow Anscombe to trace the logical relations between descriptions that imply different levels of conceptual complexity. Such descriptions often describe human action and activities. The advantage Hume brings, if indirectly, is to allow the philosopher concerned with morality ("value") to begin with more simple notions. Reflecting on the "logic" of moving from "is" to "ought" allows Anscombe to begin the quest for greater theoretical clarity on the subject matter to which the term "moral" pertains—i.e., human actions and passions. (This, in turn, leads ultimately to greater intelligibility for our cultural forms.)

The so-called "naturalistic fallacy" is based on Hume's argument that it is logically illicit to pass from the judgment that something is the case, to a conclusion that something ought to be done—i.e., from "is" to "ought." The problem has also been articulated in terms of a gulf between "facts" and "values." While Anscombe claims to be unimpressed by Hume's argument for such a position,[7] she nevertheless believes that reflecting on Hume's objections can be fruitful.

She uses the following rendition of a Humean claim to illustrate the points she sets out to make:

> Suppose I say to my grocer "Truth consists either in relations of ideas, as that 20s. = £1, or matters of fact, as that I ordered potatoes, you supplied them, and you sent me a bill. So it doesn't apply to such a proposition as that I *owe* you such and such a sum."[8]

Anscombe notes that the relation between such facts as "I ordered potatoes, you supplied them, and you sent me a bill" and "I owe you such and such a sum" is an interesting one, and begs further attention. She calls this relation that of being "brute relative to." The connection

---

not on their role in practical knowledge. For comparison, see Julius Kovesi's use of "notion" in *Moral Notions*.

7. She claims that he simply "defines truth" in a way that suits his argument and construes "passions" as an agent's aiming at anything, indiscriminately, about which Anscombe also intimates suspicion. Truth, which consists in judgments of facts and relations among ideas, and passions, which are primitive moving forces, are divorced from one another. We will deal more fully with the problem in this conception of passion in the section of this chapter on the book *Intention*—particularly when we consider Anscombe's thoughts on the role of desire in instances of practical reasoning.

8. Anscombe, *Ethics, Religion, and Politics*, 28.

between descriptions that are "brute relative" to one another is subtle. In a sense, the descriptions that are brute relative to "A owes B such and such a sum" provide the conditions making this latter description possible. In Anscombe's terms, "if xyz is a set of facts brute relative to a description A, then xyz is a set out of a range of facts some set among which holds, if A holds . . ."[9] Yet, she adds, the holding of xyz does not *entail* A, for some further facts, themselves brute relative to xyz, may imply an "exception" to the holding of A. Thus, whereas xyz ordinarily justifies A—the facts about the ordering and supplying of potatoes and the fact described as "I owe the grocer such and such a sum"—there can always be circumstances that render the connection void. Moreover, it is not possible to give an explicit account of the circumstances that make for an exception, either in theory or in our habits of speech. The most one can do here is to offer a few examples of sets of circumstances that constitute an exception. Anscombe's point is also that it is impossible to obtain a *mastery* of the relation of being brute relative *a priori*—only experience and immersion within a language gives us competence in such matters. We are thrown from our theoretical perch back among the descriptions and institutions that characterize ordinary life. She therefore concludes, allowing a partial concession to Hume, "though it would be ludicrous to pretend that there can be no such thing as a transition from, e.g., 'is' to 'owes,' the character of the transition is in fact rather interesting and comes to light as a result of reflecting on Hume's arguments."[10]

Through the concept of "brute relativity," Anscombe shows that movements from descriptions of how things are in the world to more complicated descriptions that seem to contain a normative dimension do not require "the addition of a further fact" or of something non-factual (i.e., a "value"). The description "I owe the grocer 10 shillings" does not consist in any facts over and above the ones in "I ordered

---

9. Anscombe expounds on the relation between the descriptions involved in the scenario of the transaction involving potatoes in her paper "On Brute Facts." Here she stresses that the movement from the descriptions about her ordering of potatoes and her grocer's supplying them to the description "I owe the grocer 20s." depends on certain institutions—e.g., that of the use of money in our society. Furthermore, in justifying the description "I owe the grocer such and such" the set of brute facts mentioned here belong to a range of sets of facts. Some set in the range must hold if "I owe the grocer" holds. *Ethics, Religion and Politics*, 22–25.

10. Anscombe, *Ethics, Religion, and Politics*, 29.

potatoes, he brought them to my house, and left them there." We may want to say, "It consists in such and such facts holding in the context of our institutions."[11] But Anscombe is careful to remind us that the description "I owe the grocer 10 shillings" does not *itself* contain a description of those institutions. Such complex descriptions as "I owe the grocer 10 shillings" are not mysterious in the sense of requiring that we posit a realm beyond that named by the world of facts. On the other hand, these relations are indeed complex to the extent that it is impossible to formalize them—all one can do is point to some examples from everyday life. The relations of such descriptions, as well as the logical license to move from the simple to the complex among them, depend on social practices embodied in a common language.[12]

Anscombe goes on to note that the description "I owe the grocer 10 s." might itself be brute in relation to the description "I am a bilker"—and bilking may be translated as a species of "injustice." She then points out, however, that a typical modern student may feel inclined to ask whether a man who acts unjustly is a (morally) bad man. Anscombe responds that one way to answer this question—the only sensible way, it seems, for her—is by providing some account of a "virtue."[13] A virtue, we may say, is a psychological characteristic of some kind, and its possession enables a person to act justly. If we can articulate what type of characteristic a virtue is, and how it relates to man *qua* man, we at the same time are able to say something about why a man who acts justly is good. Anscombe claims, however, that we are far from having the conceptual resources to do this at present. Yet these questions lead Anscombe into a further meditation on Hume's objections to moving from "is" to "ought." For she notes that the same objection would apply to moving from "is" to "needs."

From "Is" to "Needs": Hume Continued

Under the heading of "is" to "needs" Anscombe reinforces her earlier comments on moving inferentially between descriptions of relatively

---

11. Ibid., 22.

12 The problem, in consequence, with many of the attempts of modern philosophers to give an account of the sense of specifically "moral" judgments lies in their tendency to abstract the moral realm away from this background. In trying to single out the moral in this way, such an approach inadvertently confuses (I might say, "mystifies") the logic of normativity.

13. Anscombe, *Ethics, Religion, and Politics*, 29.

lesser to those of relatively greater complexity—or, from facts that are more "brute" to those that are relatively less "brute." Here, however, she focuses on the relations between characteristics of an organism and what they imply is "good for them," or what they "need" by way of environment. In her meditations on both topics—"is" to "owes" and "is" to "needs"—Anscombe's deeper interest is in displaying the logic of moving from "is" to "ought," for her more ultimate concern is with human action.[14] She recognizes that establishing a connection between "is" and "needs" does not fully explain human actions. For, as Hume points out, that will depend on whether the agent "wants" what they judge is good for them.[15] The intelligibility of the move from "is" to "needs" is again provided by an order among descriptions embedded in our ways of life. In what follows I expand on Anscombe's relatively brief comment on this topic.

Like the relation of "is" to "ought," the relation of "is" to "needs" is an interesting one. How do we typically make this move? Anscombe turns to plants for an example and we may broaden her choice by considering machines as well. When we say of a machine that it "needs oil" we mean that without oil the machine will not function well. To give the machine oil, then, is "good for it." Machines have certain characteristics which explain why this is the case. Similarly, a plant, due to its characteristics, needs water and sunlight. In these examples, certain characteristics (what *is* the case) seem to determine what is required, or what *ought* to be.

But how do we explain the logical relation between descriptions concerning what "is" the case about a thing or organism and those expressing what it "needs"? Or, in other words, what here plays the role that Anscombe's notion of being "brute relative" played in her discussion of transitions from "is" to "owes"? The concept at play here is the functional[16] one of "flourishing," or the perfection of a particular living

---

14. Certain of these descriptions, then, are psychological, and thus Anscombe here begins the defense of her first thesis. Yet not all are concepts of a psychological kind, and the boundary between psychological concepts and those referring to other aspects of the cultural world is somewhat fluid.

15. In the section to follow on *Intention*, I will discuss how wanting can be brought within a similar logic of descriptions. For the present, it will be instructive to note how Anscombe outlines the logic of moving from "is" to "needs."

16. The paradigm of this concept seems to be psychological: the idea of a person doing well. It is perhaps derivatively applied to other organisms.

or artificial thing. The "perfection" of a living or artificial organism—the plant, the machine—in the sense of the fulfillment of its nature, is something we see immediately, though aiding in its fulfillment may require deliberation. When we speak of the perfection of a thing, we often derive it from a picture of what that thing does (its function) when it is doing well, or flourishing. The notion of flourishing (or, "perfection") provides the background for intelligible inferences from "is" to "needs." It *shows* why certain characteristics imply certain needs, and we can discern these needs by imagining how a particular thing would fair in the absence of what is required for the fulfillment of its needs.

When a machine does not get the oil it requires, its movements become labored and noisy. A plant that has not received sun or water wilts. The machine functions well when it gets the oil it needs—it "flourishes." As does the plant when it receives sun and water. So at least with machines and plants, the relation between "is" and "needs" seems stable. The notion of flourishing makes the inference possible.

Now Anscombe notes that judging that a plant needs water and sunlight—that they ought to have them—ordinarily entails giving such judgments influence on our action. But here again Hume's objections are of interest. Hume's beliefs about the disjunction between fact and value—a disjunction inscribed within his conception of human psychology—lead him to insist that no judgment concerning what "is the case" could possibly move one into action. "It all depends on whether you *want* what is good for the plant!" he will say.

Regarding human action, Anscombe admits that while judgments of what is needed—what ought to happen—ordinarily do influence our actions, the logical relation is not one of necessary entailment, for it is not always so. Hume's objection points us to the fact that "it is possible not to want something you judge you need." "Wanting" here, in relation to human action, symbolizes the subtlety of the move from "is" to "needs"—that is, of the sort of description implied in the former to that implied in the latter—because it indicates the complexity of the concepts involved. How can we move easily from certain characteristics of a living being to a description of what ought to happen, when that being is also free not to conform its behavior to what such characteristics imply? To illumine the nature of human action will require more explanatory work, whereas to say that a plant needs water and ought to get it is in a certain sense irrespective both of a judgment of what the plant wants and of what you want.

Anscombe admits that the transition between what *you* need and what *you* want is problematic. For, "it is possible not to want something you judge you need. Yet, on the other hand, "it is not possible never to want *anything* you judge you need."[17] As we will see more fully when we discuss *Intention*, the proper order among descriptions in ordinary language implies *limits* on what human beings can reasonably want, and at the same time licenses the move from "is" to "ought." There we will see that to remain intelligible, statements about wanting must conform to a certain form—i.e., the object of want must fall under a certain kind of description. We cannot want something without having a reason that those who share our form of life would find intelligible. The idea that it is possible to want *anything* at all is nothing more than the beginning of a classroom exercise for philosophers.

Thesis 3: English Moral Philosophy and "Absolutely Prohibited" Actions

The third thesis stating that the differences between English moral philosophers from Sidgwick to the present are insignificant is sustained by the claim that their theories all lead to recommendations that fly in the face of the ethical teachings of the Hebrew-Christian tradition, which teaches that some actions (e.g., "procuring the judicial execution of the innocent") are to be avoided no matter what consequences beckon.

Anscombe connects this characteristic of the philosophy she criticizes with the way it understands a certain element of moral psychology—namely, intention. The mistaken conception of intention to which such philosophy is beholden, in turn, stems from its mechanistic conception of practical reasoning. Anscombe coins the term "consequentialism" referring to the importance this conception of practical deliberation attributes to expected consequences.[18]

What is the nature of "consequentialism" as a form of practical deliberation? We may again extrapolate from Anscombe's brief discussion and say that it has two fundamental components. First, an agent must imagine (or envision) states of affairs that might follow from doing or refraining from action "A" or "B." Second, a kind of weighing or

---

17. Anscombe, *Ethics, Religion, and Politics*, 31.
18. Ibid., 36.

balancing of these possible outcomes must be carried out with respect to a measure of "utility." The activities of imagination and weighing and balancing are perhaps indispensable parts of any psychological account of the moral life. Iris Murdoch, for example, has stressed the role of "vision" in her own account of moral discernment. But as Anscombe notes in regard to Mill, the folly in this approach lies in its assumption that the notion of utility is sufficient to allow us to identify an action as being of a certain kind and thereby allowing us to evaluate it. The conception of discernment implied in utilitarianism is in fact empty as far as relevant action descriptions are concerned. This is because the idea of evaluating human actions according to utility implies the moral agent may always remove herself from a situation. Moral decisions would be made formally in a disengaged posture, or, perhaps better, in retrospect rather than in the moment of response.

A further problem to which Anscombe leads us has to do with the tendency in such theories to see weighing and balancing as an algorithmic operation and treat it as though it were the essence of moral deliberation. When practical deliberation is depicted on this mechanistic model, the deliberator him or herself is seen as a kind of computer, coldly adding facts into distinct columns. The model is thus tied to a disengaged conception of practical knowledge. The agent—the person her or himself—is ultimately separate from what she or he contemplates doing.

Anscombe anticipates that her readers may feel she overlooked real diversity in the group of philosophers she is criticizing. We can perhaps respond to such readers by explaining why she is not simply siding with the partisans of "deontology." Consider Anscombe's reflection on the "objectivists" among post-Sidgwickian moral theorists such as Ross. These theorists propose that one of the things a moral theory must weigh in the balance is the "intrinsic" value of certain discernible types of action. While to speak of "action-types" at all does come closer to what Anscombe has in mind, the underlying model of practical deliberation according to which "intrinsic values" are one more item to be added into a calculating process prevents the "objectivist" school from holding a position substantially distinct from other varieties of consequentialism. The variety here does not disarm Anscombe's third thesis because all the theorists under consideration refuse to recognize that some actions are wrong regardless of consequences.

Anscombe's larger concern regards consequentialism's effect on moral responsibility. This effect can be explored by considering an example found in Anscombe's text. Consider a certain man who has in his charge a small child. He is responsible for maintaining this child, and so to deliberately abandon the child would be a bad thing for him to do. It would be bad, Anscombe notes, both in itself and in that it would compel another person to do something (i.e., take care of the child). "But now," she asks us to imagine, "he has to choose between doing something disgraceful and going to prison."[19] If he goes to prison, it will result that he gives up caring for the child. What form will the man's moral reasoning take?

On Sidgwick's view, we are responsible for the foreseen consequences of our actions, whether we intended them or not. In this case, the man's responsibility for abandoning the child is the same whether he does it "for its own sake or as a means to some other purpose, and when it happens as a foreseen and unavoidable consequence of his going to prison rather than doing something disgraceful."[20] This suggests that the man ought to reason by calculating which action will produce more bad consequences: going to prison (and leaving the boy) or doing the "disgraceful thing." It may be that intentionally abandoning the child would constitute a more vicious act than the "disgraceful thing." Yet, the notion of "disgraceful" or "laudable" *kinds* of action, with their usual function in discernment, will cease to have any role in what goes on in this man's deliberations. Anscombe stresses that once one gets onto the track of calculating consequences, such consequences will quickly become the only thing relevant to our responsibility.

Consequentialism has a radical impact on how one comes to conceive of practical deliberation. As she writes, "Sidgwick's thesis leads to it being quite impossible to estimate the badness of an action except in the light of *expected* consequences."[21] More important still are consequentialism's implications for how we conceive the fabric of the moral life which is evacuated of established meanings.[22] And for Anscombe

19. Ibid., 35.
20. Ibid.
21. Ibid.
22. Furthermore, given that our moral meanings are socially and linguistically encoded, fully implementing the consequentialist model would cause a profound transformation in how we talk about such things. The meanings of such terms as "disgraceful" and "temptation" are unimaginable outside of a particular community's way of life.

this is an alarming prospect. It becomes quite possible to do something *more vicious* than deliberately abandoning a child, if you can make out the consequences as being less damaging. Anything is justifiable![23]

The consequentialist model of deliberation also produces a form of individualism and the ultimate failure to take responsibility for one's actions. The special emphasis Anscombe places on "expected" in the quote above highlights the essentially individualistic conception of practical deliberation at play in Sidgwick's account. The agent is effectively distanced from the world in which she or he acts. Anscombe draws out the implication of Sidgwick's notion of responsibility as follows: "*you* must estimate the badness in the light of the consequences *you* expect; and so it will follow that you can exculpate yourself from the *actual* consequences of the most disgraceful actions, so long as you can make out a case for not having foreseen them."[24]

Anscombe claims that Sidgwick's view of practical deliberation—and here he is a representative of consequentialism—and the implications we have just seen to stem from it flow from an aspect of his moral psychology: his conception of intention. As the example above shows, the agent's responsibility for leaving the child to someone else's care is the same whether he chooses it as an end or whether it is a consequence of avoiding something vicious. He "foresees" the result of abandoning the child, and for consequentialism the distinction between foreseeing and intending has no moral significance. Anscombe argues that the conception of intention on which this view is based is distorted. Consequentialism equates intending with foreseeing. It does so because a mechanistic model of practical reasoning causes it to lose sight of the action descriptions that ground moral deliberation. Consequently, the engaged nature of practical knowledge is lost from view, or reduced to a disengaged, spectating activity carried out by an alienated subject.[25] That is, picturing moral deliberation as an impersonal process of

---

23. "The overall similarity is made clear if you consider that every one of the best known English academic moral philosophers has put out a philosophy according to which, e.g., it is not possible to hold that it cannot be right to kill the innocent as a means to any end whatsoever and that someone who thinks otherwise is in error" (Anscombe, *Ethics, Religion, and Politics*, 33).

24. Ibid., 35, emphasis original.

25. It is helpful to note her own conception of responsibility by contrast. "I should contend that a man is responsible for the bad consequences of his bad actions, but gets no credit for the good ones; and contrariwise is not responsible for the bad consequences of good actions" (ibid., 35–36).

weighing expected consequences causes us to lose sight of the engaged knowing implied in the concept of intention. The following section will show with Anscombe that, properly understood, intentions (known through practical knowledge) are closely related to the action types or action descriptions that a form of life sustains, as discussed above.

To summarize the point of this section, the English philosophers grouped together here pass over the descriptions embedded in our common language (and justify deplorable behavior) because their model of practical reason substitutes an impersonal procedure—an algorithmic one that fails to note established action types—for a realistic conception of deliberation that recognizes the limitations of human reasoning.

Intention and the Logic of Human Desire

In *Intention* Anscombe is able to show that human practical reasoning is characterized by desire for an end that the agent takes to be desirable (good). This distinguishes practical reasoning from speculative reasoning—the kind Sidgwick seems to confuse with practical reasoning—and thus implies an account of moral responsibility distinct from that found in consequentialism. How does she accomplish this?

In analyzing the book's argument for my purposes, I will try to honor as much as possible Anscombe's method of interrogating ordinary language and experience. This method is epitomized in her use of the question "Why?" In order that this analysis serve my larger purpose of showing how moral theories depend upon accounts of human agency, I streamline her discussion into the following four themes: 1) "reasons for action," 2) "descriptions," 3) "practical knowledge," and 4) "practical reason and desire." As we will see, none of these topics can stand alone. Each makes sense only in relation to the others, so that their explications will sometimes overlap.

By clarifying the concept of an intention in her book, Anscombe helps us understand the notion of a "reason for action." Reasons for action represent a particular kind of reason-giving activity characteristically distinct from what goes on in giving explanations. To illuminate her notion of a reason for action, Anscombe introduces the reader to a distinct mode of knowing. "Practical knowledge" refers to the knowledge an agent has of what she or he is doing *in* the performance of that action. Sidgwick's neglect of this mode of knowing leads to his equating intending consequences and foreseeing them. Further, Anscombe shows that the exercise of practical knowledge is intimately tied to "descriptions" sustained in a community's form of life, and in this way answers certain of Hume's problems about the logical movement from statements about what "is" the case to those about what "needs" to be.

She further explores the form of "practical reasoning"—beginning with Aristotle's practical syllogisms—in such a way as to respond to Hume's claims about the incommensurability of passions and reasons. Action implies desire insofar as it requires a source of original movement. Anscombe argues that the form of practical reasoning implies a relationship between a reason for action and an end that is desired by the agent in whom the reasoning takes place. The desired end is contained in the first premise of such a syllogism. Only here Hume will object that because it is possible to want anything at all, reasons in this sense are virtually boundless. Yet Anscombe shows that since what is wanted must be perceived by the agent "under a description," and these descriptions have an inter-subjective or social source, the very character of practical reasoning is evidence that desire is neither individualistic nor arbitrary. Her investigation thus shows up the notion popular among philosophers that anything is a possible object of wanting.

The Question "Why?" (Reasons for Action)

Intentions are constituted by a particular kind of reasoning. To offer to someone what my intention was in some action I performed is to explain that action to him or her in a particular sense—it is to answer the special question "Why?" with regard to it.[26] Yet Anscombe is aware that reasons come in all varieties, and even reasons given in the context of a single human action may reveal important differences in character. She therefore sets out to specify the *kind* of reason-giving that is constitutive of the agent's intention. How does Anscombe go about showing that an intention is a special kind of reason—that is, that it is a reason with a unique form?

---

26. "What distinguishes actions which are intentional from those which are not? The answer that I shall suggest is that they are the actions to which a certain sense of the question 'Why?' is given application; the sense is of course that in which the answer, if positive, gives a reason for acting. But this is not a sufficient statement, because the question "What is the relevant sense of the question 'Why?'" and "What is meant by 'reason for acting'?" are one and the same" (Anscombe, *Intention*, 9).

To understand Anscombe's procedure, it is important to be aware of one of her major worries. She wishes to avoid the temptation to picture intentions as things "in the head"—i.e., a species of mental entity that is only contingently related to visible human behavior. With Wittgenstein, she believes this temptation is due to the "mythological" influence Cartesian psychology has had in shaping our picture of the mind. The way Anscombe's method seeks to avoid this pitfall is by locating her search for reasons in the context of *actions* themselves. Beginning our study with *intentional actions* helps us as investigators to avoid endless ruminations about intention as some mysterious and private entity.[27]

Anscombe's approach to elucidating the nature of reason for action (intentions), then, consists in beginning with concrete examples of intentional actions and proposing the question "Why?" with respect to them. We might imagine interrogating someone who says, "I am going to be sick." When asked "Why?" she tells us that she has begun to have a nauseous feeling in her stomach which always precedes a bout of sickness. By pointing to these signs, she offers evidence. Afterwards, she may offer further reasons, such as "that yogurt I ate must have been bad." Here, the reason names a *cause*.[28]

On the other hand, suppose when we asked the same woman, before her bout of sickness, she replied, "I have to make a major report at work tomorrow, for which I am unprepared. If I feign sickness that day, it will give me time to get the report in shape." The reason given in this

---

27. Having briefly explored the verbal expression of intention, she announces that "We need a more fruitful line of enquiry than that of considering the verbal expression of intention, or of trying to consider what it is an expression of." And, after some further musings, she decides to "turn to a new line of enquiry: how do we tell someone's intentions?" "Well," she answers, "if you want to say at least some true things about a man's intentions, you will have a strong chance of success if you mention what he actually did or is doing" (Anscombe, *Intention*, 6–8).

28. The question "Why?," it should be noted, can elicit different kinds of reasons in response insofar as there are a number of distinct contexts for its use. To appropriate one of Anscombe's examples, imagine being on a tour and asking your guide why he claims a civil war battle took place here. He answers that letters at the time seem to refer to it as a site of a planned battle, and excavations show signs of the conflict. Imagine further that your spouse asks you why you gave that sudden jerk while you were drifting off to sleep, and, being a physiologist, your reply refers to a certain chemical reaction in the body. In both cases, the respondent offers a reason, but in neither is the reason the kind of reason that gives an intention. In the first case, the guide's response mentions evidence. In the second, you respond by offering the cause.

answer is what we might call a "reason for action." How does it differ from the previous reasons?

Insofar as it asks the *agent* about her or his action, the procedure utilizing the question "Why?" zeroes in on the agent's perspective. Part of what sets off reasons for acting is that they involve the agent in a deeper way than other kinds of reason-giving. Yet it would be a mistake to confuse the notion that the agent's perspective is important with the idea that it is a fundamentally privileged perspective. For it is not the case that the agent can simply invent the answers. As we shall see, these must conform to a type of reasoning that is in an important sense public.

When the question "Why?" elicits a response that mentions something future or offers an interpretation of the action, then a reason of the requisite kind is being offered. What distinguishes this kind of reason-giving from the kind that gives a cause is that it presupposes that the agent plays some role in making true what she is talking about. What distinguishes it from the kind of reason-giving that mentions evidence is the presupposition that the action bears some significance for the agent. In short, a reason for action can be defined by the notion that intentional actions have an object that matters for the agent. It articulates some goal or end that the agent seeks to bring about through her or his own power.

Mentioning something future implies that the agent has some end or goal in mind that makes sense of what she or he is doing. A neighbor asks me, "Why are you closing up all your shutters?" and I respond, "A hurricane is coming through." My reply suggests that there is some future state of affairs to which my action will be meaningfully related—in this case, as a "response" to what is going to happen. That is, what I do will shape this state of affairs, even if only in a reactive way.

A reply to the question "Why?" may also offer an interpretation of the action. "Why did you go and sit through his hearing before the military tribunal?" "I so admire his courage in standing up against the regime." To say with this answer, in effect, "I did it out of admiration," tells us the spirit in which the action was done.[29] (It is not, as we may be tempted to think, to *explain* the action causally, by giving its root cause or motive.) In expressing the spirit in which it was done, it also reveals

---

29. Anscombe gives the example of signing a petition out of admiration for its promoter. See Anscombe, *Intention*, 20.

that the action bore meaning for the agent. The action was purposefully chosen by the agent as one fitting to show the feelings harbored. It might be seen as the result of a deliberation of the form, "What could I do that would appropriately express the admiration I feel for this person?"

"Descriptions"

In the previous section I followed Anscombe in isolating the kind of reason that is a reason for action—as opposed to naming causes or giving evidence—using a particular sense of the question "Why?" I now turn to a second theme of *Intention*—namely, the presupposed descriptions in our talk of intentional actions that make reference to the agent's point of view.

The agent's knowledge of her action presupposes a particular description of that action. For instance, when asked, "Why are you doing X?," the agent might respond, "I was not aware I was doing *that*." Her reply refuses the description ("X") of what she was doing. If the question "Why?" referring to an intentional action applies at all, she knew her action under a different description. This section seeks to show a connection between an agent's reasons and a particular kind of description of his or her action. Establishing this connection furthers the claim that philosophical psychology informs practical reasoning and ultimately moral theories. It is possible to elucidate the character of these descriptions through further investigation using the question "Why?"

We might consider the following example to get at the difference between an observer's knowledge and an agent's knowledge. On a quiet Sunday morning in the city, I am watching traffic lights turn from red to green as a pedestrian steps out into an intersection where the lights are controlled automatically by a mechanism that senses pedestrians. Catching up with the person, I ask her, "Why are you making the lights change like that?" But she gives me a baffled look, unaware that the lights were pedestrian-sensitive. To her, what she was doing—that is, her intention—came under the description "crossing the street." ("Crossing the street," that is, was the description under which she knew her action. My question, of course, shows an unusual degree of unfamiliarity with this sort of behavior.)

Reasons for action correspond to a particular form of description, and that form is informed by the character of the agent's knowledge.

Just as reasons for action were identified by their significance for the agent, so the descriptions of intentional actions are informed by the character of the agent's knowledge of them. For example, if asked by my wife why I jerked with a spasm while I was drifting off to sleep, it is hard to imagine how my reply would give the kind of action description we want to isolate here. In such a circumstance, I would probably interpret the question "Why?" as a request for an *explanation*. Explanations tend to rely on a different sort of description of an event, e.g., "chemical reaction 'C' triggers response mechanism 'M' which sends a pulse down the left side of the body." This kind of description is at home in a physiology laboratory, but not in the context of intentional actions. How could such a reaction have significance for me?[30]

If the kind of description we are after is a description under which the agent knows what he is doing, the question may arise whether any action has just one description. This question is important because we have spoken of "knowledge" here, albeit the particular kind called "practical knowledge." But, the skeptic will say, can the agent know what he is doing under several descriptions at once? In a widely noted example, Anscombe gives us a case where a man is performing an action that may come under a variety of descriptions. For our purposes, then, her example gives rise to the question, "What is *the* description of what the man is doing?"

> A man is pumping water into the cistern which provides the drinking water of a house. Someone has found a way of systematically contaminating the source with a deadly cumulative poison whose effects are unnoticeable until they can be no longer cured. The house is regularly inhabited by a small group of party chiefs, with their immediate families, who are in control of a great state; they are engaged in exterminating the Jews and perhaps plan a world war.—The man who has contaminated the source has calculated that if these people are destroyed some good men will get in power who will govern well,

---

30. Another way to put the point about the form of descriptions typical of intentional actions is the following. If a reason for action implies an object that the agent hopes to achieve or bring about through her action, such objects come under a certain kind of description. That the object named in a particular "reason for action" must be "under a description" is because the reason must have some form in order to be intelligible—that is, it must be a reason for doing *this* or *that*. The very structure of "action" implies such limits.

or even institute the Kingdom of Heaven on earth and secure a good life for all the people; and he has revealed the calculation, together with the fact about the poison, to the man pumping . . . The man's arm is going up and down, up and down. Certain muscles, with Latin names which doctors know, are contracting and relaxing. Certain substances are getting generated in the nerve fibers—substances whose generation in the course of voluntary movement interests physiologists. . . .[31]

As mentioned, there are several descriptions here, some of them superfluous for our purposes. Anscombe notes that such descriptions as, "He is generating those substances in his nerve fibers" can be weeded out by the previously developed notion of "reasons for action." For instance, "[T]he description in 'Why are you generating those substances in your nerve fibers?' will *in fact* always be ruled out . . . unless we suppose that the man has a plan of producing these substances (if it were possible, we might suppose he wanted to collect some) and so moves his arms vigorously to generate them."[32]

Yet, after narrowing the field, there remain multiple descriptions that are both true and fit the form of intentional actions, i.e., "he is pumping," and "he is replenishing the cistern." A skeptic may object here that our inability to reduce these descriptions to a single action description casts a shadow over our talk of "knowledge." If we are going to say that there is a description under which the agent knows his action, we have to show that there is a form that unites the several descriptions. This form is given by the question "Why?" itself.

For example, if we ask our man "Why are you making that motion with your arms?" he may reply "I am pumping." "Why are you pumping?" we then ask. "To replenish the water supply of the house." "If this was his answer," Anscombe writes, "then we can say 'He *is* replenishing the water supply'; unless of course he is not." Here we have two action-descriptions, vis., "pumping" with the intention of "replenishing the house's water supply." Yet there is something unifying them. Once we have come to this point in our imagined dialogue it becomes appropriate to say he *is* replenishing the house water-supply. "This will appear a tautologous pronouncement," Anscombe goes on, "but there *is* more to it. For if after his saying 'To replenish the water-supply'

31. Anscombe, *Intention*, 32.
32. Ibid., 38.

we can say 'He is replenishing the water-supply', then this would, in ordinary circumstances, of itself be enough to characterize *that* as an intentional action."[33] That is, we no longer need to refer to the more primitive components which simply tell us in what "replenishing the water-supply" consists.

The relation of a series of true intentional action descriptions is often expressed verbally by speaking of the intention "with which" an action, or actions, is done. When the question "Why?" is applied to an action under a given description and answered by the intention with which it is done, the role of the new description to the former description is that of "end" to "means." The intention with which something is done, as the ultimate end in a series, "swallows up" the intentions implied in the previous descriptions. We can see the relation between each member in the series A–D by noting that, with reference to the ultimate term D, A, B, and C provide answers to the question "How?" E.g., "How are you poisoning the inhabitants?" "By replenishing the water supply with poisoned water," and so on. This way of understanding the relation also points up the limits of a proper action description. As Anscombe notes, "... the less normal it would be to take the achievement of the objective as a matter of course, the more the objective gets expressed *only* by 'in order to.'" Consequently, she continues, "though in the case we've just described there is probably a further answer, other than 'just for fun,' all the same this further description (e.g., to save the Jews, to put in the good men, to get the Kingdom of Heaven on earth) is not such that we can now say: he is saving the Jews, he is getting the Kingdom of Heaven, he is putting in the good ones."[34]

Anscombe helps us understand the unity between descriptions of intentional actions by steering us around a common error.[35] If we think of a series of such action descriptions A–D, where each is dependent on the previous one yet independent of the following one, we may be tempted to think that A and B are related in that B (e.g., he is pumping) is another description of A (e.g., he is moving his arm up and down) in the sense that both descriptions are verified by the same "happenings." Anscombe argues rather that what relates the two are *circumstances*:

33. Ibid., 39.
34. Ibid., 40.
35. Ibid., 41.

i.e., given the circumstances, moving his arm up and down just is operating the pump. "Operating the pump," given further circumstances, is replenishing the house water supply. There is no foundational event on which all the other characterizations are based (i.e., of which they are descriptions). Noting the role played by circumstances here also frees us from believing that to unite these descriptions requires locating a mental entity that accompanies both of them.[36]

Now, our skeptic may remain unconvinced. To him, the notion that a series of action descriptions gets its limits through a common sense of what is appropriate to say in the circumstances will seem arbitrary. The rule for making such judgments ought to be capable of formulation in abstraction from such cases if we are to speak of knowledge here. From Anscombe's perspective, however, this just shows the extent to which the agent is involved in the knowledge called practical.

Practical Knowledge, Knowledge in Action (Performance), Guiding Reasons

In the last section we saw that reasons for action imply a certain form of description to be intelligible. In this section we will explore the kind of knowledge that is knowledge of intentions.

It has already been made clear that the reasons that constitute intentions are necessarily reasons of an agent. A reason for action makes reference to an objective (or, "end")—which the agent knows under a description. Intentions are shaped by the way in which the agent knows them. Following others we might call this mode of knowing "agent's knowledge."[37]

Anscombe seeks to show us what agent's knowledge is because she believes it is largely neglected in modern philosophy.[38] We may link

---

36 The role played by circumstances here reminds us of Anscombe's discussion of the "brute relative" relation between facts. See Anscombe, *Ethics, Religion and Politics*, 22–25.

37. The notions of "agent's knowledge" and "practical knowledge" are interchangeable and I will use them as such. Working from Anscombe's terms, we might also have used "non-observational knowledge."

38. One of the real difficulties for understanding the notion of a distinct mode of knowledge that is practical knowledge stems from the notion that such knowledge must have its own object. Early in *Intention* Anscombe explores the distinction by speaking of "observational knowledge"—characteristic both of the way we know something we see, and of knowledge produced by inference—with "non-observational

this neglect to the problem with Sidgwick's moral philosophy raised earlier. Because Sidgwick is unable to recognize agent's knowledge—or because he has substituted a more contemplative mode of knowing in its place—his moral theory recommends judgments so out of step with common wisdom. In this section I hope to show how discernment of the mode of knowing called agent's knowledge makes attention to the action descriptions embedded in a common form of life more likely.

In the example of the previous section, the form of description marked out as characteristic of intentions was implicitly related to agent's knowledge. In addition to being true descriptions, they were ones under which the agent was aware of what it was doing. Yet we must note that to speak of an "agent" here is not just another way of talking about the human subject. For the very term 'agent' implies the context of action. Practical knowledge is knowledge that guides action.

A widely discussed example Anscombe employs in section thirty-two helps illuminate the nature of action-guiding reasons by distinguishing agent's knowledge from that of an observer. She has us

---

knowledge." A main example she uses of the latter is the knowledge we normally have of the positioning of our limbs. The intuitive problems seem to arise with more complex examples, such as "I am painting the wall yellow." This is the description of an intentional action, yet does it make sense to say that I know am doing *that* non-observationally? But then, what else could my knowledge be about but that there are such and such movements with such and such consequences?

It is here that one is tempted to imagine that an intention is an extra-physical (e.g., mental) entity of some kind. Yet Anscombe pits herself strongly against this temptation. Efforts to uncover the separate object correlative to non-observational knowledge, she notes, sometimes push backward toward the very beginning of an action. The idea is that we know without observation the initial contracting of the muscles, or the "willing" of the act, and the *results* are known observationally, like most things we know. But this approach falls prey to the kind of infinite regress—is there a separate action that gets the willing motion by willing it?

Whereas the approaches just mentioned try to fuse an "internal" entity such as "will" to a set of "external" results, Anscombe's alternative seems to involve eliminating the contradiction that arises in our minds between the notion of an intention and that of a public occurrence. "I do what happens," she writes. (Anscombe, *Intention*, 53) Furthermore, Anscombe implies that there is no incompatibility between practical knowledge and knowledge based on observation, inference and so forth. The two kinds of knowing can co-exist without becoming blurred. As she puts it, "when knowledge or opinion are present concerning what is the case, and what can happen—say Z—if one does certain things, say ABC, then it is possible to have the intention of doing Z in doing ABC; and if the case is one of knowledge or if the opinion is correct, then doing or causing Z is an intentional action, and it is not by observation that one knows one is doing Z. . . ." (Anscombe, *Intention*, 50).

imagine "a man going round town with a shopping list in his hand." "Now," she goes on, "it is clear that the relation of this list to the things he actually buys is one and the same whether his wife gave him the list or it is his own list;[39] and there is a different relation when a list is made by a detective following him about." In other words, we are to imagine a man with a shopping list being followed by a detective noting what he does.

Now she suggests that we compare these relations by asking how we would describe an error—i.e., a discrepancy between what the list says and what is in his basket—in each of the cases. Her answer: "[I]f the list and the things the man actually buys do not agree, and if this and this alone constitutes a *mistake*, then the mistake is not in the list but in the man's performance . . . whereas if the detective's record and what the man actually buys do not agree, then the mistake is in the record."[40]

To speak of a "mistake in performance" implies that, sometimes, when there is a discrepancy between what an agent says and what an agent does, it is what is done that becomes the subject of correction. The action itself becomes the target of our scrutiny for failing to correspond with what is said. This implies that some descriptions are meant for bringing about something in the world through one's own agency, rather than for reporting on what has happened. The claim contained therein is "on active duty"; its purpose is to come into being. When such a description and "what happens" fail to correspond, we don't change the description but say that what happened was done in error. Anscombe notes that, "if his wife were to say: 'Look, it says butter and you have bought margarine,' he would hardly reply: 'What a mistake!

---

39. "If he made the list itself, it was an expression of intention; if his wife gave it him, it has the role of an order" (Ansombe, *Intention*, 56).

40. Anscombe approaches this problem in another way by asking how an intention is *contradicted*. She compares the contradiction of an intention with the contradiction of an order, finding an example of the latter in a reported case of a soldier who was court-martialled for insubordinate behavior during his medical exam. Upon receiving the order, "Clench your teeth!"—the man removed them from his mouth and placed them on the table before the examiner. The point is that the court-martial is probably inappropriate because the order itself is problematic—a set of circumstances in the case make it fall to the ground, not the man's behavior. In a similar way, the contradiction of the expression of intention, "I am replenishing the house water-supply," is not, "no you aren't, for there is a whole in the pipe." Rather, it is "Oh no you aren't," said by a man with an axe poised to cut a hole in the water pipe. Ibid., 55.

we must put that right' and alter the word on the list to 'margarine.'"[41] Such are the descriptions of a person's intentional actions. Knowledge of such descriptions is distinct in kind. It is engaged knowing, or "knowing how." Anscombe describes this by contrasting it with "observational knowledge" whose essence is a disengaged and reflective point of view.

How does all this relate to Sidgwick? Sidgwick's picture of practical deliberation seems not to recognize that practical knowing is a special kind of knowledge geared toward performance. By saying that our intention in doing something amounts to what we "foresee" coming about as a result of the action, Sidgwick imagines our knowledge of what we are doing to be analogous to the way an impartial observer contemplates an event. Yet this picture of practical deliberation yields a figure characteristic of modern philosophy—i.e., the disengaged subject. As Anscombe noted above, the disengaged subject has a curious ability to exculpate itself from responsibility for what it actually does.

Further, because of the close relation we have now seen between intentions (as reasons for action) and descriptions that refer to agent's knowledge but are given first in an inter-subjective form of life, Sidgwick's account of moral deliberation tends to ignore the action descriptions sustained in ordinary language use. Thus, we find Sidgwick's agent giving serious consideration to the most vicious of actions available to him with the idea that in the larger picture things will turn out for the best. To properly take intention into account in a theory of moral judgment implies that action descriptions matter.[42] Moral judgment is not merely about contemplating a world where the good is maximized.

The Form of Practical Reasoning and the Logic of Desire

We have seen in the last sections that intentions (reasons for action) are constituted by a certain form of description and, in turn, constitute a particular mode of knowing. We now turn to the issue of desire or motivation. This topic was already implicit in the discussion of reasons for action, insofar as some account of how we are "moved" into action

---

41. Ibid., 56.

42. For an illuminating discussion of the radical ("up-rooting") nature of modern moral theories in regard to their ignoring ordinary moral language, see Pinches, *Theology and Action*, 199–203.

is necessary. Desire is included implicitly in the form of description and mode of knowing we have been outlining.

As we recall from our discussion of "Modern Moral Philosophy," Hume raised the problem of desire when he noted that whether judgments of need will have any effect on action depends upon what the agent "wants." He thus called our attention again to the nature of psychological concepts and their complex logical relation to other kinds of concepts and descriptions.

The conception of practical knowledge we developed in the previous section may already be of some help in responding to Hume's puzzle. For it suggested that practical knowledge, while being knowledge of reasons, is tied to action in some essential way. Its reasons, we recall, are on active service in an actual or anticipated performance. The idea of practical knowledge challenges the penchant in Hume's psychology to dichotomize reason and passion, and may help bring to light the logic of passing from judgments concerning needs (i.e., what someone needs) to intentional action itself.

Here we will examine the resources Anscombe finds in the logical form of practical reasoning for responding to Hume's puzzles regarding desire and human psychology. Hume objected that no judgment about what is the case could by itself lead to an action. Anscombe further showed that even when the logical permissibility of moving from something's characteristics to a judgment of what it needs (e.g., from the nature of plants to the judgment that they need sunlight) is displayed, a follower of Hume will interject that action can only be explained by adding that the agent "wants" what is necessary. One way to articulate the upshot of Hume's psychology and of the gap it places between desire and reason, is that it becomes difficult to say what limits or directs desire, so that the specter of desire as an untethered capacity comes into view. If it does not take its direction from reason, can it be directed at anything at all?[43] This becomes an urgent question.

Anscombe tries to show how the logical form of practical reasoning itself helps us understand where desire is limited within intentional action. And in showing how desire participates in a practical kind of logic, she at the same time begins to reveal a psychology that bridges the divide between reasons and passions present in Hume.

---

43. It is hard to imagine that Hume wanted this. His notion of moral sentiments seems to assume an order and intelligibility within human passion.

How does the form of practical reasoning help uncover the logic of, or the reasoning inherent in, desire? Can we show that psychological concepts of intention and practical knowledge offer any insight into the nature of desire's reasonableness? That is, do these concepts show us the way desire is integrated in the forms of human reason-giving, and thus rescue it from isolation and arbitrariness? Through her examination of practical reasoning, Anscombe shows that it is the very nature of such reasoning to attribute to desire a certain shape.

There seems to be agreement among theorists that practical reasoning leads to action, and this implies that it includes desire within its form. But how is desire included? To answer this question we must examine how the character of practical reasoning differs from that of typical demonstrative reasoning.

Anscombe turns to Aristotle here because he seemed to discern the distinctive character of practical reasoning in relation to other kinds of reasoning.[44] His practical syllogisms, Anscombe implies, demonstrate his sensitivity to the distinctive character of practical reasoning. We therefore turn with her to these in our consideration of the question above—how does desire participate in practical reasoning? The following example of a practical syllogism comes from the *Nichomachean Ethics*.

> Dry food is suitable for any human
> Such and such food is dry
> I am human
> This is a bit of such and such food...

Anscombe notes that Aristotle often leaves the conclusion off these syllogisms, but also assumes that the conclusion is an action—e.g., taking some of the dry food. In this, Aristotle's syllogisms reflect that practical reasoning takes place where there is deliberation that leads to action.

Her discussion implies that desire enters in Aristotle's first premises where something desirable is mentioned. That desire is included in the form of desirability characterization is itself important. It means that the desire is already formed as the end or objective for someone (or class of persons) in particular. In Anscombe's terms, this end is the

---

[44] Anscombe, *Intention*, 58ff. For the classic discussion of the distinction of practical and theoretical wisdom, see Aristotle *Nichomachean Ethics* 1139a, 35–1141b, 20.

object for which we calculate.[45] This is distinct from having a separate premise that merely asserts "wanting." If desire's inclusion were represented by a premise of the form "I want X," we are more likely to conceptualize desire as raw feeling—i.e., the very picture of desire we found problematic in Hume's psychology.

And what does Aristotle's way of including desire—i.e., through the characterization of something as the end of a particular agent in the first premise—tell us about how practical reasoning differs from demonstration? A good way to answer this is to turn to the ways in which modern commentators have tried to make sense of the practical syllogism. Again, it is largely agreed that the conclusion of such syllogisms is an action. "But how does an action follow from an argument or series of inferences?" these commentators ask. The presupposition of such commentators, as well as their driving concern, is that a conclusion only follows from premises when it is entailed by them, as in, "All men are mortal, Socrates is a man . . . ." In other words, the one who accepts the premises *must* accept the conclusion or be guilty of inconsistency.

A first way of constructing the premises of a syllogism with the hope that the conclusion—an action—will follow by way of entailment is to add a premise asserting the reasoner's desire, e.g., "I want X," or "Let me attain X." This ploy stems from the thought that the conclusion is entailed by the premises only when these include everything necessary for the conclusion to follow. So, if the reasoner goes through the steps in the syllogism above, and adds further, "I want what is good for me," the conclusion of taking some of the food in front of him would seem to be entailed. To accept all the premises and not take some of the food would be inconsistent.

Yet Anscombe suggests that giving the agent's desire the role of a premise in this way distorts, rather than illuminates, the form of practical reasoning. Clearly desire must have some role in a bit of reasoning that leads to action. Yet when we compare a premise modeled on this tactic—e.g., "I want dry food"—to Aristotle's own—"Dry food is suitable for human beings"—we notice that in the former, "wanting," is a somewhat random concept or operation. In other words, it is not located in a specifiable agent. We have "I" as the subject, but unlike Aristotle's syllogism, we do not know in what aspect this "I" wants what

---

45 Anscombe, *Intention*, 65.

it wants. In Aristotle's first premise, the agent is reasoning according to its nature as a human being—i.e., according to what is good for it.

Other first premises found in Aristotle mention that some thing or situation "is suitable for" or "is pleasant to" some person or class of persons. For instance, in my rendition, "A cow of type X is suitable for Idahoan farmers." Such premises describe the desirability of the object in relation to the agent who desires it. The desired thing is desired in light of its being desirable by someone in particular—that is in light of its significance as someone's end. By contrast, the tactic of adding a premise of the type "I want . . ." as would Hume, suggests that desire can be made intelligible independently of who wants it and why. In Anscombe's words, "the role of 'wanting' in a practical syllogism is quite different from that of a premise. It is that whatever is described in the proposition that is the starting point of the argument must be wanted in order for the reasoning to lead to any action."[46]

That is to say, wanting is not an additional fact that, together with those named in the other premises, accounts for a bit of reasoning's concluding in an action. Rather, wanting is integral to the very form of practical reasoning. If a bit of reasoning does not come to fruition in an action, it is not practical but reasoning of some other sort. In short, the trouble with adding a premise of the kind, "I want X," is that it achieves entailment at the cost of implying that desire is an additional fact and not integral to the reasoning itself. The form of reasoning represented here leads to the conception of desire as essentially arbitrary, the problem with which Hume got us started.

A second way that modern commentators have sought to make the conclusion follow by entailment involves giving the premise an imperative form with the implication of a rule that applies without regard to moment or circumstance.

To illustrate this tactic, we might turn to an Aristotelian syllogism. (It is Anscombe's attempt to bring Aristotle's "dry food" syllogism up to date.)

> Vitamin X is good for all men over 60
> Pigs' tripes are full of vitamin X
> I am a man over 60
> Here's some pigs' tripes . . .

46. Ibid., 66

The conclusion assumed by Aristotle is the action of taking some of the pigs' tripes: in verbalized form, "So, I'll have some." Yet what is *entailed* by the premises is not, "So I'll have some," but rather, "this bit of food is of a type good for me." This conclusion, in other words, is not an action, but the truth of a proposition.

In order that the action ("So, I'll have some") be entailed, the second tactic recommends changing the first premise to read, "Every man must eat all the pigs' tripes he ever sees." Given this premise, the conclusion "So I'd better have some" does indeed follow by way of entailment. The person who accepts it, together with the other premises, will be inconsistent if he or she does not go on to eat the pigs' tripes.

Anscombe shows how constructing a premise such as this distorts the character of practical reasoning by drawing out what would be implied in an agent's accepting such a premise. Consider the following example.

> Do everything necessary to avoid having a car crash
> Wearing one's spectacles while driving facilitates avoiding crashes
> I am driving
> Ergo: I'll put on my spectacles

A little reflection reveals that for a person to hold such a premise in ordinary life will yield myriad and incompatible conclusions, such as "driving immediately into the private gateway on your left and abandoning your car there, and driving into the gateway immediately on your right and abandoning your car there."[47] The agent who accepts the premise must also accept the conclusion. But the agent who accepts the premises is also insane.

This problem, however, helps us see the role of circumstantial context in practical reasoning. Only in a narrowly defined context of deliberation—such as in the case of a special art (e.g., cooking)—can a rule of the form "Always do such and such" sensibly operate. Thus, Anscombe suggests, we ought to interpret Aristotle's further example of a first premise, "Always taste sweet things," as, say, a rule among undercooks. In other words, it is the sort of rule that holds only in a narrowly defined context. For when the same premise is given as one

---

47. Ibid., 59.

for life in general, we can only imagine a person "having a sweet tooth to the point of mania."[48]

Practical syllogisms that give an imperative first premise in order to achieve entailment suggest that the rules of practical deliberation can be more general, and independent of circumstantial context, than they can be in fact. Only when further circumstances are brought in do rules of this sort become intelligible. We ought, further, to see the form of Aristotle's syllogisms—their resistance to the temptation to make the conclusion logically compulsory—as a reflection of his ability to recognize the distinct character of practical reasoning.

To sum up, Anscombe draws from Aristotle's practical syllogisms two related points about the form of practical reasoning. First, its inclusion of desire in first premises that mention a desirable end, rather than a mere assertion of wanting, implies that practical reasoning is always the reasoning of some particular agent. An agent's perceptions of what is significant for it constitute the desired object as such. Second, by resisting the temptation to draw up first premises that are indiscriminately binding in order to achieve entailment, his syllogisms imply that circumstantial context is essential to the form of practical reasoning.

The necessity of context raises a question about how practical syllogisms are made valid. Insofar as proof syllogisms can gain their validity without going outside the premises, the implication is that practical syllogisms represent a distinct kind of reasoning. Yet the question of how the practical syllogism is made valid is only fatal if we assume with the modern commentators that the validity of a conclusion is equal to entailment by the premises. That Aristotle resists the temptation to construct the premises such that the conclusion is logically compulsory reflects his discernment that practical reasoning by its very nature requires being located in a particular person in given circumstances and with a particular objective. These last are what make the reasoning sound.

We might summarize the distinction of practical reasoning in relation to standard demonstrative reasoning succinctly. Whereas the validity of the latter is described in the formula "he who accepts the premises must accept the conclusion," the former accords with the dictum, "he who does the conclusion must accept the premises."

---

48. Ibid., 65.

But let us return to our starting point by asking, What does the structure of Aristotle's syllogisms tell us about the concept of wanting (the nature of the thing desired)? That is, what do we learn from it about how desire is incorporated into practical reasoning and thus into ordinary inferential practices? Further, how does this discussion help us overcome a Humean psychology where reason and passion are incommensurable?

The problem, as Hume posited it for us, was that wanting seemed to be something without form or limit. (If one can want anything, how can the concept of wanting submit to an order of reasons?) The preceding discussion has shown us that wanting crucially depends upon a context. The form of the practical syllogism, with premises describing something as suitable or pleasant for someone, implies that practical reasoning depends upon a particular practical reasoner. The agent gives desire its intelligibility.

Anscombe shows us another method for bringing to light the character of practical reasoning and how desire is incorporated into it. In a sense, this way examines more closely what is involved in Aristotle's first premises.

Here Anscombe looks to the basic formulation of practical reasoning as "calculating what to do." She finds such calculation to be implicit in the descriptions of intentional actions we treated above. There we discovered that reasons for action depend upon a kind of description that gives something as the "end" or "object" (objective) with a view to which the action is done. We further followed Anscombe in finding that multiple descriptions of this kind that apply to a single action are related as means to end—a further description in the series expresses the intention "with which" the previously described thing was done. Furthermore, a series of description so constituted serves not only to unite the descriptions (intentions) involved but also to place a *limit* upon them. As she put it, in asking for the description of an intention with which an action was done we eventually arrive at "a break." At this point, a further question about the action at hand ("why?" or "what for?") simply changes the subject. It embarks on a new series.

What makes these descriptions a type of calculation is their teleological structure. To have an "end" for one's action means more than responding in a spontaneous way to a stimulus. It is to see your action as something calculated to bring about what you affirm to be a good—

that is, to see it as a "means." To see one's action as "fitting" in order to bring about some desired end is to choose it through deliberation.

To break all this down once more, we may say that the descriptions, and the serial order among descriptions just mentioned, reflect two basic features of practical deliberation. First, practical reasoning is essentially reasoning with a view to action, and therefore presumes desire on the part of the agent. Second, the descriptions and their means-to-end order reflect that practical reasoning is essentially teleological. In other words, they reflect the form expressed by "in order to . . . ," and always point to some object or end that the agent wishes to achieve. These two features are importantly related in that the desire implied by the descriptions is the desire for some "end," the object of calculation or deliberation.

The inclusion of desire in the descriptions and their ordering as outlined above can be seen in the close resemblance of the question that furthered the series—"Why?"—to a question referring to desire—"What for?" or "What do you want to do that for?" Consider how easily, in a typical series, one can be substituted for the other.

> Why are you pumping?—to replenish the cistern . . . What do you *want* to do that for?—so they have plenty of water in the house.

The presence of desire indicates that practical reasoning is not mere speculation, or a classroom exercise. Rather, it is reasoning inseparably connected to action.

On the other hand, the teleological character of such a series of descriptions highlights the fact that the desire here is desire for an end taken by the agent to be good (i.e., "desirable" or worth desiring). That is to say, such a desire presupposes deliberation and choice on the part of the agent. It is not desire in the sense of unspecified feeling.[49]

In this light, we can see that the first premises of Aristotle's syllogisms offer something like the ultimate term—the "break"—in a series

---

49. Here Anscombe's explanation of how primitive "reasonings" of the form "I admire him, so I shall sign his petition" require further formation in order to specify an object of desire ("I admire him . . . what is the best way to express that . . . by signing") make the point clear. Once you have the concept "expression of admiration," the agent's desire *under that description* can be the object of practical deliberation. "We must always remember that an object is not what what is aimed at *is*; the description *under which* it is aimed at is that under which it is *called* the object" (ibid., 66).

of such descriptions. For example, if you ask me what I am doing, and I reply "Eating some bran cereal," you might go on to ask "What for?" Suppose I respond, "Because it is dry food." You may then reasonably ask, "Why do you want to eat dry food?" At this point, drawing on Aristotle's first premise, I reply "Because I am human and dry food is suitable for my kind." Here, a further question, "What do you want to eat suitable food for?" starts a new set of questions about new issues. My answer at this stage has been a desirability characterization. It makes no more sense to ask "Why do you want what is suitable for you?" than to ask "Why do you desire what is desirable?"

When desire is taken up into practical reasoning, it is no longer raw, spontaneous energy. It takes on a certain order or form. And we have just seen how the form of practical reason is reflected in descriptions characteristic of everyday life. Desire is not something "added on" to the life of action. The naturalistic fallacy—that it is impossible to pass from judgments of "is" to "ought"—is predicated upon a falsely narrow conception of "nature."

It is perhaps useful to note, moreover, how the way we have been describing the logic of desire is different from giving it a theoretical "foundation." The very nature of the first premises in Aristotle's syllogisms—offering "desirability characterizations"—implies that the logic of desire is not reducible to one form or order of inference that can be abstracted from particular instances. The admitted vagueness of these premises ("desirability characterizations") means rather that what makes these syllogisms valid lies partly outside what can be made explicit in their premises. That is, it lies in the background context of social practices. The undeniable role of background is implied in the means-to-end series of action descriptions discussed above as well. Identifying where the "break" in a series of descriptions comes requires an appreciation of what convention and circumstance require. This is why Aristotle believed practical reasoning to be bound up with practical wisdom (*phronesis*) or skill at relating general rules to particular cases.

Rather than supplying a foundation for desire in a rational model, we are better off saying that Anscombe's view of the nature of practical reasoning integrates desire into reason by locating it within the context of a social form of life. This social "home" is both constituted by our actions and gives them intelligibility. In other words, desires gain their form from participating in practices of reason-exchange that are irreducibly social, as well as by persons who inhabit roles of a socially recognized sort.[50] At the same time, Anscombe gives us a more holistic picture of the person where the boundaries between the operations of reasoning and desiring are less fixed.

Conclusion

We are now in a position to grasp the kind of problem that provides the lens through which I will be examining subsequent moral theorists in this book. Simply stated, theories of moral judgment are influenced by the way they conceive of practical reason, and accounts of practical reason, in turn, are both informed by and rest upon a conception of the psychology of agency. This is the significance of Anscombe's first thesis, where she asserts that it will not be profitable to do moral philosophy until we can work out a more adequate philosophical psychology. She means, in other words, that before investigating moral judgment we must get an adequate account of what a human being is in its practical, "moral" life. Such, after all, is the kind of being for whom moral judgments pertain. As I go on in the next chapter to consider Charles Taylor's anthropology and account of practical reason, I will ask how these relate to the social nature of human being and rationality—i.e., in Anscombe's terms, whether it attends to the descriptions of actions sustained in a socially particular form of life. In other words, I will ask whether his accounts of these matters are "political." In a related sense, I will ask whether Taylor's view adequately appreciates the distinct "practical knowledge" to which Anscombe drew our attention.

In the following chapter I hope to show that Stanley Hauerwas's work represents a response to the challenges Anscombe raises for ethics, and that he has in fact learned what Anscombe has taught about practical reason. Her significance for theological ethics as regards practical reason connects through him.

---

50. There is a further way in which Anscombe finds a "home" for desire in her discussion in *Intention*, and it is also quite helpful. She notes that replies to the question "What do you want?" or "For what do you want X?" can be given a more particular form when they are grounded in concrete situations of observable actions. She notes repeatedly in sections 36–37, that "the primitive sign of wanting is *trying to get*." Thus, there is a sense in which expressions of want are open to public scrutiny through ordinary observation. This is thus another way to show that there is a social pressure on "wanting" to be intelligible.

CHAPTER 2

Charles Taylor: Practical Reason as Becoming Articulate

INTRODUCTION

Anscombe has helped us to establish the concepts of human agency (moral psychology), practical reason, and politics and their relation. Even more than Hauerwas, Taylor has been in a position to respond to Anscombe's challenge. In several ways, I claim, he does so adequately in his conception of practical reason. The criteria for testing Taylor's moral philosophy in this chapter will be his conception of practical reason. And this in turn will be assessed according to how it employs these three concepts and embodies the relations among them. Yet in addition to appreciating Taylor's accomplishments in this regard, I will also raise challenges for Taylor along the lines of the following questions: Does Taylor fail to do justice to the distinctive character of practical reason, neglecting its close relation to action and allowing it to become overly abstract? Is the reason for this that his accounts of practical reason and agency are insufficiently political (that is, bound up with a polis)?

How, then, will Taylor's account of practical reason inform our concern about theological ethics? There is something of a friendly debate among theologians going on currently about Taylor's influence on theology, so I will resist foreclosing it by coming down too strongly on one side.[1] Nevertheless, I hope to show that the difference between Taylor and Anscombe are similar to those between him and Hauerwas, and that what makes Hauerwas's practical reasoning different from

1. See for example: Hauerwas and Matzko, "Sources of Charles Taylor," 286–89; and Long, "How to Read Charles Taylor," 93–107.

Taylor helps to display why his work is good for theological ethics today. In other words, I am in part using Taylor contrastively to set the backdrop for Hauerwas.

Since, however, this difference, which naturally has to do with the character of practical reason, can be named by Anscombe the philosopher, I will in chapters 4 and 5 return to the philosophical challenge of practical reason in conversation with Alasdair MacIntyre.

The Self and the Good

Returning to the three concepts, Anscombe implies that their accounts of these aspects of moral psychology will lead us to debunk some of the most prominent modern moral theories. In her critique of consequentialism, she shows that one way of drawing out a philosophy's conception of the person is by concentrating on how it conceives of practical reasoning. At the same time, in its picture of the person—i.e., in its anthropology—we are able to more clearly judge the conception of reasoning the theory seeks to model. How we picture the agent, furthermore, will have far-reaching implications for our conception of the life of action—that is, the moral life. In the case of consequentialism, this meant a blind neglect of inherited moral descriptions as the natural home for human agency. The moral agent, in effect, faces a world without signposts or a horizon of the familiar and the foreign. It all devolves on him or her.

In this chapter, I take Charles Taylor's moral philosophy as exemplary insofar as it endeavors to place the human agent back into such a "home." In much of his work he argues for a portrait of the human agent wherein the agent is constituted in relation to some conception of the "good" or what matters to it. In *Sources of the Self*, he explains that the agent stands in relationship to what matters after the manner of a traveler within a land that has certain locations marked out as special, with the most special location providing order for all the less special ones through their own relationships to it. The agent's conception of these locations on her map of the good serve as sources of motivation: they provide the meaning and intelligibility for the various activities of the agent. To take away this horizon or landscape of the good would render the agent paralyzed or worse. When certain modern theories of morality attempt to do without these landscapes of the good—or, Taylor might say, strip them away from the agent—they at the same time throw up a distorted picture of the human agent and of practical reasoning. Moreover, the agent's access to her or his moral sources, the goods that give shape to a moral landscape for her or him, depends at least in part on her or his ability to articulate what they are. The principled reticence of many moral theories is thus doubly damning.

But important to understanding Taylor's work on human agency is recognizing his belief that he has had to argue for the very rights to raise the questions he wants to raise. This is because, he claims, one of the most influential currents of modern thought, "naturalism," has sought to altogether suppress such questions—the questions to which his conception of the situated agent is the answer. Those under the influence of naturalism would prefer to think of agency in the terms of mechanism—or the view of "nature" often associated with natural science. One of the important features of this view, or ontology, is that it generally finds no place for a horizon of what matters. Taylor, however, shows how naturalism has nevertheless issued in a family of views of the good. These moral theories are peculiar in that they are unable to articulate what inspires them. He gathers such theories under the heading "the ethics of inarticulacy." In any case, Taylor's polemic against naturalism is necessary in order to make space for the project of articulating the horizon of human significance or mattering. We may see this correction of such theories for a basically misguided approach to agency and practical reason as the therapeutic moment in his work.

We will therefore see that Taylor's essays often push forward on two fronts simultaneously. He attempts to push back the forces of naturalism to make a space for his questions, while at the same time advancing a constructive argument for a view of human agency. This has made Taylor especially aware of the issue of how social sciences understand themselves and has motivated him to emphasize the distinction between "human sciences" and "natural sciences" with regard to the nature of their activities. As we will see, some have charged that Taylor, driving on the first front, has pushed this distinction too hard, creating reified conceptions on both sides that distort how reasoning goes on in such disciplines.

I noted above that part of Taylor's account of an agent situated within a horizon of the good is that the agent's access to that horizon depends in part on his or her ability to articulate it. To be articulate with regard to some matter means to be able to talk about it, or publicly enact or embody it in some manner. To become articulate is to make the implicit explicit. Taylor's emphasis on articulation goes deep into his understanding of language in relation to human nature.[2] He argues for a view he calls "language as expression," which entails that it is in the expression of something that it becomes manifest and real for us. So, the goods that form our horizon of what is important for us as agents can be truly present, and thus guiding, when we are articulate with respect to them. Contrariwise, when we become inarticulate, or unable to expressively reveal them, they become dim or altogether absent.

This means that Taylor believes that our fondness as modern people for a naturalistic, or morally neutral, metaphysic has led us to a condition of being inarticulate. Naturalism is not merely a metaphysical or theoretical problem, but also a moral or cultural problem. Taylor is convinced, that is, that our naturalist-inspired condition of being inarticulate is a problem for us insofar as it hampers our access to the goods on our horizon of mattering. We therefore, as agents, stand on shaky legs, and our ability to act is compromised. To draw on our earlier metaphor, the agent is again homeless. To become once again articulate is to recover a language about the good, and only in this way can we recover morally. This is his description of the "conflicts" within the modern identity.

This explains why one of Taylor's primary objectives is to get us beyond what he calls "the ethics of inarticulacy." As mentioned above, this is the name he gives to a collection of the most prominent modern moral theories, whose common characteristic is that they tend to be self-defeating: they promote ideals of behavior while at the same time denying any ground for such ideals in reality. To recover morally as agents we must "recover from" a condition in which moral theory not only fails to provide a space for conversation about what matters, but actively suppresses such matters.

One primary way that Taylor attempts to help us in this recovery is by telling the history of how we got to where we are. By telling the story we can at least come to see more clearly what the obstacles are to moral recovery. A second way is found in his attempt to show up these theories as inadequate. He does this by showing contradictions built into them. They must at the same time affirm what they deny, deny what they affirm.

---

2. See Taylor, *Human Agency and Language*.

I will show that Taylor's project of putting us on the right track morally can be seen to culminate in a picture of a kind of practical reason based on recognizing the fundamentally basic nature of articulation within the human life form. Articulation is central to Taylor's practical reasoning. While Taylor claims the modest aim of increasing our self-understanding in *Sources of the Self*, it may be said of him that he believes a form of practical reasoning that recognizes the expressive nature of human being can help us get beyond our moral and cultural impasse. For the nature of this impasse is that neither of the major voices commenting on what we have become help us to a) understand ourselves fully, or b) get in touch with the best that we might become. Practical reason, understood in Taylor's way, is enacted both in the historical recovery operation through which Taylor discloses the sources of the modern identity—itself a kind of articulating work—and in the describing and assessment of who we are now, understood in terms of the hypergoods which give our lives purpose. There is thus a fitness between Taylor's historical narrative of the modern identity and his portrait of practical reason as articulation.

In addition to displaying the relation of human agency and practical reason in Taylor's work, however useful that may be, I wish also to challenge him, using insights gleaned from Anscombe as a guide. Like Anscombe, Taylor is concerned that our picture of practical reason correlate to a properly conceived agent, and not the frictionless subject of modern moral theory. In wishing to recover an agent whose life is intelligible only in relation to a framework of the good Taylor is commendable. Yet Taylor's historical conception of the modern agent is problematic. In short, the fit between his construction of the modern identity and his conception of practical reason is too neat. Practical reason as Taylor conceives it, I will argue, does not allow us to challenge the picture of the modern agent that Taylor constructs. That is to say, it is not clear how Taylor's practical reason could allow a confrontation in reasoned argument between his own narrative of the modern identity and a counter-narrative.[3] It does not allow us, in other words, to fully

---

3. In a moment of criticizing views of modernity that either celebrate it unreflectively or knock it comprehensively, Taylor argues that "not only are these one-sided views invalid, but many of them are not and cannot be fully, seriously and unambiguously held by those who propound them. I cannot claim to have proved this, but what I hope emerges from this lengthy account of the growth of the modern identity is how

cope with the contingency of conceptions of the good, insofar as we come to own them through membership in communities for whom what matters is distinctive and may be incommensurable with what other communities espouse. Indeed, it is hard to see how, on Taylor's account of practical reason, we could ever come to the realization that our self-understandings are not simply incomplete, but in significant ways mistaken. Because of its inadequacy regarding incommensurability and error, Taylor's conception of practical deliberation opens the door for the re-entry of the insubstantial modern subject within his own thick account of the same. I argue that this is because Taylor does not adequately discern the political character of practical reasoning. I hope to go on to show that affirming the political character of practical reasoning allows us to better account for ruptures in our self-understanding.

My claim, derived from my reading of Anscombe, has been that the practical reasoning of human agents stands in unbreakable relation to the descriptions carried by a community. My Anscombian challenge will thus ask whether the ambitions of Taylor's account of practical reasoning cause him to risk missing something important about the nature of the moral life. This "something"—the role of a particular community—I hope to be able to articulate more fully in the following chapter through my treatment of Hauerwas.

In the structure of this chapter, therefore, I begin by exploring how Taylor refutes naturalism in order to begin to see a picture of the human being for whom being situated in respect to a horizon of mattering is basic. I go on in the next section to explore how this picture of the agent informs Taylor's view of how social/human sciences should understand themselves as distinct from natural science models. It is difficult to keep separate Taylor's refutation of naturalism and his arguments for the situated nature of human agency from his claims about the form of practical reasoning and the historical sources of the modern identity. So the reader will indulge a bit of cross over even here.

I will go on to consider more directly Taylor's analysis of the "ethics of inarticulacy" and its relation to our current predicament, which he dubs "the conflicts of modernity." Practical reason, the subject of the next section, I will claim names Taylor's effort to show the way forward

---

all-pervasive it is, how much it envelops us, and how deeply we are implicated in it…" (Taylor, *Sources of the Self*, 503).

in this predicament, primarily by re-framing the debate over the peculiarly modern understanding of ourselves as agents and the goods that orient us. In my conclusion, I will set out my own criticisms of Taylor in a way that relates them to the overall thesis of this book regarding practical reason and to what I hope to show in the chapter that follows.

Human Agency and the Good: Rationality and Human Action

We begin our study of Taylor's account of practical reasoning in relation to anthropology with the two essays that open the first volume of his *Philosophical Papers*. In these essays, Taylor attempts to construct an account of "a responsible human agent," or the kind of agency that distinguishes humans from other agents (i.e., animals). He avers that it is necessary to pay close attention to what he calls "the subject of experience." Taylor finds that establishing this account requires fighting against "one of the fundamental prejudices . . . of modern thought and culture"—that is, the reductive tendency of the naturalist ontology. In the end, his view of the human agent implies steering a middle course through the landscape of current conceptions of language. What Taylor accomplishes in these two essays is to push back the forces of naturalistic reductionism in order to make room for a scientific account of human experience, and to go on and develop a normative conception of human agency.

I will start with the second of the themes named above, the question of subjective experience, as treated in "Self-Interpreting Animals." Here Taylor works out his account of the subject in contrast to models of the human organism found in reductive human sciences such as mid-twentieth-century behaviorism's attempt to explain human responses in terms of an organism composed of discrete mechanisms and given to discrete operations.

Taylor's first task in "Self-Interpreting Animals" is to show that there is a "world" constituted by human purposes and desires—a world inescapably bound up with the experience of a subject—that the "objective," or "naturalist," ontology inspired by modern science cannot account for in its own terms. He goes about this by analyzing the structure of human emotions.

Emotions are a primary form of subjective experience. They are, Taylor argues, experiences related to objects in a "strong," rather than "weak," sense. To understand what Taylor is after in this distinction between strong and weak subject-object relations we might consider the following example. To make a statement of the sort, "There is a black object rolling toward me and I am growing afraid," is to identify the object of the emotion fear in a weak sense. The implied logic is that it is simply a contingent fact that the aforementioned object approaches and I am growing afraid. A strong sense of relation to an object requires a *judgment* relating the object to the emotion. For example, "Look at that *huge, black thing*; it's headed straight for me!" Here, in stating that I grow afraid at the approach of that dark rolling object I imply that I judge that object to be a fear-inspiring one. I ascribe the quality "fearsomeness" to the object as the *import* that this situation bears for me.[4] Yet a world that includes human imports is one that naturalism has difficulty accepting.

That emotions contain import-ascriptions, or descriptions of an object in terms relating it to the desires or purposes of a subject, means that they can be, in a sense, "wrong." The subject, in other words, can ascribe an import to a situation, say "fearsome," that does not really merit the ascription. For example, the snake in my path I judged poisonous turns out to really be of another type. For the same reason, Taylor explains, it is also possible, "to feel shame or fear irrationally, where for instance we are intellectually convinced that the situation is not menacing or shameful, but we cannot help feeling afraid or ashamed." If the emotion were not affirming a judgment it would make no sense to speak of its being "irrational." In short, because import ascriptions describe some object they can be held to a standard. The fact that we judge emotions as rational or irrational in relation to their objects implies that we treat such imports as real and independent of human fancy.

Thus the structure of emotions, even relatively simple emotions like fear, is such as to make reference to an object, or perhaps better a "situation," and thus to the purposes of a subject. That human emotions have this structure, Taylor argues, also causes problems for attempts to

---

4. In coining the term "import-ascription" here, Taylor, it seems, wants to emphasize the way the objects of human experience unavoidably make reference to the subject him or herself. "By 'import' I mean a way in which something can be relevant or of importance to the desires or purposes or aspiration or feelings of a subject; or otherwise put, a property of something whereby it is a matter of non-indifference of a subject" (Taylor, "Self-Interpreting Animals," 48).

understand them within the model of behaviorism. That model wishes to understand the self in terms of discrete operations. The very structure of human emotions, with import ascriptions that imply that the subject's experience matters, open up a space of experience with which these models are ill equipped to deal.

Yet the behaviorist may be unperturbed by an account of the structure of emotions such as Taylor's. One way a theorist committed to a naturalist ontology may seek to overcome this obstacle is by re-describing emotional experience in neutral terms (i.e., terms that do not depend on the experience of the subject). So, for example, import-ascriptions that presuppose a fearsome object in the environs of an agent can be re-described in medical terms.[5] Thereby we are again able to explain emotions in objective—that is, subject-neutral—terms. The new description would show that the judgment of something as a fearsome object boils down to the recognition by a complex mechanism that certain aspects of a situation signal its probable bodily injury or even death. One does not have to be familiar with the experience of a subject in order to understand that certain features of a situation point to an organism's injury or destruction.

There is, however, a rebuttal to this sort of strategy. This is to point out that there are emotions that will not allow translation into subject-neutral terms. To translate such emotions is to change them. But if one's theoretical translation changes the emotions it seeks to explain, then it no longer has in view what it sought to understand.

The reason that certain emotions cannot be translated into a subject-neutral language is human emotions are themselves *constituted* by language, and in some cases the language that describes emotions is inescapably bound up with subject-referring imports.[6] The feeling of shame, for example, is possible only for a subject "in whose form of life there figures an aspiration to dignity," or "to be a presence among men

---

5. "Now the import of a menacing situation could be defined in terms of these medically defined states: it would be a situation which in virtue of well-understood causal mechanisms had a certain probability of bringing about one of these states; hungry tigers are likely to sink their teeth in nearby flesh, angry human beings in the mass are likely to beat whoever provokes them unrelentingly. Our model of human beings as capable of experiencing fear would then see them as beings capable of recognizing situations with these causal properties, that is correlated with a high degree of probability with the negative medically defined states" (ibid., 52).

6. Ibid., 68ff.

which commands respect." "Dignity" and "respect" are terms that form part of a vocabulary that figure a world in which the subject matters. In particular, they refer to the importance of how we appear before others and stand in relation to them. Our emotion of shame is linked to the way that brute aspects of our lives (e.g., a man's shrill voice) communicate meanings within this world; they have an "expressive" function there. This vocabulary is not translatable into the experience-neutral terms favored by the behaviorist.

As human emotions depend upon a sense of one's form of life, they also depend upon language. This implies that human subjective experience depends on articulation. Evidence for this is that we often find ourselves searching for the "right words" to express what we are feeling, and, when we arrive at a formulation the feeling itself is sometimes changed. Articulation is a *constitutive* element in certain emotions; describing them plays a role in determining what they are. Human emotions, by their very nature, refute naturalism.

We can now see why Taylor believes that the project of understanding what it is to be a self in "objective" terms—i.e., free of subject-referring properties—has formidable obstacles to surmount. For such attempts will inevitably strive to compress, or even collapse, the space in which the experience of the subject is found. Yet since Taylor has shown that this space is essential to human life as we know it, to attempt to understand the human being in objective terms risks mis-identifying what it was meant to explain. Or, we may now say that such attempts cannot but do violence to the language in and through which the life of the subject is already experienced. Wholesale acceptance of a naturalist ontology leads to gross misunderstandings of human agency.[7]

---

7. On the other hand, this account shows why another form of explanation fits naturally with the study of the human self. Just as emotions are constituted by judgments relating the subject to a situation, illuminating them requires drawing out more formally what these are. The integral role of language helps establish the rationality of human experience on a continuum with its own explanation. Both our primitively articulate understandings and theoretical understandings, and all in between, are the result of articulation. Furthermore, the human self is purposefully engaged with the world and inescapably social. For all of these reasons, the subject of experience, what Anscombe called the agent's point of view, is essential to what a self is. Yet theoretical understandings of this self are possible when theory is understood as a continuation, or a further drawing out, of the activity that constitutes the subject in the first place. Moreover, evidence that this point of view is social can be found in its dependence

The conflict Taylor is engaged in here can be seen from a different perspective. I have said that Taylor's view of human agency and practical reason are connected to his philosophy of language. His view can be dubbed "language as expressive," since Taylor holds that the possibilities of human agents are constituted in and through the language they employ. But Taylor knows well that there is an alternative philosophy of language to emerge and, in some corners, hold sway in the modern age. This is the view that language can be seen as an instrument employed to carry out tasks by an agent whose identity is secured apart from the language it speaks. This is the "disengaged" self Taylor claims arises in the modern world in step with an understanding of the world as mechanism in addition to what he calls in *A Secular Age* the "drive to reform." The disengaged self identifies with its own powers of self-control in a way that mirrors its domination of "nature" through natural laws. Such an identity, Taylor shows, is bound to recoil from the expressive view that language is best pictured as a web of meaning that shapes and limits what we can say and limits our very being. We have just seen how inheritors of the tradition of the disengaged self will strive for a reductive explanation of human behavior precisely by seeking to remove it from the ordinary language that is its setting.

We may view Taylor's analysis of the responsible human agent in "What is Human Agency," as providing another angle on practical reasoning in relation to anthropology. Here he begins by asking, "What is it that we attribute to ourselves as human agents which we would not attribute to animals?"[8] Noting that desire, or motivation, while a basic component of agency in general, fails to capture what is unique to human agents, he turns to Harry Frankfurt's notion of "second order desires."[9] While desires are affective engagements with the world necessary for action, I can be said to have a second order desire "when I have a desire whose object is my first order desire." For example, as a human being I can desire that my desire (read: "impulse") to drink too much after work each night be subdued or wiped away. I can also desire that I have a desire that I do not now have—i.e., to spend quality time with my family evenings when I get home from work. Taylor reads

upon a vocabulary that always already has been established to name and make judgments about human experience.

8. Taylor, "What Is Human Agency?" 15.
9. Frankfurt, "Freedom of the Will," 5–20.

Frankfurt's definition of the human as pointing to the activity of *evaluating* desires. Not only do we choose between desires, or sometimes suppress a certain impulse in order to act on a contrary one. We also judge some of our desires as desirable and others as undesirable.[10] This capacity of self-reflection seems to define us as human agents.

Taylor asserts that there is more to say about the evaluation of desires, insofar as there are competing accounts of what uniquely human self-evaluation consists in. He defends an account according to which humans engage in an evaluative activity he calls "strong evaluation." We can see what this is by contrasting it with another account which, following Taylor, we may dub "weak evaluation."

Views of the evaluation of desires are connected to conceptions of deliberation. For instance, one might find oneself confronted with the choice of ordering a cheeseburger or a calzone from the menu at a local restaurant. One may reflect on the choice for a few moments, asking oneself, "What do I want more?" Or, to take one of Taylor's examples, one may have a present desire to eat lunch (hunger) but also the wish to go for a swim. The pool, however, does not open for another hour. One could go and eat lunch now, satisfying immediately one's hunger, but then have to forgo the swim (say, he may only leave for a single break per day). So, the choice is either lunch now, or lunch with swim later.

In both examples, the evaluation is necessary because both desires cannot be satisfied. In the case of ordering lunch, deciding for the burger or the calzone means simply reflecting on which of the desires feels stronger. In Taylor's example the deliberator tries to quell the urgency of one desire in order to achieve a greater sum of satisfaction at the end. The important point is that the evaluative activity here seems simply a matter of weighing preferences, and not much can be said to explain the choice, e.g., "I was just in the mood for a calzone, I guess," or "I thought if I could just concentrate on reading for another hour, I could get that swim in."

Without denying that human beings undertake the activity of simple weighing, Taylor argues that this picture of evaluation misses an important aspect of human agency. Humans also engage in "strong evaluation," or the evaluation of desires according to their *worth*. In contrast to the mere weighing of preferences outlined above (now, "weak evaluation"), strong evaluation both distinguishes desires in kind and operates

---

10. Taylor, "What is Human Agency?" 16.

according to necessary contrasts between motivations. And in contrast to the inarticulate quality of the choice above ("I just feel like a calzone today"), strong evaluation involves being able to say something about, or articulate, the superiority of one desire over another.

What does Taylor mean by stating that through strong evaluation human beings reflect on the quality of their desires themselves and weigh them according to a system of necessary contrasts? As opposed to the tendency, seen especially in the utilitarianism of modern economics, to reduce all desires to a single and commensurable standard, strong evaluation supposes that there are necessary contrasts between kinds of desire. To grasp this point, it may be helpful to look again at Taylor's example of "weak evaluation" mentioned above. We saw there that the two motivated actions in question, "lunch now" or "lunch with swim (later)," were incommensurable in that acting on one rules out acting on the other. Yet if a certain circumstance were modified—e.g., the pool opened earlier—the incommensurability would disappear. There is nothing intrinsic to the two motivations, or their relation, that weighs in favor of acting upon one rather than the other.

To paraphrase another of Taylor's examples, we may now imagine that I am put in a position where I have a choice between doing a cowardly act or risking injury or even my life (say I have been sent to the front by my superior in a desperate battle and I can stand and fight or run away). While the choice here may in part be the product of contingent circumstances (my superior could have sent someone else at this time), it is not merely so. The very term "cowardly" implies that we are in the territory of strong evaluation here. To run away is wrong because it embodies living in an ignoble way as opposed to a life of courage. Put the other way around, to be courageous just is to overcome such temptations to cowardice.[11]

The terms employed in this example ("cowardly," "courageous") bring us to Taylor's next point, which is that strong evaluation is integrally related to employing a vocabulary of qualitative contrasts (e.g., "noble," "base," "dignified," "maudlin," etc.) It is only through such a vocabulary that strong evaluation is possible. We find further that this is to say that strong evaluation essentially involves articulating

---

11. Taylor writes, "[R]unning is to be eschewed because it is 'cowardly,' a word which carries a sense of a non-contingent conflict with honorable conduct" ("What is Human Agency?" 21).

the significance of our motivation—the desirability of their objects—in such a language.[12]

This, in turn, leads to Taylor's summary definition of strong evaluation as "a condition of articulacy" such that "to acquire a strongly evaluative language is to become more articulate about one's preferences."

The simple weigher model of deliberation, Taylor suggests, corresponds to a certain model of practical reasoning. In claiming that the evaluation of desires is a matter of calculating how best to satisfy most of them, or the strongest among them, rational choice utilitarians take desires to be raw feelings; they cannot be given more elaborate characterization because calculation requires commensurability. We ought to do whatever we want to do most—whatever satisfies our strongest desire, or concatenates the largest number of discrete desires.

Because of its role in defining the quality of motivations, how our desires are evaluated helps determine "self-interpretations" and thereby plays a role in how we conceive of the "responsibility" of the human agent. Taylor here has us imagine that he is "addicted to over-eating" and leads us to examine the personal conflict this causes him from two different perspectives. First, he may think "that someone who has so little control over his appetites that he would let his health go to pot over cream-cake is not an admirable person." That is, he interprets his situation in the strongly evaluative terms of "admirable" versus "base" and perhaps "self-indulgent." Then, Taylor asks us to imagine that he has "stepped away from the contrastive language of strong evaluation." It is now simply a question of "quantity of satisfaction": by eating too much he automatically foregoes the pleasures of being able to climb stairs, take hikes and worry less about his overall health. But shifting from one perspective to the other will change his very experience of what it is to be obese by changing his interpretation of his motivated behavior.

Taylor implies that one can see more clearly how the view of deliberation as strong evaluation differs from its rivals by considering moral

---

12. "I cannot tell you perhaps very volubly why Bach is greater than Liszt, say, but I am not totally inarticulate: I can speak of the 'depth' of Bach, for instance, a word one only understands against a corresponding use of 'shallow', which, unfortunately, applies to Liszt. In this regard I am way ahead of where I am in articulating why I now prefer that éclair to the mille feuilles; about this I can say nothing (not even that it tastes better, which I could say, for instance, in explaining my preference for éclairs over Brussels-sprouts; but even this is on the verge of inarticulacy—compare our replying above that Bach 'sounds better')" (ibid., 25).

theories that picture deliberation in terms of a "radical choice." In a certain way, such theories are indebted to strong evaluation, though they also contain a fatal misunderstanding of the nature of such evaluation. The defining feature of radical-choice existentialism is that the font of moral action is a choice of the will, which in itself "creates" the action's value. How is this theory indebted to the conception of human nature represented by strong evaluation? We said that the latter implies that the process of deliberating on a course of action is guided by interpretations of our motivations. Yet evaluating interpreted motivations can yield a conflict wherein strong value supports two incompatible courses of action. The arising of such a "dilemma"—composed of conflicting moral visions—suggests that there is nothing but the radical choice to opt for one or the other. And if this is so, then the choice itself seems to determine value.

According to Taylor, such a theory attributes an over-inflated role to choice (or, the will). For it seems to say that the choice itself somehow creates the evaluations that we understand as motivating moral actions. But if choice itself really did play this role, the gravity surrounding such determinations would quickly disseminate. For, if choices created values, the choice whether or not to go out and get an ice cream cone could be just as significant as Sartre's famous example of the young man who must decide whether to join the resistance, or stay with his ailing mother.[13]

Taylor argues that the theory of radical choice in fact turns out to be something much like weak evaluation, or the simple-weighing model of moral deliberation referred to above. For the agent implied in these accounts seems to deliberate on the basis of inarticulate preferences.[14] The anthropological picture that sees human beings as strong evaluators could never conceive of radical choice as the key to moral action, for such a view greatly oversimplifies what is involved in moral deliberation. It does not account for the "depth"[15] of human beings—

---

13. Ibid., 30.

14. "The agent of radical choice has to choose, if he chooses at all, like a simple weigher. And this mean that he cannot properly speaking be a strong evaluator. For all his putative strong evaluations issue from simple weighings" (ibid., 31).

15. Taylor claims to uses the term "depth" as a "metaphor" for getting at that dimension of human nature implied by strong evaluation, or the self's ability to articulate the significance of its desires in a vocabulary of necessary contrasts. He writes, "Strong evaluation is not just a condition of articulacy about preferences, but also about the

that is, the way in which the quality of their motivated behavior is inevitably bound up with the kind of agent they take themselves to be. A truthful account of practical deliberation must take into consideration these necessary contrasts between self-interpretations as well as the language in which they are formulated.

Taylor therefore asks us to reconsider whether the existence of dilemmas truly supports the theory of radical choice. In the Sartrean version, the appearance of incommensurable motivations in conjunction with a situation that unavoidably calls for action makes the notion of radical choice tempting. Yet Taylor's point is that such dilemmas imply that moral deliberation and choice take place within a context ("horizon") of strongly evaluated motivations. These motivations, and the course of action to which they point, are strong precisely because they make a *claim* upon the agent. They *call* a person, and this contradicts the notion of their being a product of a person's choice. It is the strength of these proposed routes (motivations) that constitute the experience of a dilemma—i.e., being morally pulled in two different and incommensurable ways at once.

But there is another way Taylor concedes that the theory of radical choice, though ultimately deceptive, points to something important about the nature of the moral self. The theory particularly strives to account for the sense of "responsibility" inherent to human action.[16] The profound reach of human responsibility, Taylor explains, is such that we sometimes make judgments about an individual's character, which is shaped by their strong evaluations.[17] When we judge someone an insensitive person—in the sense that they act over time in such a way as to

---

quality of life, the kind of beings we are or want to be . . . And this is what lies behind our ordinary use of the metaphor of depth applied to people. Someone is shallow in our view when we feel that he is insensitive, unaware, or unconcerned about issues touching the quality of his life which seem to us basic and important. He lives on the surface because he seeks to fulfill desires without being touched b the 'deeper' issues, what these desires express and sustain in the way of modes of life. . . ." (ibid., 26).

16. Ibid., 28.

17. Ibid., 38. Taylor writes, "because our insights into our own motivations and into what is important and of value are often limited by the shape of our experience, failure to understand a certain insight, or see the point of some moral advice proffered, is often taken as a judgment on the character of the person concerned. An insensitive person, or a fanatic, cannot see what he is doing to others, the kind of suffering he is inflicting on them. He cannot see, for instance, that this act is a deep affront to someone's sense of honour, or perhaps deeply undermines his sense of worth."

reveal a lack of sensitivity to the dignity of others—we imply both that the person in question is shaped by a particular set of strong evaluations and that he "ought" not to be so shaped, or that he ought to change. In other words, we imply that he is responsible for who he has become—responsible for the fundamental evaluations out of which he acts.

But in the end, Taylor concludes, the idea that we are responsible in some sense for our fundamental evaluations lends little support to radical choice. He suggests that responsibility enters into our moral deliberation precisely because we recognize that our evaluations are articulations of an inchoate grasp of its object, and as articulations they must be in some way amenable to revision.[18] Articulation contrasts with responsibility understood as (radical) choice in at least two ways. First, articulation implies that most of our deliberations are carried out in terms of other evaluations and deliberations that are already in place. It is not an a-contextual matter. Second, responsibility understood in terms of articulation implies that that the articulation articulates *something*. Deliberation is always deliberation about, or with respect to, something. In that it is a response to something, this conception of deliberation contrasts with the notion that choice itself creates value.

So we learn from Taylor's treatment that an account of human beings must make reference to the quality of their motivations. The kinds of motivations we take human beings to have, which shape the actions they perform, are internally related to the model of practical deliberation that seems to us fitting. Taylor's claim that motivations are shaped by strong evaluation implies that practical reason cannot faithfully be modeled on a simple procedure of weighing desires. And much less is it a matter of standing back and calculating possible outcomes. Furthermore, the temptation of a moral theory that posits a radical choice taking place behind and beyond all evaluative judgments can only misguide us. Our understanding of human agency must begin with desires and their evaluation. This evaluation of desires amounts to articulation of their objects in a language of qualitative contrasts that selects out certain motivations as incomparably higher for us. Because

---

18. "Because of the character of depth which we saw in the self, our evaluations are articulation of insights which are frequently partial, clouded and uncertain. But they are all the more open to challenge when we reflect that these insights are often distorted by our imperfections of character. For these two reasons evaluation is such that there is always room for re-evaluation" (ibid., 39).

of the very nature of human deliberation, then, the notion of articulation—elucidating our experience through language—ought to play a more important role in our modeling of practical reason than calculation. Put differently, practical reason, because it is based in human desire, is engaged reasoning mediated by language. It is reasoning for beings who act in terms of a world-view made possible by language.

Reason in the Human Sciences: Taylor on "Social Theory"

In the foregoing we have seen something of Taylor's account of the reasoning agent as it appeared in his discussion of emotions and motivated behavior. In turning now to his reflections on social theory we will be able to see how he relates such practical reasoning to a kind of theorizing. Here Taylor goes beyond Anscombe's marking of the distinction between reasons for action and observational knowledge or reasoning. For he shows how articulation—the activity of making what is implicit, explicit—relates the activities of practical reasoning and theoretical reasoning (at least of a certain kind). In doing so, he shows also how social theories can better grasp what they are trying to explain, i.e., human practices. Or at least he shows how they can avoid mistaking the very "object" under study. In these next two sections we begin to see how Taylor's account of practical reasoning emerges from his normative conception of human agency. We also see where argument comes into Taylor's account of practical reasoning, and what it might mean to test the validity of such argument or to speak of a "gain in reason" as the result of such argument.

In "Social Theory as Practice,"[19] Taylor states that he will try to convince his reader of the value of conceiving of social theory as a *practice*. But what does it mean to say that social theory is a practice? And why is this so important?

To begin with, Taylor suggests that we ought to examine more closely in what the *activity* of social theorizing consists. Here Taylor warns that social scientists are tempted to confound their own theorizing with that of natural science.[20] Natural scientific theory conceives

19. See also, Taylor's "Understanding and Ethnocentricity," 116–33.

20. This is the first reference in my discussion of a central theme in Taylor's work. Much of Taylor's (early) philosophical corpus is directly, or less directly, preoccupied with the theme of the relation of the human to the natural sciences. A general characterization of this theme in Taylor would note that he finds it necessary to do battle

of the object under study as *independent* of its own activity. Thus, its theoretical activity consists in creating models that would describe or mirror the object being studied. Such science seeks to find descriptions that correspond to the object, or phenomenon, under investigation.[21] Social theory, on the other hand, understands, or ought to understand, its activity as having a more intimate relation to what it studies. This is because while natural science investigates "nature," social sciences study human practices. The special nature of the object in social theory, according to Taylor, is that it is already an "interpreted" object—i.e., social practices are constituted by common understandings.[22] The reasoning (self-interpretation, articulation) we saw to be part of all human action in the previous section underlies what Taylor means by a social practice. He offers voting, or making political decisions by majority vote, as an example. When an agent within a society that has this practice votes, it has some awareness of what counts as proper and/or improper. While the norm governing the voter's behavior may not be explicitly articulated, she or he understands implicitly that her or his own decision is supposed to be determinative and that when someone else determines her or his vote (or, by extension, others' votes) this is "foul play."[23] Theories of voting, furthermore, tend to have an impact on these implicit understandings of propriety (Taylor will employ the terms "constitutive understandings" or "self-understandings" in what follows). This they do by placing the practice in a new framework of

---

with the imperialistic tendencies of the natural science model. To combat this impulse is to make a space for the distinct human sciences, which have often been in danger of encroachment. For an examination of how Taylor's understanding of the relation of natural and human sciences impacts on some of his arguments, we will consider below an article by Clifford Geertz on this issue that appears in Taylor's *festschrift*.

21. Whether natural science can do this without somehow achieving an Archimidean standpoint with respect to its own use of language is a question we will take up with Geertz.

22. "There is always a pre-theoretical understanding of what is going on among the members of a society, which is formulated in the descriptions of self and other which are involved in the institutions and practices of that society. A society is among other things a set of institutions and practices, and these cannot exist and be carried on without certain self-understandings" (Taylor, "Social Theory as Practice," 93).

23. Taylor explains that this awareness constitutes the practice as such. "If no one involved had any sense of how their behavior checked out on this dimension, then they would not be engaged in *voting*. They would have to be engaged in some other activity that involved marking papers, some game that we do not yet understand" (ibid., 93).

significance. For instance, Marxism attempts to show the voting agent that her belief that she is participating in a process whereby a majority of individuals freely determines the course of policy is in fact mistaken. For the causal matrix that underlies capitalist democracies insures that the voter will only have those choices that insure the continuance of profitability.[24] When its false consciousness is unveiled by the Marxist theory, the voter may determine that revolution is a more appropriate way to exercise political freedom then holding its nose and choosing the lesser of evils at the polls. Thus, theorizing here can be said to modify the object it seeks to interpret, and thus instigate change in the practice itself.[25]

Understanding in natural science is also often manifest in practice—that is, in a new way of coping with the natural phenomenon it helps us understand. Yet here the object under consideration—the laws governing the transference of heat, for example—is not believed to be affected by our understanding of it. To theorize here is to make a model that corresponds to an object (e.g., a matrix of physical causes and effects) that stands independent from the theory itself. When such a theory is used to alter a practice this is understood as an "application" of the theory.[26] This means, Taylor further points out, that employing the natural scientific model in the study of social practices—i.e., by taking the activity of study to be merely instrumentally related to practice or, "the object"—will lead to misidentification of the object to be understood itself. As Taylor puts it, it is a case where the *explanantia*, or theory, risks overrunning the *explananda*.[27]

---

24. Ibid., 95.

25. "[Political theories] can undermine, strengthen or shape the practice that they bear on. And that is because (a) they are theories about practices, which (b) are partly constituted by certain self-understandings. To the extent that (c) theories transform this self-understanding, they undercut, bolster or transform the constitutive feature of practices" (ibid., 101).

26. "Theory relates to practice in an obvious way. We apply our knowledge of the underlying mechanisms in order to manipulate more effectively the features of our environment" (ibid., 92). Elaborating on this relationship later in the same essay, Taylor writes: "We can say that while natural science theory also transforms practice, the practice it transforms is not what the theory is about. It is in this sense external to the theory. We think of it as an 'application' of the theory. But in politics, the practice is the object of the theory. Theory in this domain transforms its own object" (ibid., 101).

27. Taylor, "Understanding and Ethnocentricity," 118–19.

Our most primitive engagement in social theory, Taylor goes on, "arises when we try to formulate explicitly what we are doing, describe the activity central to a practice, and articulate norms which are central to it."[28] To theorize in this sense involves making explicit the norms implied in our ordinary behavior. Taylor anticipates the objection that if this is so, social theory fails to really produce a better understanding of what is actually going on. And he is quick to add, the fact that such theorizing is always grounded in the self-understandings of agents does not mean anything goes. There is a form of validation particular to social theories. A theory is validated by making the practice it interprets more effective.

The motive for engaging in social theory is in fact often "the sense that our implicit understanding is in some way crucially inadequate or even wrong." When two theories compete for our assent regarding a certain practice, they frequently make competing claims about the point of the practice. To return to the example of voting, what Taylor calls "atomistic" theories view this practice as a mechanism whereby the majority of citizens' desires are satisfied by public policies. The "republican" tradition, by contrast, imagines voting as a practice that at once both forms and embodies a "public spirit" signifying a general will. In offering competing interpretations of a practice, two social theories offer rival accounts of the ends for which it is meant, and thus cannot but impact the self-understandings of the practitioners. Here, we may say, their common object concerns what free participation in government amounts to and thus how best to realize our desire for it.

This leads naturally to the notion that the validation of social theories—their test as the best account of the practice they are meant to describe—takes a dialogical form. Because we cannot turn to some uncontroversial basic description in order to arbitrate disagreement, we turn to one another and begin by drawing out formally our perhaps hazy judgments. Our view regarding a particular practice can then be tested to see if it is coherent, and if not whether the standpoint of the interlocutor can more successfully hold together what our position cannot. If it can, then the move from our position to theirs can be considered a gain in reason. And of course more directly, a social theory can be tested by checking in with how we feel after we have adopted it.

---

28. Taylor, "Social Theory as Practice," 93.

Cross-cultural understanding provides a paradigmatic example of the activity of social theory. In "Understanding and Ethnocentricity," Taylor recommends picturing cross-cultural interpretation as using a language of "perspicuous contrast" in order to "formulate both their way of life and ours as alternative possibilities in relation to some human constants at work in both."[29] Taylor turns here to how we might understand the "magical" practices of primitive societies, such as dances for producing rainfall, as it is taken up in Peter Winch's "Understanding a Primitive Society."[30] There, Winch takes umbrage with studies that configure primitive practices of this sort as failed efforts at what we call "technology." In contrast, he proposes they be understood on a separate model as "symbolic" practices whose function is to integrate collective meanings, and recommends that social theorists take the stance that foreign practices cannot be judged in our terms (i.e., the "incorrigibility thesis"). Taylor argues that the proto-technology versus symbolic-expressive dichotomy itself indicates ethnocentricity, for the separation of scientific understanding and spiritual concern is characteristic of the culture of the modern West. What is needed is a language that places the primitive society's understanding of the relation of expressive and technological functions in juxtaposition to that of the modern West. "Now," Taylor writes, "identifying these two possibilities—respectively, the fusion and the segregation of the cognitive or manipulative on one hand, and the symbolic or integrative on the other—amounts to finding a language of perspicuous contrast. It is a language that enables us to give an account of the procedures of both societies in terms of the same cluster of possibilities."[31]

Here, furthermore, attempting social theory by adopting the natural science model can have particularly sinister consequences. For if we believe that we are comparing the culture in question to a truly independent and neutral theoretical model, we are likely to remain unaware of

---

29. Taylor, "Understanding and Ethnocentricity," 125.

30. Winch, "Understanding a Primitive Society," 307–24.

31. Taylor, "Understanding and Ethnocentricity," 128–29. One might, however, be concerned here that Taylor is betraying his own principles. In his refutation of naturalism, Taylor has insisted that we conceive of the self in relation to the good and always situated within a horizon of strongly valued ends. But, one may ask, who is the self that undertakes social theory of this kind? In his talk of a language of "perspicuous contrast," it seems that the subject has migrated again to the periphery of all moral frameworks.

our imperialistic motives for giving an unfavorable evaluation of the foreign culture at issue. So we end up with a "colonialist" version of the case where the *explanantia* mistakes, and thus overruns, the *explananda*.³²

Because the phenomena we are talking about are practices, and practices are constituted by self-understandings, an important implication of cross-cultural theorizing is that it puts our own understandings in play and at risk of change. This reinforces the point that Taylor's account of practical reasoning, at both the implicit and theoretical levels, is tied to the theme of agency (anthropology).

Taylor concludes that the validation of a social theory is to be judged *in practice*—that is, in the practice as modified by the theory. This is as true of theorizing that compares competing conceptions of the significance of a practice or places it within an unseen causal matrix as it is of an individual's self-clarification of why they carry out certain actions. Social theories that offer competing accounts of a practice, Taylor suggests, can be seen as offering "rival maps of the terrain" upon which we carry our actions out. "The proof of a map," he continues, "is how well you can get around using it." So the question we must ask of ourselves is whether our practice has become more effective, or a stumbling block surmounted, through the application of the theory. If our practice as modified by the theory is "freer of the stumbling, self-defeating character which previously afflicted it," the theory has succeeded.³³

Taylor goes on here to show why "validating a theory in its self-defining use" comes before "establishing it as explanation/description." For example, he suggests, the debate over the merits of Marxism as a social theory often turns on the question of whether it has been adequately

---

32. "A good example is the theory of development dominant until recently in American political science. This was based on the notion that certain functions were being performed by all political systems, only in different ways by different structures. But these functions, for example interest aggregation and articulation, are only clearly identifiable in advanced industrial society, where the political process is played out through the articulation of individual and group interests. This identification of functions pre-supposes a degree of individuation which is not present everywhere. The importance of understanding another people's language of self-understanding is precisely that it can protect us against this kind of ethnocentric projection" (ibid., 126).

33. Taylor, "Social Theory as Practice," 111. "Put tersely, our social theories can be validated, because they can be tested in practice. If theory can transform practice, then it can be tested in the quality of practice it informs. What makes a theory right is that it brings practice out in the clear; that its adoption makes possible what is in some sense a more effective practice" (ibid., 104).

tested in experience. Opponents will claim that the Soviet Republic was the crucial test, proving the theory to be a failure. Proponents, claiming that the conditions for its historical embodiment have not yet come to pass, describe the Soviet experiment as a "grotesque caricature of socialism."[34]

In any case, we can now make sense of Taylor's proposal to view social theory *as practice*. Rather than striving for the correspondence between a hypothetical model and an inert object, social theorizing consists in attempting to make explicit the inchoate, common-sense understandings encoded in social practices. Their validation consists in asking whether they bring greater "clairvoyance" to these practices from the internal point of view. If the answer is yes, the transformation the theory instigates within the practices can be counted retrospectively as a gain in reason.

We can further see how Taylor's account of social theory as a distinctively human science both builds upon and furthers the construction of the accounts of human agency and practical reason traced in the previous sections of this chapter. Those accounts posited an insoluble connection of human agency to language understood as expressive, and in particular the language in which agents are oriented toward the higher good. We can now appreciate that practical reason is socially embodied and dialogical as we seek through theory to help one another overcome problems inherent in our practices and self-understandings.

As I mentioned earlier, exploring the distinctive character of the human sciences also forms part of Taylor's effort to push back naturalist encroachment to the extent that space is made available for the questions Taylor wants to raise—questions about the good. It will be well at this point, therefore, to consider briefly whether Taylor's fight on this front may have backfired. Clifford Geertz has sought to make problematic the initial dualism Taylor posits between natural science and human science. He argues that the reductive ontology of a "neutral universe" Taylor pictures does not, or does no longer, underwrite sci-

---

34. Taylor continues, "How do you decide this kind of question? Presumably the answer turns on how you interpret the historical record. But this is relevant precisely as a record of *stumbling or clairvoyant* practice. The conservative claim is just that the failure of previous attempts amounts to a case of the self-defeat that attends a practice informed by a wrong theory. The radical answer will always be that the failure springs from other sources, external factors, lack of propitious economic, or educational, or military conditions and so on" (ibid., 112).

entific endeavor. He therefore claims that this dualism in fact leads to a distorted view of natural science, and, perhaps more surprisingly, of human science as well.[35]

Removing the frame of dualism allows us to see that "natural science" names not a single form of inquiry, but a great variety of theoretical activities, each operating with its particular presuppositions and dogmatic starting points. This vision of scientific activity as taking place in diverse "communities" of investigation may already suggest understanding science as a practice rather than as a supreme technique applied relentlessly to various, independent subject matters. If the activity of natural scientific inquiry is made possible by belonging to a particular scientific community, accepting its self-understanding, and adopting its theoretical practices, then it seems to follow that scientific knowledge itself is constituted by particular, communal self-understandings. This would seem to place natural scientific theory on a par with social scientific theory in that validation in each would be inescapably caught up with the particular practices of the community of inquirers.

Geertz further helps us imagine an alternative model of reasoning in (and between) communities—that is, practical reasoning—that does not propose rival ontologies. Interestingly, Geertz concludes that the effect of Taylor's sharp line between human and natural sciences is to make it more difficult to see the way all examples of reasoning depend upon the authority and standards of communities, whether, he adds, the community be of Orthodox Jews or chemists.

The Ethics of Inarticulacy

We have been reviewing Taylor's basic arguments concerning what it means to be human and in what does a "human science" consist. The real importance of this work is that it lays the groundwork for Taylor's engagement with the "big" problems of meaning and of moral direction in modern Western societies. In a way, Taylor's work can be seen as a reply to what Anscombe and Murdoch have said about modern

---

35. Geertz writes, "Taylor's resistance to the intrusion of 'the natural science model' into the human sciences seems in fact to accept his opponents' view that there is such a model, unitary, well defined and historically immobile, governing contemporary enquiries into things and materialities in the first place; the problem is, merely, to confine its proper sphere, stars, rocks, kidneys and wavicles, and keep it well away from matters where 'mattering' matters" (Tully, *Philosophy in an Age of Pluralism*, 95).

moral philosophy—namely, that such theories do not give us direction or understanding for our lives because they do not address the question of human moral meaning head on. Further, the topic of practical reasoning has much to do with Taylor's sense of what kind of activity is needed if we are to surmount our current impasse. In the remainder of this chapter, therefore, I will treat, 1) the character of the modern crisis as reflected in moral debate and contemporary moral theories, which are symptoms of the problem; 2) the deeper problem which Taylor refers to as "the conflicts of modernity"; and 3) how practical reason should be conceived and how it can help in this crisis.

I start here with 1) the character of the modern problem as reflected in its moral debates. Taylor speaks of an important facet of the scene of contemporary moral debate, as well as the philosophical one, using the phrase the "ethics of inarticulacy." By this phrase he wishes to call attention to the fact that the debate itself is a shallow one, in the sense that it skates along the surface of a pond of meaning whose depths it ignores. There is much that is relevant to the debate that waits just below the surface, if only we would probe. The key then is to improve the character of these debates themselves, and the way to enrich them is precisely by becoming more articulate.

One of the characteristics of these debates is that they pit two inflexible points of view against one another. Taylor suggests as an example the question of the value of "being true to oneself" in the way many moderns express what is most important to them in life.[36] For him this is the debate over "authenticity" as a general stance, or orientation, of the self, or the modern human agent, in moral matters. What strikes him about this debate as he sees it being carried on is how divisive it is, with one side able to see no good in this developments (the "knockers") and the other unwilling to criticize anything in it (the "boosters"). These terms, "boosters" and "knockers," themselves suggest that the two positions are rooted in gut reactions or affective responses to the subject in question.[37] What troubles Taylor about this kind of debate is that it motivates neither side to examine more carefully what they are debating about. The object itself is taken for granted and remains uninterpreted. It is not difficult to point out how each side is deficient. The knockers have a point in suggesting that some manifestations of authenticity in

36. Taylor, *Ethics of Authenticity*, 15.
37. Ibid., 72.

contemporary life reflect a shallowness of moral outlook. But in their blanket condemnation of authenticity as mere egoism they fail to consider that authenticity represents a legitimate vision of the good with a complicated history. Not all versions of an ethic of authenticity can be captured by the net of "mere egoism." For their part, in un-reflexively rooting for authenticity in all its forms, the boosters do not help to bring to view the more rich conceptions of authenticity that might give the knockers pause. Rather than help us understand better what is at stake, the debate itself causes the moral stance of authenticity to recede further behind a cloud of confusion. So, such debates merely further our confusion about moral matters because they fail to engage us in the work of interpreting or articulating the ideals that inspire and shape us.

Therefore we see that inarticulacy produces perspectives that dig in their heals and denies us any deeper insight into what is at stake in the debate. It further prejudices us against the very viability of practical reasoning, or reasoning about the worth and priority of moral ideals in our lives, as we shall examine a little further on. But what are the roots of inarticulacy? Taylor explores two sources of our hesitancy to become articulate, and thus of the shallow nature of our debates about moral ideals.

The first is the influence of a model of explanation in relation to the real (ontology) in moral philosophy. The model in question rejects a priori those modes of explanation that presume the subject of experience. We saw how this functions earlier. These models of explanation suppose that the viewpoint from which an object is properly understood is one that prescinds from any human perspective. It is "the view from nowhere" that counts. Correspondingly, those objects, e.g., values, which would not be what they are apart from human beings who hold (or reject) them are said to be shadowy, unreal, or "queer." If we have been encouraged to believe that "the good" does not exist, it is no great surprise that we have ceased to talk about it.

On the basis of this model, theorists have tried in at least three different ways to "explain" what we mean when we use the vocabulary of the good. "The first . . . tries to assimilate our moral reactions to visceral ones."[38] This allows us to adopt a "naturalistic" approach to morality. "The second represents our notions of the good as opinions

---

38. Taylor, *Sources of the Self*, 56.

on an issue which is ultimately optional . . ." In other words, moral ideals are a kind of adornment on human life as such, and the latter can go on just fine without such ideals. "The third is the thesis that value terms have descriptive equivalents."

Taylor's refutation of each and all of these is anthropological, and might also be called phenomenological. He is challenging the whole picture of human agency they assume. He asks what it would be like to try and live one's life while holding any one of these theories about morality. Part of his point here is to note that adopting the terms of any one of these theories would require radically altering the understanding that accompanies our daily lives now. For example, alternative three would require getting rid of virtue terms like "courage" in our activity of describing and deliberating about what to do. In place of the virtue, it would substitute some sort of "neutral" description of the context where fear confronts us. Perhaps, as we said earlier, we could use terms referring to the probability of bodily harm, or emotional discomfort. But think of how awkward this would be? How could we in the moment capture all of the physical, social, and imaginative elements that go into the word courage without relying not only on it, but the range of virtue terms which help establish its meaning? Taylor concludes that we could not, and therefore the proposal of this "empirical" theory does not in fact explain courage at all, but something else.

But this awkwardness, and ultimate failure, of employing such a theory in our lives of deliberation counts decisively against it. For a crucial aim of constructing moral theories is to make our lives of action more clairvoyant by shedding light on them. Taylor makes this point by showing that the languages by which we explain human morality and the language with which humans carry on their moral lives—interpret, deliberate, comprehend their behaviors—are continuous with one another, and not separated by an impassable gap. In the life of action, in other words, the language with which we deliberate and comprehend carries over into the language in which we reflect on the meaning of our lives. Placing an artificial boundary between these languages—of theory and practice—may seem attractive from the point of view of a desire to have mastery of ourselves. However, such a separation tempts us to believe that a privileged theoretical terminology has the authority to trump the terms in which we actually live out our lives. Taylor points out to us the perversity in this, arguing that no theory, just because it conforms to a certain model of what theories should look like, has the right to trump the terms of our self-understanding. Explanations of any phenomenon vindicate themselves by making the best sense of those phenomena. The criterion for theories of morality then must not be conformity to a particular model of theories but whether they offer the best account of the moral life. Such a standard places prima facie trust in the languages in which we actually live and reflect upon our moral lives. Any terms that make a contribution to this "best account" ought to be permissible.

This conclusion has further implications for what ought to be considered part of "the real." The objects that correspond to those terms with which we are able to give the best account of our moral lives, and correspondingly lacking reference to which our explanations become less good, count as real. "What is real," Taylor writes, "is what you have to deal with, what won't go away just because it doesn't fit with your prejudices. By this token, what you can't help have recourse to in life is real, or as near to reality as you can grasp at the present."[39] Thus, the "best account" approach to explanation comes along with a different ontology.

One cause of the suppression of becoming articulate about the good, then, is the ontology of naturalism. But in addition to naturalism, there are moral theories that contribute to this suppression. Moral theories contribute to our inarticulate condition when they try to repress, or simply avoid, all talk of "the good." One group of theories achieves this by making a hard and fast distinction between "the good" and "the right." They claim that "the right" refers to "duties" or what is actually required of us in the way of action. "The good" then has to do either with what motivates an individual to act rightly, or with the explanation of behaviors that go above and beyond what morality requires. It is sometimes noted that one can achieve societal agreement on "the right" while allowing for diverse conceptions of "the good."

One motivation Taylor finds behind such moral theories is the very naturalist outlook we have just reviewed. Because the good appears "queer" from a certain epistemological and ontological standpoint, it is best to concentrate upon actions and principles of actions, as though the latter could be identified without reference to the good. But, as Taylor notes, the dominance of moral theories of dutiful action

---

39. Ibid., 59.

also has *moral* motives. In the case of one modern theory, utilitarianism, that motive is the sense that special value attaches to "ordinary life," or the pleasures and pains of daily living. Utilitarianism, to describe it crudely, is the theory of morality that claims human actions are, or ought to be, guided by principles whose aim is to produce lives that maximize our ordinary pleasures while minimizing our ordinary pains. Historically, Taylor argues, the sense of the value of ordinary life results from a "reform," wherein an older way of seeing things according to which "higher callings" like monastic life were seen as better or more special than the life of a craftsman was rejected and inverted.[40] The affirmation of ordinary life, which drives utilitarianism, has itself become a moral ideal toward which we aspire. It is what Taylor calls a "hypergood," or a good whose superiority gives it authority to prioritize the lesser goods we acknowledge.

Utilitarianism illustrates well the basic problem theories of the right run into. Namely, the right and the good cannot be neatly separated. The hard and fast separation results in confusion for those who propound the theory. It leads them to be unable to recognize the hypergood that underlies the arising of the theory in the first place. This means they are at a loss when it comes to saying why anyone should adopt the utility principle(s) in the first place. Moreover, Taylor would add, since our very access to hypergoods is routed through our articulations of them, consistent utilitarians will tend to lose touch with the grounds of their moral motivation. A parallel problem plagues Kantian-inspired theories of the right that emphasize autonomy. Their emphasis on the principles of right action causes them to lose touch with the hypergood of moral freedom that provides the *raison d'être* of these theories.

The inability of proponents of action-based theories of morality to come to grips with this source of inconsistency is facilitated by what Taylor refers to as a "procedural" conception of practical reason. When pressed to give an answer to the question of why one ought to embrace their account of morality, proponents of the theories of dutiful action have responded with a picture of practical reason that highlights a method or series of steps to be taken. What Taylor means by a procedural conception of practical reason is that to choose an action rationally is simply to follow a certain procedure leading to a conclusion. In utilitarian thought, as we saw in chapter 1, this procedure is represented

---

40. Ibid., 213–18.

as standing back and calculating the balance of harms and benefits, whereas in deontology it is embodied in the categorical imperative. By contrast, a "substantive" account of practical reason is one in which the character of the reasoner and the good she aspires to remain relevant to our assessment of why, or the rationality, of our moral life. I will take up Taylor's proposal with regard to practical reason after bringing into better focus the modern problem as he sees it.

The Conflicts of Modernity

The purpose of Taylor's attack on the ethics of inarticulacy and the naturalist assumptions that buttress it is not simply or even primarily to undo the damage has been wrought by the predominance of a set of ontological assumptions beholden to the supposed self-understanding of natural science by clarifying the boundaries between one academic discipline and another (i.e., human sciences and natural sciences). By helping us understand what is at stake in the largely uncomprehending debates that have taken over our cultural and religious institutions, Taylor hopes to clear off the pathway to a new common ground in the Western identity.

Taylor understands the debates between the boosters and knockers of authenticity to be symptomatic of a deeper moral crisis. The "crisis of modernity" as he calls it in *Sources of the Self* is an identity crisis, by which he means a crisis of meaning. Because for Taylor identity and meaning are rooted in the basic orientation of human beings toward and within a horizon of strongly valued goods, an identity crisis for him means that we are morally adrift, or soon to be so.

This also explains why articulation is the first step and is at the heart of Taylor's project. The primary access of human beings to their map of the good is through expression or articulation, whether this be in words or some other expressive form. Our inarticulacy prevents us both from seeing what is at stake in our major cultural debates about identity and prevents us from doing the work that might carry us beyond the current crisis, into a new, "reconciled" relationship to what is ultimately important. We have been content to affirm a basic agreement about "life goods" such as equality and the elimination of suffering, but our inarticulacy prevents us from seeing that our very motivation to act in pursuit of these depends upon being in touch with their sources.

So, in addition to being a crisis of meaning, the crisis of modernity is a practical crisis as well. The two cannot be separated on Taylor's account.

At this point we need to ask what the crisis of the modern identity is. The answer to this question presupposes that we have an idea of what makes the modern identity unique. The place to begin to understand the modern identity is in Taylor's conception of authenticity, mentioned already. Authenticity serves as a kind of all-purpose general term for the moral source of modern Western identity, or the "self." It connotes that a basic concern of modern persons is that their life be self-determined, such that the shape of that life displays that what matters most to him or her and is at the same time an expression of his or her uniqueness. Authenticity implies that freedom, understood in a particular way, is an important orienting ideal for modern persons. But it is also true, as Taylor's genealogical study of the modern identity makes plain, that the modern identity and its ideal of authenticity encapsulates an array of distinct but related ideals. Three such ideals are the affirmation of ordinary life, disengaged reason, and romantic self-expression.

These ideals help us see what authenticity requires in terms of our moral behaviors in the world. The importance placed on ordinary life explains our commitment to eliminate suffering for all human beings, which becomes an ethic of benevolence toward human beings as such, regardless of class status or geographical location. Movements like Medecins Sans Frontieres give concrete embodiment to this ethic. Disengaged reason often works in tandem with ordinary life insofar as modern leaps forward in terms of instrumental control over nature and the human body are seen as directed toward the goal of alleviating ordinary suffering.

Crucial to Taylor's narrative of the modern identity are the transitions it traces in our relations to these sources. The story revolves around our history and in particular the passing on of two conceptions of agency and language, one rooted in the naturalist metaphysic and emphasizing control of self and world and the other in the romantic response to naturalism and emphasizing a natural continuity, or participation, between world and self.[41] Both of these were at one time

---

41. It is also important to see that, for Taylor, the moral sources of these modern conceptions of agency arise from a rupture with the ancient conception of agency and the good. He describes this by saying that the good is "internalized" in the modern

motivated by what seemed to us a moral gain. In particular, naturalism has its moral roots in a discovery of the value of "ordinary life," including the absence of suffering, family intimacy and benevolence. All this is against a hierarchical view of the "chain of being," which modern Europeans threw off. Romantic expressivism is rooted in the value of being connected to order that transcends "me," the individual. Taylor's argument is that the ascendancy of naturalism has caused us to be unable to access the framework of the good that empowers us to pursue the good as "universal benevolence" understood in terms of the value of ordinary life. The lack of connection between the commitment to benevolence and some sense of a larger order into which we fit is the modern crisis. Practical reason is meant to bring to the fore what is of value in both facets of the modern identity so as to facilitate our becoming able to envision and articulate a new horizon of the good. In so doing, it will enable us to place the agent back into a "home" of situated agency and make her able to go on, perhaps better than ever before.

In his explication in the final chapter of *Sources of the Self*, Taylor names three basic tensions in this modern identity. First, while moderns can be said to be in broad agreement on what morality requires of us—namely, universal benevolence—we hold to diverse conceptions of the moral sources that provide sense-making background for them. There is an ambivalence as to what sources empower us to meet our own moral standards. Second, there is a tension over instrumental reason and its place in our lives. At root, we are on the one hand inspired by the image of humanity as disengaged reason, and on the other by romantic protest that instrumentalism's ascendancy has robbed us of something essential to humanity, namely our interconnectedness with nature. Third, we suspect a lack of fitness between our moral sources and our moral standards. This breach is in part created by the very demandingness of morality as universal benevolence, which itself would seem to threaten our own fulfillment.

These three tensions are indeed related, and perhaps number two best illustrates what concerns Taylor and consequently motivates him to undertake the kind of study he undertakes in *Sources of the Self*. Taylor asks the interpretive question of what the conflict over instrumentalism between the proponents of disengaged reason, and of

---

way of seeing it, and that this change infuses agency with a new sense of, or emphasis on, "freedom."

romantic self-expression looks like from the standpoint of the picture of the modern moral identity, the "self," composed of the hypergoods of affirming ordinary life, disengaged reason and the value of self-expression. His hope is that the picture of ourselves he has created will at least give us a clear grasp of the tensions within us.

Still, Taylor doesn't pretend to be neutral in the conflict over instrumentalism (2). He rather takes the side of romantic self-expression in its ongoing skirmish with disengaged reason. "The attack has been on two levels: that the disengaged, instrumental mode empties life of meaning, and that it threatens public freedom, that is, the institutions and practices of self-government." The experiential and civil come as a package insofar as "an instrumental society, one in which, say, a utilitarian value outlook is entrenched in the institutions of a commercial, capitalist, and finally a bureaucratic mode of existence, tends to empty life of its richness, depth, or meaning." In a society based on individual consumption and bureaucratic efficiency we learn to see others and ourselves as merely statistics that have needs to be met. There is nothing transcendent to command our allegiance and nothing worth dying for.

Yet when the proponents of disengaged reason have been called upon to answer these charges, they have responded by simply calling them illusions.[42] They claim that the complaint that a disenchanted world is bereft of meaning reflects a lack of courage to face the world "as it really is." They may admit that a real ecological crisis has been created by our practice of exploiting the earth to meet our needs and our wishes, but to fix this we need deeper forays into technological manipulation rather than nostalgia for an outmoded way of life.

Taylor's dissatisfaction with such a rejoinder focuses not merely, or even primarily, on its adequacy as a practical response. He focuses instead on the mentality that governs it, for this mentality plagues all sides and cripples the debate itself. It is manifest in an unwillingness to acknowledge a real dilemma in the modern predicament. It is determined to deny a real, substantive good animating one's opponent's stance. The rightness of one's stance requires the absolute wrongness of that of one's opponent. The right path forward is clear and unambiguous.

---

42. He writes, "The protagonists of disengaged reason are often totally dismissive of these complaints. The alleged experiential consequences are illusory. Those who complain lack the courage to face the world as it is, and hanker after the comforting illusions of yesteryear. The supposed loss of meaning reflects merely the projection of some confused emotions onto reality" (Taylor, *Sources of the Self*, 504).

This habit is present not only in the disengaged camp but their antagonists fall prey to it as well. Taylor sees a whole line of thought descending from Nietzsche and Heidegger that takes the noble cause of reconnecting the disengaged subject to a natural and social web too far. Witness how the subject in Heidegger can sometimes be so secondary to the call of being as to disappear, or how Foucault's rigorous analyses of the totalizing power systems of contemporary societies fail to own how they are inspired by the ideals of freedom and even autonomy.

Taylor's real point here is that goods that conflict with one another do not thereby refute each other. When we feel that maintaining our position requires simply denying that our opponent has in view a genuine good we are assuming value must be black or white. If two goods are contingently incommensurable, such that achieving one requires sacrificing the other here and now, then the one to be sacrificed must not be a real good after all. Against this, Taylor argues that we read such conflict differently. The fact that goods come into conflict in our lives suggests not that one of the "goods" is unreal and its proponent suffering from an illusion, but that the goods that move us are plural and in the moral life we sometimes come across genuine dilemmas. Taylor can therefore write that "the trouble with most of the views that I consider inadequate, and that I want to define mine in contrast to here, is that their sympathies are too narrow."[43]

The second zone of tension in the modern identity, revealed by Taylor's historical account of it, is intimately connected to the third and the first. The third raises the question of whether the moral sources or constitutive goods of the modern identity are adequate to the moral standards it acknowledges. It asks, "Does the ideal of instrumental reason (disengaged reason) or that of inner nature expressed through the self constitute a sufficient motivation to practice benevolence toward all humanity?"

The original theistic source of benevolence grounded our obligations toward others in their worth as creatures "made in God's image." It provided a positive affirmation of their worth. It's motivation was something akin to, and perhaps even a form of participation in, the original "seeing good" of God's affirmation of his creatures in Genesis 1. Taylor suggests that when the demand for universal benevolence is experienced negatively as a duty that falls upon me, the individual, it

---

43. Taylor, *Sources of the Self*, 502.

tends to breed contempt both toward myself and the ones I am duty bound to help. Gradually the norm of benevolence is transformed into a spiteful pity toward the other, saying in effect "you are contemptible to me . . . but I guess I must help you." In another version, the evil or inadequacy I find in my own thoughts is projected outward so that whole groups of people are seen as simply "beyond helping."[44]

Nietzsche's life shows how this issue of the inadequacy of our sources can become an argument for complete rejection of the morality of universal benevolence. In light of the self-stultifying guilt such morality imposes on the person, the path to a new self-affirmation must travel over the grave of a slain morality and of the god of such a morality. "Is this our predicament?" Taylor wonders. Must we sacrifice the morality of benevolence in order to regain a sense of meaning? Or, he asks, is there a way to articulate sources that affirm the worth of humanity in the wake of theism's collapse? With this question we can see that Taylor's inquiry into the second and third zones have always been in the orbit of the first zone, the relation of our sources to our moral standards.

Underlying all this is our history of relations to the goods that underlie authenticity and its transitions.

Practical Reason

Having focused the big problem that I claim must be practical reason's challenge in Taylor, we may now return to practical reason and concentrate on Taylor's conception of it. If it is to help with our modern crisis, we may suppose that it includes the articulation of those sources or hypergoods that provide the necessary background or home for our ability to exist as human agents. It also includes the kind of narrative-making Taylor performed in order to describe the modern crisis, a crisis which itself names a point (the present) in an ongoing story of our transitions between moral sources. Seeing that that story has brought us to a place of conflict in which plural sources vie with one another,

---

44. He interrogates the modern notion of ordinary life, and its development in terms of inner nature, in the same way, asking whether a conception of the worth of human beings "that derives its affirmation [of human being] through rejecting an alleged negation"—i.e., religion's supposed depreciation of nature—is "fundamentally parasitic." He wonders, that is, whether such a source can survive the absence of its enemy (ibid., 517).

we are led to ask, "How are we to go on?" Or perhaps, since our lives as agents are what's in play here, we might better ask, "Who are we to become?" In one sense, this perhaps goes beyond Taylor's scope in *Sources of the Self*, which he claims is to interpret the modern identity. He has sought, that is, simply to help us get a clearer grasp of what we are. We did also see, however, that the clearer interpretation of the self his historical study intended to provide is meant to improve the debate between those who celebrate the modern identity and those who knock it. It is meant, in other words, to clarify what is at issue between them, and perhaps what they must accept as the common background of the debate if they are honest with themselves. For the proper interpretation of this identity, we may say, both makes possible the ongoing debate and puts it on firmer, more productive ground. As we saw earlier, the prevalent inarticulacy prevents both the boosters and the knockers from even knowing what it is they are arguing about, and in that sense articulation makes the debate possible. Further, the debate over the modern identity that he hopes will now proceed more clairvoyantly depends on the notion that the goods that serve us as sources can be argued over in reason, or are the province of practical reason.

What then is practical reason on Taylor's account? He offers his fullest description in an essay, "Explanation and Practical Reason."[45] Taylor begins the essay claiming that an inadequate conception of practical reason leads to skepticism about what it can accomplish. Because the range of practical reason covers the area of voluntary action, moral skepticism is quick to follow. The latter is manifest in such theories as "subjectivism" (or "emotivism" as Macintyre pejoratively put it)—i.e., the belief that moral values are the product of the subject's projection of their internal impressions onto objective reality and nothing more— and in "relativism"—the theory that states because different cultures appear to have incommensurable moralities, and because there is no way to arbitrate between their sometimes radically conflicting moral beliefs, truth in morals does not exist. To rebut such theories, which he finds exaggerated, Taylor claims he must first restore confidence in practical reason by constructing a more acceptable picture of what such reasoning entails.

Taylor argues that our conception of practical reason has been diminished by the hegemony of a certain epistemological model, which

45. Taylor, "Explanation and Practical Reason," 34–60.

he calls "apodictic." According to the apodictic model, reasoned argument unfolds through proving to a competitor that her basic premises are not true—that is, they do not correspond to the facts they are meant to represent. Commenting on Karl Popper, Taylor points to the image of argument as a "championship." Rival theories "play off" against one another according to external criteria. If theory X scores two goals and theory Y scores one goal, X clearly wins. Two "absolute" judgments form the basis of proving one theory superior to another.[46] (In contrast, Taylor's alternatives will stress judgments that compare the theories to one another.) Such reasoning supposes, of course, that the rival positions agree on what counts as criteria for arbitrating between them—the "facts" in question are out of dispute. But this is exactly what our most trenchant moral debates seem to lack; how does one prove to someone who believes that a fetus is clearly not a human being that in fact it is? Even more, the apodictic model presupposes that the positions being compared are fully explicit—there is no doubt as to their interpretation. Therefore, in establishing his own account of practical reasoning—an account whose aim is to "extend the range of rational debate"—Taylor questions a) whether practical reasoning always presupposes criteria that rivals agree upon; and b) whether the proponents of a theory ought to be assumed fully aware of all its implications.

In fact, his questioning of b) leads to a). Because our beliefs are never fully explicit, it becomes possible to look for commonalities that don't on the surface seem to be there. For example, imagine that one is confronted with someone who seems to completely eschew one of our basic moral beliefs (e.g., a Nazi).[47] This person seems to reject the prohibition against the killing of conspecifics. How can one hope to persuade such a person, or even reason with him? His fundamental moral premise makes him so different from, and so much at odds with, our way of thinking that it is difficult to imagine what means we could use to persuade him. This example is used by Taylor to draw attention to the unreasonable demands of apodictic models of moral argument. For such imply that showing the Nazi wrong would require pointing to facts that neither he nor we could deny. But this common ground seems to be precisely what is lacking here. If such models exhaust our

---

46. Ibid., 43.
47. Ibid., 35–36.

resources for argumentation, morality itself seems finally "relative" or the product of subjective projection.

But, Taylor asks, is this really the predicament in which we find ourselves regarding moral debate? In fact, he suggests, we can also turn to the Nazi's own set of moral beliefs, assuming that he shares "at least some of the fundamental dispositions toward good and right which guide me." We then turn to face our interlocutor on the assumption that he does not actually reject the prohibition against killing conspecifics. Rather, we hypothesize, he is confused about what that belief entails regarding the treatment of Jewish human beings. Practical argument takes the form of helping him to clear up the confusions and inconsistencies that sustain his incoherent moral beliefs (e.g., that killing persons is murder, and that he should endeavor to help exterminate the Jews), or in this case cutting through the "special pleas" such ideologues use to support their exception to a widely recognized rule. This turning directly toward the interlocutor is the essence of the sort of practical argument Taylor dubs *ad hominem*.

At this point in his account, Taylor takes a now familiar detour to explain why the *ad hominem* argument has such a rough path to tread. *In nuce*, it is that our epistemological and ontological assumptions are deeply shaped by naturalism, which privileges a world unsullied by the peculiarly human *ad hominem*.[48]

Because skepticism about rational argumentation in morals is tied tightly to the prevalence of the apodictic model, and because this model is underwritten by a naturalist ontology, combating it requires uncovering alternative models of practical argument and alternate ontologies. Taylor's introduction of *ad hominem* kinds of practical reasoning, all of which focus upon the positions actually espoused by the

48. Elsewhere, Taylor contrasts "procedural" versus "substantive" accounts of practical reason. (See *Sources of the Self*, 87ff.). Procedural accounts emphasize the procedure according to which reasoning is carried out rather than the end toward which the reasoning is directed: good reasoning is a function of *how* one reasons rather than *what* one is reasoning about. He gives John Rawls' "original position," where the emphasis is on creating the right circumstances for deliberating about principles of justice, as an example. By contrast, Taylor favors substantive accounts which suggest that we must ultimately come to grips with what we want to achieve (the good), and not just how decisions are made. He recognizes, furthermore, that a primary motivation for procedural accounts is the potential for conflict in conceptions of the good. His account of practical reason presented here can be read as a way of demonstrating how such conflicts might be resolved. See also Taylor's "Motivation behind a Procedural Ethics."

interlocutors in a debate, is intended to do just that. He lays out these forms of argument in ascending degree of "radical departure" from the apodictic standard.

In general, *ad hominem* kinds of practical argument imply that much reasoning is about the *transitions* from one position to its rival. In assessing the philosophical impact of Thomas Kuhn's work on revolutions within the history of science, Alasdair MacIntyre argued that the incommensurability of frameworks that displace one another throughout science's history does not require eschewing our belief in progress but reforming our conception of scientific reasoning.[49] The skeptical conclusion that tends to follow our realization that there are no common criteria with which rival frameworks are to be judged can be avoided when we choose to focus on the transition from one scientific outlook to another (e.g., from Aristotelian to Galilean physics). We do this by constructing narratives of the passage from one framework to its rival. In constructing the narrative of the transition from Aristotelian to Galilean frameworks we are able to judge the transition itself a gain in reason. Were we to reverse the narrative order, the story would not work. An asymmetrical relation between the two has thus been established.[50]

Taylor outlines three alternative patterns according to which practical reasoning can be better conceived. What is common to all three is that they emphasize comparative judgment rather than validation in relation to facts taken as brute. What makes this possible is the assumption of a broad ontology that includes goods of human subjects among the real. Further, it is often the transition between one theory and another that plays the central role in the comparison. As already mentioned, a theory is said to outdo its rival when the story of the transition from the one to the other can in some way be judged as a gain in reason.

According to Taylor's first model of *ad hominem* argument, there is some common ground on which to adjudicate between the rival positions, yet this is not fully explicit. Here he draws further on MacIntyre's example of the story of the transition from the pre-Galilean to the post-Galilean understandings of motion. The important point of mutual

---

49. MacIntyre, "Epistemological Crises," 453–72.
50. Taylor, "Explanation and Practical Reason," 42.

recognition between the two sides lies in the fact that the pre-Galileans knew that they were struggling to fit certain phenomena within their system. Starting from the Aristotelian principle "no motion without a mover," the Paduan philosophers looked desperately for a way to explain violent motion—i.e., the causes of the continued movement of a projectile. Post-Galilean theories of inertia show clearly why this problem will remain irresolvable within the terms of the earlier theory. At the same time, it supplants the Aristotelian explanation with a wholly different one. According to the perspective of the new theory, the continued movement of the projectile is no longer the *explanandum*, for the principle of inertia takes such movement for granted. Focusing on the transition between the positions reveals that there is a semi-conscious confusion or anomaly in the first theory, which the second theory illuminates and then overcomes. While the transition entails a shift in paradigm, both sides can be expected to acknowledge it as a gain in reason since it refers to a problem that both sides recognize as such.

For the second model, Taylor pictures a divide that runs deeper than in the first. There, the superior framework overcame a problem that its competitor was consciously striving to solve. Here, each science has a different conception of its own activity. This difference is reflected in its conception of the standard of scientific knowledge. For the Platonic-Aristotelian framework, Taylor claims, the kind of understanding that comes from placing things (including ourselves) within a meaningful order is privileged. This kind of understanding then becomes a standard within science; success is attributed to theories when they are able to place things within a meaningful order. Yet not all scientific paradigms value this sort of knowing. For example, our modern natural science, on Taylor's view, makes paradigmatic the kind of knowing that enables us to "make our way about" in an environment. But if the standard conception of knowing can differ between different sciences, how are we to choose between them?

Taylor admits that, if the argument between such rivals were to take place "on Mt. Olympus" the standoff would be insurmountable. And yet, turning to the history of how these conceptions of science play out can make decision possible. When it can see that modern science has utilized its standard of "knowing one's way about" to produce not only spectacular technological payoffs but the universal body of laws undergirding it, Platonic-Aristotelian science must, Taylor argues, "stand up and take notice." Moreover, the *success* modern science achieves on its own terms becomes a criterion for its superiority over the Platonic-Aristotelian view. For on the latter's view, knowledge pertaining directly to material objects would never amount to much. Stable and lasting science must concentrate on the eternal "forms" or exemplars on which ordinary objects are based.[51]

In the end, a narrative construal of transitions can again be decisive here. For a story written from the perspective of Platonic-Aristotelian science has great trouble explaining how modern science achieves the success it does on its own terms, whereas modern science will not fall prey to the same problem—it has no difficulty showing why Platonic science achieves success on its own terms. But this means that modern science can explain the existence of Platonic science, but not visa versa.

Taylor next introduces a model that, he claims, constitutes the "most striking departure from the canonical [read: apodictic] model." While in the others the transition from X to Y was judged a gain because Y performs better than X at some task both acknowledge, in model three one expects Y to perform better than X because one judges Y to be an improvement upon X. Model three, that is, requires no mediating commonality—be it something more or less conscious to both rivals as in the first case, or implicit and requiring further articulation as in the second—to stand as judge between the two competitors.

Take the "simple case of perception." Taylor imagines walking into his classroom on a typical afternoon and seeing a pink elephant with yellow polka dots standing at the back. He stops, shakes his head and rubs his eyes. "Is this what I am seeing?" After thus checking himself, and finding that his perception of the elephant turns out to be just that, and not say a large piano with a decorative covering, he concludes:

---

51. "There is a mode of understanding which consists in knowing your way about. This is universally recognized. In making another mode the paradigm for scientific explanation, pre-Galilean science drew on a set of assumptions which entailed that this manipulative understanding would never have a very big place in human life. It always allowed for a lower form of inquiry, the domain of 'empirics' who scramble around to discover how to achieve certain effects. But the very nature of the material embodiment of Forms, as varying, approximate, never integral, ensured that no important discoveries could be made here, and certainly not an exact and universal body of findings" (ibid., 47).

there is a pink elephant with yellow polka dots in my room! Someone must be playing a practical joke.

The transition from the first perception to the second, Taylor argues, is intrinsically error-reducing. His increased confidence in the second judgment consists simply in its being an improvement on the first. In another example, Taylor has us imagine a certain "Joe" who is confused about whether he loves his "Anne" because he also resents her. After being brought to see that his resentment did not necessarily inhibit his loving her, Joe concludes that he does in fact love Anne. His present self-reading elicits more confidence than its predecessor since arriving at it entailed overcoming confusion: he believed, mistakenly, that you cannot love someone you resent because the two emotions are incompatible. We have all experienced transitions of this sort, and in fact we know how to carry them off. These, furthermore, are *ad hominem* transitions of the most essential kind. Taylor emphasizes the kinship between practical reasoning so-modeled and autobiography. We all live with convictions that take their strength from being the products of overcoming some confusion or frustration that bedeviled an earlier stance of ours.

The third model thus uses the error-reducing transitions individuals enact in their perceptual and emotional lives as paradigmatic for comparative judgments in reason. The question likely to be raised of this model, however, is in what sense it can be considered "reasoning" at all. That is, when the rival positions are held at separate moments by the same person, why call it "argument"? Taylor therefore reminds us that we carry out this form of argument interpersonally all the time. If I am Joe's friend, for instance, I am likely to respond to his confusion by offering him interpretations—"your feelings of resentment and love are not incompatible, you know"—that, if accepted, would catalyze just such an error-reducing transition.

In sum, the despair over the prospects of moral argument stem from the hegemony of the "apodictic" model of rational proof, which is itself tied to a naturalist ontology of a neutral universe. Ad hominem arguments, Taylor claims, extend the range of what we conceive of as rational argument primarily by overcoming the apodictic bias that sees argument as a contest between positions uncontroversially and explicitly held. Much practical argument, Taylor argues, goes on when we try to bring inchoate evaluations to the surface and test them in its light.[52] Further, in ad hominem forms of argument the superiority of one position to another is seen in the transition between them, and this transition is read by constructing a narrative of the passage from one to the other. Thus, the role of articulation, or the activity of drawing out what is implicit and making it explicit in a narrative form, is crucial to practical reason. This ultimately is what ties the three models explored here together.

Concluding Assessment: Taylor's Conception of Practical Reason

Where do we go from here with practical reason? We have seen that Taylor's account of practical reason provides a more ample and generous vision of how such reasoning might be pursued. To what use will it be put? Taylor began his treatment of practical reason with the problem of arguing over moral matters, especially where the debaters seem to hold incommensurable positions. But Taylor's particular use for practical reason focuses on reconciling the plural sources beneath the modern identity—ourselves as human agents. Practical reason's subject matter for Taylor is the narrative history of the transitions between goods and hypergoods that is our moral history. That is, Taylor is using practical reason to show us how to go on with that narrative that accounts for *us*.

But if practical reason both informs this narrative and promises to be the vehicle forward, we would do well to question this narrative—what kind of narrative is it?—together with his explanation of the form of practical reason.

Let's begin by raising a critical question as regards the form of practical reason. May it be that Taylor, in his zeal to avoid the naiveté of apodictic models of practical reason, has gone too far in the other direction? Alasdair MacIntyre has suggested just this—that Taylor, striving to avoid naturalist reduction, overemphasizes implicit and embodied forms of understanding.[53] Doing so may be the cause of Taylor's neglect of another model of practical reason that both avoids apodictic naiveté and at the same time refuses to succumb to the slide toward solipsism that beckons Taylor's third form of ad hominem reasoning. It

---

52. Ibid., 55.
53. MacIntyre, review of *Philosophical Arguments*, 94–96.

also avoids the way this form overlooks the political character of practical reason. This is Aristotelian *phronesis*, a characteristic and virtue that attaches not only to individual human agents as they deliberate about what is good for them but also to legislators as they frame laws meant to direct action to the common good in a society. *Phronesis* covers both an individual's "making her way about" in an environment and practices of deliberation directed toward the common good. The latter deals dialogically with explicit rules ("rules-as-represented" in MacIntyre's parlance). We can see that MacIntyre's drawing attention to this form is precisely drawing attention to the political character of practical reason, which Taylor's account threatens to cover up. To buttress MacIntyre's intuition, we might recall Geertz's criticism, which also suggested that Taylor's account overlooks the communal structure of reasoning in all disciplines of thought.[54]

Let us now turn to Taylor's narrative of the modern identity. Is this a narrative that is political, in the sense of being the story of a community that carries it across time as a means to knowing they remain in continuity with their ancestors such that they know they remain themselves?

On the surface at least, it is a story of a community, as there is a "we" here that Taylor has in mind. But what sort of "we"? Taylor's method of narrative construction separates the sources of modern agency from the concrete manifestation of these sources or their outworking in the lives of their adherents.[55] The "life goods"—his term for concrete practical aims—such as unrestricted benevolence and universal justice receive broad acknowledgment in modern societies, whereas there is fierce disagreement about sources. Taylor hopes for reconciliation with regard to sources, as practical reasoning allows the narrative to unfold. Yet there is an eerily compulsory dimension to this narrative that seeks to merge a great many streams in its flow. It does not invite counter-narratives or easily reconcile itself to incommensurability or difference. (Taylor's framing of the debates over authenticity provide evidence of this.) The separation of sources from life goods in the narrative's construction allows Taylor to avoid the question of

---

54. See above.

55. I owe this way of putting it to a review of Sources of the Self by David Matzko and Stanley Hauerwas. "Sources of Charles Taylor," 288.

whether one's sources will cause one to interpret justice or benevolence differently.[56]

For instance, while, say, the Christian evangelical and the Marxist-Feminist undoubtedly share sources and self-understandings, the overall shapes of their narratives are importantly different. This is evident in their different notions of what "liberation" means. While both ought indeed to seek justice and equality, these narrative differences will make a difference when it comes to how one is to pursue that goal.

Such communities are the agents of practical reasoning. In their review of *Sources of the Self*, David Matzko and Stanley Hauerwas raise the question in regard to Taylor's effort to interpret the modern identity, "who is the 'we' that Taylor is describing?" They go on to show that in many ways this is an abstract "we" or a "universal we." Put differently, although they admit that Taylor's narrative describes the way many of us are, they point out that Taylor seems unaware that by creating this "we" he also creates a "non-we." By disregarding this fact, Taylor "writes

---

56. Political philosopher Stephen White observes how Taylor "wants to distinguish ... the necessary space of agency from its fuller and variable historical manifestations" (*Sustaining Affirmation*, 48–49). He refers to Taylor's basic assertion that agency is constituted by strong evaluation as his "template" of human agency in distinction from "its fuller and variable historical manifestations" [i.e., its sources]. White's purpose is to use Taylor as a theorist whose work illustrates his own concept of a "weak ontology." Such differ from strong ontologies in that they open themselves up to being contested and, rather than determine a particular morality and politics, they merely "prefigure" such. I believe White is right to see Taylor to be separating the self as the identity of a modern agent from a particular politics of the modern agent. However, what White seems not to have seen, while Matzko and Hauerwas have, is that the particular and historical sources Taylor identifies for the modern identity are also abstract, in that they are separated from a politics of practical life. We see this is so when we see that Taylor separates practical norms and standards—a third level to accompany the strong evaluator and the constellation of peculiarly modern sources—from moral sources. This is why he can claim that moderns can agree on standards while at the same time disagreeing about sources. Whereas White takes Taylor's insistence on separating out agency and sources from politics as a virtue of his work, I side with Matzko and Hauerwas in seeing it as a vice. White seems to be operating on the assumption that the only way for one's framework of the good to be truly open to challenge is for it to be apolitical, or not immediately political. My own quite different claim is that it is only through acknowledging the political character of our (admittedly historical and contingent) frameworks of the good that we can be ontological realists where morality is concerned and can avoid the shallow view of the agent found in modern moral theories. Cf. White, *Sustaining Affirmation*.

[the 'non-we'] into the narrative of modern culture without the recognition that the process is hegemonic."

If Taylor were to begin with the empirical—the putting in practice of these moral sources—the unity of the modern identity would likely be harder to attain. How do today's Americans perform by the standard of universal benevolence? Well, we allow ourselves to kill Iraqis without mourning for their deaths. Ironically, Matzko and Hauerwas point out, we use the notion of such a "universal we" in order to justify ourselves in this.

To come at this point about narrative and the political from a different angle, we might shine the spotlight on autobiography as the narrative form most akin to Taylor's third model of ad hominem practical reasoning. After listening to Taylor's account of this model, we might retort that autobiographical narration, if it can lead to improved self-understanding ("a gain in reason"), can also lead to self-deception. For who is to insure that I am telling the story truthfully? Of course, Taylor might reply that such narrative-making is inherently dialogical insofar as we bring our experiences into articulacy in dialogue with friends, as Jim did his feeling about Anne. To this we should say, it all depends on whether your friends have the characteristic of truthfulness in friendship.

In the next chapter, I hope to present an account of practical reason and narrative whose approach is different. It avoids the abstraction that Taylor's view beckons and, also unlike his, is more robustly political. It does this by unwinding a narrative of a "we" that not only readily faces the possibility of radical incommensurability but that is itself shaped by its practices of responding to conflict and to "the other." It therefore does not hide the political character of practical reason but embraces it. Perhaps it can do this because it understands itself fundamentally as a counter-narrative or subversive story.

This, Hauerwas', account of practical reason ties practical reason to agency by showing that becoming what our sources require is itself an argument for them. It achieves this by tying practical reason to "character." Character itself is made intelligible by a narrative containing exemplary persons. The reference to character insures that practical reason be political in a rich sense because only through being shaped in community do agents come to have the ability to carry on the story.

Once again, I am not arguing that Taylor's conception of practical reason is wrong per se, or that we do not gain much by his expanding of the terrain of practical argument. For one thing, the debate between positions will be potentially richer insofar as Taylor's conception weakens the tendency to slip into inarticulacy. Goods and hypergoods will no longer be suppressed, but part or what is in contention. Unreflective boosting and knocking will be tempered by greater self-awareness regarding what we share, and conceptions of human agents will be made more truthful by connection to moral sources that make agency intelligible. Returning to our three concepts—practical reason, human agency, and politics—Taylor builds a strong link between practical reason and human agency. I am pointing to the temptation of Taylor to obscure something—namely, the political bases of all instances of practical reason.

CHAPTER 3

Stanley Hauerwas: Practical Reason as Performance

INTRODUCTION

In Anscombe's analysis of Aristotle's practical syllogisms it became apparent that, in addition to its concern with action, practical reasoning assumes the context of a *community*—a particular, historical social body. A correct moral psychology not only assumes that practical reasons are embodied in the agent's actions, but that these actions are constituted in relation to others within such a social body. In other words, what underlies such reasoning and licenses its inferences is a community. For "the good" at which intentions aim relies upon "descriptions" that can only be found in reserves of community life. In this sense, agency is embedded in the life of a particular community, and practical inferences are licensed within communities of shared goods or reasons. This is the "politics" component of the three interrelated concepts—agency, practical reason, and politics—that we have striven to articulate as well as used as a test for moral philosophies. Anthropologically, this may be taken as an affirmation of Aristotle's observation that man is a social and political being.[1]

Such communities, furthermore, are always historical and *particular*. Anscombe also drew attention to the task of constructing a better philosophy of psychology. The "a-social" character of the moral theories she criticizes tended to distort human agents by separating them

---

1. See Aristotle *Nichomachean Ethics* 1097b, 15.

from their engagements—i.e., the relationships and socially attributed roles that account for the motivation to act.

Taylor's agent is an embodied subject who cares about his relationship to the moral world and has no doubt that the moral world is real. Taylor argues persistently that the descriptions agents give of their ends and purposes are irreducible to the kind of pseudo-scientific explanations based in an impartial perspective. He has further employed transcendental arguments to argue for the reality of moral ontology; the good must have a place in an adequate conception of how things are. Further still, he developed an account of how recognizing the agent's perspective will reform the practice of social science.

Taylor's weakness as regards Anscombe's challenge is the failure to specify a concrete community that sustains practical reason by providing descriptions of ends and purposes for an agent to make her own. His tendency to consider the commitment to the good requisite to human agency in formal terms, moreover, tempts him to paint an overly optimistic portrait of moral growth. The closest he comes to such community is the modern "self." But who such persons are is not self-evident. They seem to be Christians who have wandered away from the sources of the society they have made. Put differently, we have not yet accounted for the "politics" in our three-part account of practical reason. What is needed is not another abstract philosophical account of practical reason, but someone who exemplifies practical reasoning in a particular community. Stanley Hauerwas strives to be such a community-formed practical reasoner. It is in this sense, I claim, that his practical reasoning is "political." I will argue in this chapter that Hauerwas learned better than Taylor how to receive Anscombe's challenge and go on, though he may be positioned to learn from Taylor on some counts. To make the case will require not only pointing to Hauerwas's employment of the language of a particular community ("Christianese"), but arguing that because of that employment the very form of his practical reasoning is different in crucial ways.

I believe this argument can be made by showing that Hauerwas understands himself to be an agent of the church and its witness in his ethical writings. Hauerwas understands his practical reasoning in terms of Aristotle's assertion that man is a social and political being. The influence of Wittgenstein has made Hauerwas inflect his understanding of man's social nature by stressing the importance of language. The ability to describe, as we will see, is the *sine qua non* for human action. The church carries the descriptions of ends that inform the actions of Christians; it is the social matrix that sustains the inferences that structure their practical reasoning.

There is a danger here that by describing the church as the source of Christians' language we may miss what is crucial about Hauerwas's account of practical reasoning. Many of us moderns tend to think of language as a "tool" that we employ to achieve otherwise specified ends and as something *we* shape and change as the occasion arises. Hauerwas, by contrast, follows Wittgenstein in believing that what philosophy needs is a rigorous and disciplined attention to the constraints of grammar and its life-form-shaping rules. Language, for us human beings, is as powerful a shaping force as any type of institutional authority. The language of the church is always enacted in liturgical rites and practices. Moreover, it is witnessed in the kind of people or body the church becomes. For Hauerwas, the grammar of Christian language is to be found in the church's witness to the peaceable kingdom.

It is the political nature of Hauerwas's practical reasoning that distinguishes it from Taylor's in its basic form. The primary body or agent of such practical reasoning is the church body, not that of the individual subject. The emphasis on church explains why for Hauerwas Christian ethics cannot be performed by first discerning truths about human nature as such. For such a move would betray the connection of Christian agency with the character-shaping language that sustains it, as well as deceptively imply that we can do ethics without language. Rather Christian ethics must connect the good of action with Christian convictions about the very nature of God. Because there is no "ethics for anyone," and to so pretend belies something crucial about human nature as linguistic being, admitting the particularity of one's starting place is the first step in a truthful account of self and world.

Hauerwas is also concerned with moral-anthropological issues. Stemming from his political conception of practical reasoning centered on the church, Hauerwas further follows Aristotle in emphasizing virtues. For him the virtues are skills Christians learn in community that enable them to go on being who they are—which is to say, talking as they talk.[2] Cultivating the right virtues allows Christians to pass down

---

2. For an excellent account of Hauerwas's practical reasoning as embodied craft, see Shuman, "Discipleship as Craft," 315–31.

their story through generations and thus sustain the political community called church. Every new generation needs competent speakers of the Christian idiom.

As already hinted, the notion of narrative is an important component of Hauerwas's account of agency and practical reason, for he believes Christians live by memory. Sacred Scripture is the clearest indicator that Christians are such a people and helps remind them of the connections between their history and that of the Jews. That human agents are historical (have histories) is crucial to a truthful account of human agency and this shows that, for all the value of Greek sources, the root of the Christian story is Israel.

If I am to succeed in making the argument that Hauerwas's account of practical reasoning is structurally different from Taylor's in the sense just described, I must not only convince the reader that the church, conceived as a polis, is central to his theological ethics, but also display, however falteringly, how this is so.[3] I will go about this in two stages. First, I will draw on Hauerwas's early work, which relates moral philosophy, and particularly the criticisms of its account of agency that Anscombe helped articulate, to Christian ethics. Second, I will provide a close reading of Hauerwas's attempt at a "primer" in Christian ethics, his book *The Peaceable Kingdom*. The book, which journeys from the problems of modern ethical theory to Christian casuistry regarding war and peace, with a tour across the recent history of theological ethics in between, displays the pattern of Hauerwas's thinking. In drawing attention to how the various components of the book—such as virtue, narrative, scripture and eschatology—"hang together," I hope to show how Haurewas' ecclesiology constitutes the center of gravity. To give an example of Hauerwas's reasoning is also an appropriate technique for understanding him.

Christian Ethics and the Aesthetic: Hauerwas on Facts and Values

In his early work, Stanley Hauerwas does battle with the moral theory, and its conception of the human being, according to which thought and action are fundamentally separated categories—i.e., that conception of the agent Anscombe finds in consequentialism. Such theory has great

---

3. For a helpful comparative study of Hauerwas and Moltmann on eschatology, see Rasmusson, *Church as Polis*.

difficulty accounting for the intuition that moral value stands independent from us, the agents, and therefore "calls upon" us to conform to its demands. Only "facts" exist objectively, while "values" are a function of the will or decision.

In "Situation Ethics, Moral Notions and Moral Theology," Hauerwas claims that this picture of the agent not only distorts human agency but also evacuates the world, and thus our decisions, of moral significance. For without moral notions that are shared beyond the individual will, the latter is fundamentally unguided in its machinations. Joseph Fletcher sought to address this worry when he called attention to the excessive emphasis moral philosophers place on rules and norms.[4] Such an emphasis, he claimed, oversimplifies the problematic nature of moral experience: when we try to live by applying norms deductively to situations we tend to ignore important details. Fletcher endeavors to correct this imbalance by stressing the importance of "context," or the circumstances surrounding a moral decision.[5]

While in sympathy with Fletcher's emphasis on context, Hauerwas claims that his solution rests on a fundamental misunderstanding. In his characterization of moral "situations," Fletcher unconsciously reproduces the picture of agency that his "principlist" adversaries themselves employ. Fletcher's "situation ethics" imagines the "facts" before the agent to be impersonal and open to objective description. In such a situation, the agent's "decision" can only be absolutely free and unguided. That is, Fletcher's "situations" are so free of "norms" as to lose their grip on what makes them morally significant. For if the agent is not called upon by non-subjectively binding considerations, it is unclear what makes his decision a moral one.[6]

---

4. See Fletcher, *Situation Ethics*.

5. Hauerwas, "Situation Ethics, Moral Notions and Moral Theology," 12–14.

6. "Fletcher's concentration on decision as the primary datum of moral experience reflects a kind of picture of moral experience that is shared by many people today. Those that assume this model of moral experience tend to think of the world primarily as made up of hard facts that are easily recognizable by reason. The moral life is thought to consist primarily of 'value judgments' or preferences formed somehow 'above' or 'beyond' the facts but for which our reason cannot find any grounds to justify. There is not, nor can there be, any relation between the is and the ought. . . . The idea that somehow the facts are simply there to be perceived accounts in part for Fletcher's tendency to talk about 'situations' as they are simply given apart from the human beings that make them up" (ibid., 13).

Hauerwas explains that Fletcher's error is also a misunderstanding of the nature of principles and their relation to "context." The correct understanding, for Hauerwas, is captured in Julius Kovesi's concept of "moral notions."[7] For Kovesi moral judgments are closely related to language or the terms in which they are articulated. These terms, like "good" or "murder," are ways of combining various *material* aspects of a situation—time, place, voluntariness—with a particular form, or organizing principle. Everyday moral notions combine what we often in theory distinguish as "normative" versus "descriptive" propositions. By artificially separating out these two sides of moral judgment—or forgetting their natural mixture in practice—Fletcher has repeated an error made by much of modern moral philosophy—i.e., that of allowing moral norms to become abstract entities that are made concrete in decisive moments—i.e., the moment where an agent "applies" them to a set of facts. Hauerwas argues that moral notions imply that all evaluative judgments have descriptive elements within their structure, and only in this way can we make sense of the objective significance of moral experience.

For the agent, this means that moral experience is not simply a matter of decision, but also of vision. Before decision and action, the moral life involves learning to see the salient aspects of a situation. To learn to see morally is to learn to use the terms in which our moral notions are encapsulated. It is only in the light of moral notions that there is something in our lives about which decisions can be made.

To talk about vision in terms of learning a language, furthermore, implies that we only learn to see morally by participating in a "way of life." In other words, our moral vision is a communal (political) vision.[8]

However, driving Fletcher's work is the further insight that sometimes "convention" does not do justice to the complexity of the moral life. To address this, Hauerwas turns to Kovesi's distinction between "complete" and "incomplete" notions.[9] The distinction is meant to point up that our moral language does not exhaust what we experience morally. Some parts of our moral language have been extensively developed, e.g., the term "murder" is a term falling in the class, "killing," but with a more determinative moral meaning. Yet, he notes, we do not yet have

---

7. Kovesi, *Moral Notions*.
8. Hauerwas, "Situation Ethics, Moral Notions and Moral Theology," 19.
9. Ibid., 20–21.

a term for actions that constitute lying in circumstances that would remove the imputation of blame.

These latter facts about our moral language reflect the form of life we inhabit, but they also allow us to reflect upon the very nature of moral philosophy. Such inquiry naturally takes place within a form of life and it ought to illuminate how the different aspects of a community's language, its various moral notions, hang together. This is not to suggest that moral philosophy cannot be critical; Hauerwas seeks only to remind such theorists that they are criticizing a way of life, and not a disembodied norm. Furthermore, moral philosophy so conceived is not neutral toward its subject matter but rather helps shape a particular vision of the moral life. Hauerwas therefore argues that moral philosophy is better conceived on the analogy of "an artist engaged in his work than a critic making a judgment about the finished product."

What all this means for Christian ethics is that it is a form of inquiry that seeks to illuminate, balance, and criticize the way theological notions hang together in the Christian way of life. This way of life and its language is not isolated from the ways of life surrounding it, yet the notions deemed central by Christian ethics become a center of gravity and give particular inflections to wandering terms like "joy" as they come within its pull.[10] Reinhold Niebuhr, for example, tried to re-describe worldly notions of freedom within the Christian notion of "sin." In this light, Hauerwas recommends at the end of "Situation Ethics, Moral Notions and Moral Theology," that Christian moral philosophers "should again turn to an investigation of basic religious notions such as repentance, forgiveness, guilt, in order to reemphasize their relation to the moral life." That is, they should attend to the moral notions embedded in the Christian life-form and their vision-shaping power.

10. Speaking of the moral notions common to all persons, Hauerwas writes, "[T]he moral theologian does not just accept the formal element of these notions as given, as his own special commitments may limit or expand the meaning of such concepts. This is not a process peculiar to theological ethics but is the same kind of business the philosophical ethicist is engaged in from the point of view of other commitments. Theology is at least the conceptual arrangement of religious notions in such a way that they inform, qualify and limit one another. Theological ethics is the juxtaposing of such notions in relation to our moral notions to show their ethical significance. That is why theological ethicists often try to suggest central metaphors around which our other moral notions can be explicated and analyzed. For example, joy is an inherited moral notion, but it may be that its formal element is expanded or limited within its theological context" (ibid, 28–29).

But again the incompleteness of moral notions implies that theological ethics is a kind of struggle with the limits of its own language. And given that moral notions shape the vision of participants in a way of life, the members of a community, this struggle is a kind of self-discipline. Describing the Christian life, Hauerwas writes that "[t]o be a Christian in effect is learning to see the world in a certain way, and thus become as we see." Therefore, "the task of contemporary theological ethics is to state the language of faith in terms of the Christian responsibility to be formed in the likeness of Christ."

My claim is that Hauerwas's emphasis on moral notions grounded in a form of life, together with the cultivation of vision as a self-discipline of the agent, marks out his conception of practical reasoning and agency as political. We now turn to a more detailed discussion of the role of vision in relation to community within his work.

Vision and Christian Ethics: Hauerwas on Murdoch

As the title suggests, in "The Significance of Vision: Toward an Aesthetic Ethic" Hauerwas further explores "vision" as a central metaphor for the task of living morally. He does so through a long meditation on the ethical philosophy of Iris Murdoch, and then connecting her work to the challenges of theological ethics.

The metaphor of vision for Murdoch, as for Hauerwas, concerns the central image around which a picture of the human agent is constructed. In *The Sovereignty of Good*, Murdoch carefully exposes the picture of agency that underlies the moral theory of her contemporaries (both continental existentialist and Anglo-analytic).[11] The central characteristic of such an agent is freedom. The *sine qua non* for moral life is the assumption that we are determined by nothing other than our own wills.

The picture of the human agent as decision-maker is complemented by a particular characterization of the world. The stuff of the world is neatly separated into facts and values. The role of human reason is to survey "the facts" wholly impartially, whereas the will's function is to determine values (wholly personally). The good, then, is only contingently related to "how things are." The isolated human will injects value into an otherwise indifferent world of neutral facts.

---

11. See Murdoch, *Sovereignty of Good*, 4–8.

Murdoch's problem with this conception of things is that it ignores what she takes to be a central human moral task: to see the world as it really is. The value-neutral ontology implicit in the image of man the decision-maker has allowed moral philosophers to avoid a central problem of moral rationality: the difficulty of seeing, or discerning, the good. By introducing her alternative for human agency—the moral agent as artist—Murdoch calls attention to the ongoing challenge and inherent difficulty of moral discernment: seeing the good without distortion.

This challenge stems from there being a tendency in human beings toward illusion and fantasy. Through fantasy we reduce other people to a mirror for ourselves and thereby avoid the pain of acknowledging that their relationship to us is contingent and fragile. The moral life of the agent as artist is an ongoing effort of love to pierce the veil of selfish delusion in order to attend to the other. The category of "the Good" symbolizes the self-transcendence necessary to the moral task. Our agency is engaged by the reality of the Good, which stands beyond us and claims us.

Hauerwas argues that the same conception of the human agent as decision-maker infects Christian ethics. God is deemed "wholly other," and thus indifferent to our existential situation, or He is only brought into play in order to confirm our self-creations. It can be seen in the view according to which Christian dispositions are demoted to the "inner" and private; actions are what counts and these can be judged without reference to their peculiarly Christian motivations. "On such a view," Hauerwas writes, "any life-directing attraction toward God's creative and redemptive being becomes unintelligible."[12]

Hauerwas argues that Christian ethicists mimic modern moral philosophy when they attempt to separate Christian doctrines about God, self, and world, on the one hand, from a minimal account of human moral action, on the other. Murdoch shows the way to a more robust Christian ethics because she shows why the world as the agent envisions it must matter to moral reflection. The job of the Christian ethicist, therefore, is to order the Christian vision of the moral world. It is an aesthetic task in that it confronts the difficulty of seeing the world as construed by Christian teachings.[13] The construct of man the

12. Hauerwas, "Significance of Vision," 31.

13. "Christian ethical behavior cannot be simply to assume a loving attitude; it must adhere to and locate the self in respect to basic affirmations about God and man.

decision-maker can only lead the Christian ethicist to avoid his fundamental task.

For our purposes, we must note that the metaphors of vision and art, like the foregoing discussion of moral notions, contribute to the basically political structure of Hauerwas's account of practical reasoning and agency. They entail that human action cannot be described apart from world-construing claims about the reality of the good. For Christians these claims are articulated in the (agency-constituting) teachings of the church about God and God's relation to the self. This is why, as we will see in the upcoming discussion of *The Peaceable Kingdom*, Christian moral philosophy cannot be separated from theology. The church, as a polis, is both constituted by these claims and their carrier.

Ethics as Grammar

> For Christian ethics is not first of all an ethics concerned with doing, but its first task is to help us rightly see the world.... For we can only act within a world we can see and we can only see the world rightly by being trained to see.[14]

Brad Kallenberg's study of the importance of Wittgenstein for Hauerwas provides an illuminating perspective on the manner by which Hauerwas does Christian ethics.[15] For the purposes of this chapter, Kallenberg's study issues in two principles. First by reading Hauerwas through Wittgenstein Kallenberg shows how theological ethics may be conceived as intended to transform lives through transforming subjective vision, as contrasted with its more austere posture as providing theoretical pictures of the moral life.[16] He shows this by taking the reader through Wittgenstein's own journey from what might be called the theoretical posture, where the philosopher's work is to compare the logical version of language to an abstract model or picture of the same, to the therapeutic posture, where philosophy is a matter of "working on oneself" and aiding others to do the same. Second,

---

A Christian does not simply 'believe' certain propositions about God; he learns to attend to reality through them..." (ibid., 46).

14. Hauerwas, "Demands of a Truthful Story."

15. Kallenberg, *Ethics as Grammar*.

16. Charles Pinches offers the salutary view of theological ethicist as "forester" whose role is to be intimately familiar with the territory of his forest, or in this case the moral life. See Pinches, *Theology and Action*.

Kallenberg's story of how Wittgenstein's conception of "form" from his earlier to his later work helps us understand why Hauerwas's ethics is aptly described as political. These principles are developed by Kallenberg in the first four chapters of his study, which alternately focus upon Wittgenstein and Hauerwas.

In chapter 1, Kallenberg outlines the "migration of the subject" from the periphery to the center of Wittgentstein's work. This migration is manifest before all in the aporetic form of the *Philosophical Investigations*. Kallenberg argues that Wittgenstein's remarkable work was intended not to produce a "school of thought" in relation to certain problems in logic and the philosophy of language, but rather to train his students how to "go on." Wittgenstein saw his students, and contemporaries more generally, as mystified by the kind of account of language that in part drove his own Tractatus, which attempted to provide an ultimate guide for how language could be fitted to reality. By helping them, each in her own way, to overcome this mystification, which tended to remove them from the philosophical task, he sought to cultivate in them the understanding that philosophy is a kind of skill. In this, it is not unlike the skills that help us to go on in ordinary life, such as learning to speak a language.

How then do Hauerwas's ethics parallel Wittgenstein's migration of the subject from the periphery to the center of the philosopher's craft? We have the beginning of an answer in the comparison Wittgenstein drew between philosophy and ordinary life. In chapter 2, Kallenberg argues that Hauerwas learned from Wittgenstein to treat the matter of the moral life aesthetically. As displayed in his early work, Hauerwas learned from Wittgenstein that the relation of ethical deliberation to action is not external but internal. From Aristotle, he learned to name this internal relation "character." Thus, for Aristotle the firmest basis for practical reason is simply the *phronimos*, or the practically wise person. One cannot get behind the *phronimos* in order to justify practical deliberation in some character-independent way. The relation here is internal.

Hauerwas builds on this understanding of the internal relation of practical reason and action in his more mature work with his use of narrative, which will be discussed at length below. Here to "go on" skillfully means the ability to make one's actions one's own, or a part of one's "past." This can only happen if our sufferings—i.e., our actions described in retrospect—can be given form by being engrafted into an ongoing story. To learn to go on, or become a "responsible self," is to learn to acknowledge that we all have been gifted with a story of our lives. To grasp the narrative form of our lives is to grasp that properly understood the self is "eschatological": it is both prospectively directed to the future which I co-author, and retrospectively directed toward a past which, as "past," is given to me as a gift by my story. What we need, morally speaking, are stories sufficient to give us the skills to go on with our lives. Christian ethics is about how human agents discover their selves in learning to find their selves in the Christian story. The truthfulness of that story, furthermore, is to be found in how well it enables them to "go on."

Second, Kallenberg demonstrates through his readings of Wittgenstein and Hauerwas how the transformative power of theological ethics only becomes clear when we understand the activity of theological ethics as politically grounded. Chapter 3 sets the stage for this claim in Wittgenstein by tracing the transformation of the term "form" from his early to later writings.

Just as in chapter 1 of *Ethics as Grammar* Kallenberg traced the journey of Wittgenstein from his *Tractatus* to his *Philosophical Investigations* in order to show the migration of the subject from the margins to the center, so in chapter 3 he traces the evolution of Wittgenstein's understanding of the concept of form. Kallenberg claims that this change is so significant that one cannot point to some common substance that persists throughout the change and so allows one to define precisely what remains the same and what is different. Rather, the relationship that exists between "form" in his early writing and "form" in his later writings can be best described in terms of "family resemblances." In other words, the relation can be shown and seen but not concretely defined.

In his early writings "form" for Wittgenstein meant the underlying structure of the world. Language was thought to have meaning in so far as it "represented" this world. The logical form of language had to agree, or be isomorphic with, the form of the world. By "world" Wittgenstein meant what humans experience. This led Wittgenstein to conclude that there must be only one way in which the atoms of the logical form of language, which he called propositions, could be applied to their corollary atoms of the world.

In Wittgenstein's later work, which was largely spurred by problems he found with the one-to-one correspondence theory of meaning, he began to think of form less in connection with language as structure and more in terms of its connection to language use and users. In saying this he was asserting his discovery that as human beings we cannot really get outside of language, as his earlier account with its "external" view of the relation between language and world implied. This coincided with, and was inspired by, his discovery that the ways of picturing things with language are multiple. Language ought not to be thought of so much as, through its logical structure, putting firm limits on what we can see, but as being what enables us to see something. Different applications of language open up different vistas, enabling language users to see (experience) different things.

Thus, "form" for Wittgenstein in his later work came to lie not primarily in language itself but in the human context, or life-form (*lebensform*), where language is used. The form, or as Wittgenstein as often put it, the "grammar," of words referred to the rules by which they function in this broader life form. The grammar of words includes their place in systems of language, or language games, within the life form. These provide the "local" context in which a word's meaning or inflection is given shape. The expression "all men are brutes," Kallenberg notes, means something different when spoken by a theologian and by a woman who has just been jilted. The grammar of words includes, further, their relation to the "primitive" within human life, namely gestures such as infants and toddlers employ (crying, etc.). It includes the conventions by which a community provides rules for language users that go no further than what "we" do. All together these aspects of the form or grammar of words compose a "form of life." It is the "hurly-burly" of such a form of life that Wittgenstein means by form in his later work.

We can, I hope, see how this next stage of Kallenberg's study completes the principle that helping students go on through being transformed is central to the tasks of philosophy and theological ethics. For such a conception of form implies that the speaker's skill is not separable from the form of language. Form also refers to the speaker's evolving skill as she learns to use language appropriately. Further, we should now be able to begin to see how Wittgenstein's later notion of form illumines the political nature of Hauerwas's ethics. If the task of theological ethics is to guide the transformation of students of such ethics through finding their selves in the narrative of the Christian story, then the church is the form of life that carries this story in any particular historical time and place.

Kallenberg himself addresses this question in chapter 4, where he asks us to consider the oft-heard charge that Hauerwas's manner of doing Christian ethics is, in the words of his teacher James Gustafson, "sectarian, tribalist, fideist."[17] The charge could be summed up as the claim that since Hauerwas believes that (given that language is internally related to world) one must be formed in Christian ways of speaking in order to understand Christian truth claims, Christians as a polity must wall themselves in against outsiders. But for the first part of this claim to entail the second part, it must also be that there exists no way to communicate between rival life forms apart from simply stepping outside of any form of life. Hauerwas asserts that coming to understand others is like learning a second first language. His work in the form of a body of essays is primarily directed to those who do not already think like he does. They attest to his belief that one can begin to grasp what one does not yet understand by being shown how a given language works. In his own case, he wishes to display the grammar of Christian convictions, considering the heart of Christian ethics to be not theory but witness.

Yet that only a purportedly neutral language, grounded in no particular form of life, can ensure communication is precisely what Hauerwas's critics hold, and this is the topic of Kallenberg's fourth chapter. There, Kallenberg argues that the family resemblance between Wittgenstein's later conception of form and Hauerwas's insistence on the political character of Christian ethics becomes visible in the way Hauerwas refutes the charge that he is sectarian by showing that his critics are relying upon erroneous assumptions about how language enables us to communicate. In each case they overlook the fact that language is not our tool for manipulating the world but is the forming power that enables us to attend to the world's features.

If any communication between forms of life is possible, Hauerwas reminds, it cannot bypass the political. As a corollary to this, anyone willing to attend to Christian convictions in their political embodiment—whether that person have some identification with Christianity or be a stranger to it—is already out of the starting gate on the track

---

17. See Gustafson, "Sectarian Temptation," 83–94.

of understanding the configuration of God, self, and world to which Christians cling.

Practical Reason in *The Peaceable Kingdom*

The ensuing discussion of *The Peaceable Kingdom* will provide a more detailed explication and example of how practical reasoning in Hauerwas is a church-centered activity. This section of the chapter, again, will read differently because it is not purely analysis but a description of how Hauerwas performs his task as well.

The main argument is as follows. In *The Peaceable Kingdom* Hauerwas demonstrates how aspects of doctrines of Christianity hang together, and how the doctrines themselves fit with certain methodological tools for carrying on Christian ethics. By "doctrines" I mean the short hand for those notions, both descriptive and normative, by which Christians learn how they are to see and act in the world, or God's good creation. They are the "grammar" of a form of life. These doctrinal and methodological aspects—narrative, Scripture, virtue, and Christ—point to the centrality of the church in Christian ethics. And the ethical obligation of the church, says Hauerwas, is to be the church. Therefore, Christian ethics is about aiding the church to be the church.[18]

In *The Peaceable Kingdom* Hauerwas presents his fullest expression of practical reason and its social rootedness. Written in 1983, it draws together his major ideas on moral philosophy and theological ethics from the previous decades. By representing the progression in his work from philosophy to the proclamation of the church, *The Peaceable Kingdom* exemplifies Hauerwas's peculiar way of articulating Christian convictions to make a picture of a particular form of life.

We begin by pointing out with Hauerwas the problems of the attempt to find universal foundations for ethical norms. This effort stems from the desire to secure peace by reinforcing the particular ethical systems that sustain human communities. The next step is to explore "narrative," a key tool Hauerwas employs in learning to reflect on the basis of his own tradition, Methodist Christianity. Narrative is the

---

18. "... [T]he first ethical task of the church is to be the church—the servant community. Such a claim may well sound self-serving until we remember that what makes the church the church is its faithful manifestation of the peaceable kingdom in the world. As such the church does not have a social ethic; the church is a social ethic" (Hauerwas, *Peaceable Kingdom*, 99).

basic form of practical rationality, including an account of agency, for Hauerwas since it enables the agent to appropriate the stories it lives by. It therefore plays an important role in Hauerwas's account of agency and the interpretation of scripture.

Hauerwas's polemic against foundationalism, and his introduction of narrative, helps us see why Christian ethics must embrace the particularity of its social basis. Hauerwas goes on to show that the particular people called Christians need Scripture and tradition to form the memories that allow them to identify themselves. Through the stories of Israel and Jesus Christians learn to be a community that strives to become like their God (*imitatio Dei*) in its way of life. For God's will, as revealed in the Scriptures, is to form such a community. Learning to remember these stories, which means learning to re-tell them both in their rites and their lives, requires the concrete community of the church: the school of Christian virtues. The church is essentially the place where the stories of God in Scripture are made into living practical guidance for the community. Hauerwas, together with his students, have therefore made the church a key focus for Christian ethical reflection.[19]

Having shown why any Christian ethics requires first that the church be the church, Hauerwas comes around to the question of what difference the story re-told in the church makes for the moral decisions we all see being made. The story of the church is polity-shaping and every polity has a distinctive way of life.

These steps comprise the components through which Hauerwas describes practical reasoning as learning to become a people of peace in *The Peaceable Kingdom*, and thus provides an example of practical reasoning that embraces its communal rootedness. The critical step is the church as the embodied image of God's peaceable kingdom. The centrality of the church shows that Hauerwas's reasoning is fundamentally political. Yet the other steps are crucial to Hauerwas's understanding of the church because they help us see both how the church can remember truthfully its political character and what kind of polis the church is called to be.

---

19. See Hauerwas and Wells, *Blackwell Companion to Christian Ethics*.

Making Peace: Foundationalism, Particularity, and Narrative

In *The Peaceable Kingdom* Hauerwas focuses on two types of theory—modern foundational theory and Christian narrative ethics. The form that ethical theories take and their material (political) content are intertwined: they grow out of personal responses to our felt condition. Modern theory is shaped by the political determination to achieve peace by disregarding our differences and the sense of unease it causes us.[20] Christian ethical reflection seeks a peace that teaches us not to fear our differences, and would so enable us to accept them; its politics is founded on reconciliation. The differences in these theories, manifest in their forms, stems from the different qualities of the "peace" each seeks to bring to bear in response to a felt division.

Hauerwas argues that modern moral theory, in its intimate relation to the state of our moral world, is an attempt to patch up the problem of "lack of agreement on morals."[21] At the same time, with Anscombe, he sees that this cure is part of the problem. He does not take Anscombe's line that consequentialism is "corrupting our minds," but rather assumes that consequentialism signifies that we are already out of our bodies. So, whereas Anscombe examines theories and exposes them for their capacity to distort the moral world in which we live, Hauerwas looks to the moral world itself. For him it is a world of fractured and distorted lives, and fractured *because* they are distorted. Anscombe shows us how moral theory has attempted to escape the fractured moral life, to find a foundation apart from our social forms of life. Hauerwas moves in the opposite direction. He points to a way that we can enter back into the fractured moral life by giving a truthful account of where we are. This "truthfulness" is made possible by the good news of the Gospel, which allows us to see our brokenness in the light of God's redeeming work. His way back into the moral life is through making peace. By accepting that our lives are fragmented we can resist the temptation to escape them and create peace within them.

---

20. Hauerwas use of the term "political" stems from its Aristotelian sense as pertaining to a "polis." It may therefore be contrasted with the sense Rawls gives to the term when articulating a conception of justice that stands apart from a "comprehensive doctrine." In this chapter, Hauerwas's use of political focuses the social ground of practical reasoning to which Anscombe points. For an illuminating account of the "family resemblance" between Hauerwas's concept of the political and Wittgenstein's concept of a "form of life," see Kallenberg, *Ethics as Grammar*.

21. See Hauerwas, *Peaceable Kingdom*, 22.

Ethics for Anybody

In chapter 1 of *The Peaceable Kingdom*, Hauerwas describes how the question of foundations—"aren't there any absolutes?!"—arises from souls troubled by a sense of fragmentation. They do not find the wholeness for which they long. And because we are by nature social, this sense of fragmentation—moral fragmentation—refers not to the isolated self, but ultimately to the fragmented community. It is no accident, he continues, that the ethics profession works with tools for patching holes, bridging gaps, and gluing together. Responding to the socially felt question—are there no absolutes?—ethicists seek to find ultimate foundations, procedures of justification, for those moral principles that will hold our societies together.[22]

What is the character of such bridging principles? First, they are "abstracted" from the common morality that runs through any human social body so as to achieve a broader relevance. As Kant teaches, morality is autonomous, standing apart from both empirical life and metaphysical belief. Consequently, the work of ethicists comes to be primarily about procedures for justifying actions and policies with respect to universal principles abstracted from a common life.

Secondly, the procedures of justification that come to typify ethics seek to isolate individual persons. (Only later are they invited back into a larger collective). Because we sense that the morality binding us is increasingly broken and unusable, we gravitate toward the conclusion that morality must begin, and end, with the self. "I must be author of my own moral standards and vision of the good life," is a typical expression of this conclusion. Thus, the term "freedom" becomes the standard coin of our moral talk.[23]

"Quandary ethics" also describes modern moral theory. Ethical theorists begin their inquiry by proposing a moral dilemma: an agent must choose between two incompatible paths, both representing some good. By assuming dilemmas as an incontrovertible starting point, quandary ethicists assume the autonomy of dilemmas. They exist independently of the agents who confront them.

Beginning with quandaries exemplifies the foundationalist approach in that the individual who confronts the quandary can be

---

22. Ibid., 21–22.
23. Ibid., 6ff.

anyone. The agent is a rational soul who has to choose according to some principle or other. But Hauerwas argues that this forgets that agents must be socially formed in a certain way in order to recognize a quandary as a quandary. We can only encounter a dilemma because we have learned to recognize the competing goods between which it asks us to choose. Dilemmas are not simply found. They are always dilemmas *for someone.*

Further, in its effort to provide moral principles grounded in no particular form of life, foundationalist theory naturally gives rise to the question, "Whose ethic is this?" "For whom does this ethics provide moral guidance?" An ethic based on universal principles presupposes that it is possible to have moral thoughts without, at the same time, occupying a home in some form of life, i.e., being a person with a culture. Following Bernard Williams, Hauerwas notes that the agents implied in these moral theories occupy the "midair" stance—that is, they must deliberate in a way that stands back from anything they might actually care about.[24] This disengaged agent is precisely the one to whom Anscombe drew our attention in chapter 1.

Foundationalist theories thus distort our understanding of the agent. Yet Hauerwas is equally concerned with the political motivation that he believes animates these theories, and the sense of fragmentation that underlies it. Hauerwas argues that modern ethical theory is rooted in fear—in the sense of fragmentation that bedevils the human soul and characterizes society—and seeks to secure peace by abstracting from our differences. We have a deep craving for wholeness. Wholeness, or our lack of it, is the fundamental source for how we approach the moral life and generate the kinds of theories that can help us manage it.

The political reality initiated by the life of Jesus—the promise of learning to live with our differences without fear of the other—enables Hauerwas the Christian to develop another mode of moral reflection. It enables him to begin by affirming the particularity and contingency of all moralities—that which, in his view, gives rise to the felt divisions. Most importantly, it allows him to work from an avowedly particular perspective.

Hauerwas affirms that every ethic has a "qualifier" (e.g., Christian ethics, Jewish ethics, etc.). A "qualified ethic" points to an alternative

---

24. See Hauerwas, *The Peaceable Kingdom*, 17–19.

to foundationalist theory. It operates with a set of conceptual tools that include the virtues and narrative. Together virtues and narrative compose the form of practical reasoning that, for Hauerwas, display the manner in which Christian convictions work in shaping the moral life for Christians. Hauerwas deliberately combines form and content here. Narrative properly understood entails particular stories—stories with a concrete content rather than "story" as category.[25] There is thus an intimacy for Hauerwas between the form of practical reasoning (as formation in the virtues exemplified within a narrative) he adopts and the content of Christian convictions. This means that for him there is no contradiction between an ethic's being particular and its reasonableness—i.e., its ability to make truth claims. Accepting the particularity of our moral lives, Hauerwas would say suggestively, is the first step in giving a truthful account of them.

The Importance of Qualifiers

Embracing narrative and virtue has special value for work done within Christian theology. For modernity's search for foundations has led to distortions within Christians' own self-understanding. By implying that true moral principles must be free of metaphysical presuppositions, or beliefs whose source lies outside the bounds of pure reason, foundationalism categorically excludes Christian convictions—grounded in historical revelation—from making claims to moral truth. As a result, Christians come to speak as though their convictions play the merely "functional" role of "motivating" them to do what is required by a morality to which they are indifferent.[26] But this implies that moral experience can be divided into two parts. On the one hand, we have moral truth claims or judgments, and, on the other, the agent who is otherwise motivated to act upon such claims. When adopted by Christian moralists, however, this moral psychology leads to the problematic assumption that formation in the church is not necessary to acting Christianly.

Because it distorts the nature of the Christian moral life in this way, the influence of modern theory may lead Christians to misinterpret their own convictions. For one such conviction is that their lives

---

25. See, for example, Hauerwas and Jones, *Why Narrative?* 1–20.

26. Hauerwas, *Peaceable Kingdom*, 12–15. Here, Hauerwas's heading is "The Privatization of Religion."

are subject to transformation. In fact, Jesus calls them to be a new people—the citizens of a new kingdom.

Accordingly, Hauerwas insists that Christians ought to acknowledge the contingency of their ethical reflection—i.e., the importance of the qualifier "Christian." This serves the purpose both of truthful representation of our moral experience and of getting Christianity right. For, in denying their particularity they deny who they are. Being truthful about their particularity may seem merely to exacerbate the fragmentation they feel in their selves and in their world. Yet Christians believe that what they need in order to cope with their fractured moral lives is a truthful story that acknowledges their lives as they are.

Thus, a political story of peace-making, of reconciliation over and above our differences, fear and brokenness is the form of Christian moral reflection. Christians learn to be part of it by living with others who live by the same story in the church. It is in the church that they become skilled in the habits of accepting their particularity, what Hauerwas calls truthfulness.

Narrative and the Virtues

We now turn directly to the conceptual tools (narrative and virtues) that Hauerwas deems so appropriate to a Christian ethics, and their distinction from "foundationalist" ones.

The main tool that Hauerwas seeks to develop here is that of "narrative." Broadly construed, "narrative" can be seen as an account of the nature of human beliefs and their relation to the practical life. It supposes that our moral lives are fundamentally dependent and particular. Narrative is an especially important alternative theoretical tool for Hauerwas because it is an integral part of the conceptions of self and action requisite to the Christian story, which construes human beings as creatures of a gift-giving God who require help in recognizing their dependence on God.

Narrative essentially describes the form by which beliefs compel actions. Foundationalist, or rule-based, theories seek to explain the relation of belief to action by pointing out how the judgment embodied in a particular action is justified by more general rules. Narrative ethics responds to this "vertical" picture of the justification of actions with a horizontal or historically comparative approach. The agent justifies his or her action both by comparing a current judgment with the wisdom embodied in the history and traditions carried by his or her community, and by comparing them with the pattern established in his or her personal history. Narrative thus recognizes that the moral life is historical. Its unity is that of a "pattern" in the story one tells about oneself in one's world: a story with a beginning, a middle, and an end. Reasons are offered by persons who are rooted in a past, look forward to a future, and are confronted with the necessity of acting in the present circumstances.

This distinct view of deliberation has implications for the question of the motivation to act morally as well. For on the narrative view, the agent's deliberation mainly entails evaluating current choices in the light of his or her history—what he or she has done and why (i.e., in relation to the rationality or pattern of his or her action). Because deliberation is rooted in the agent's history and sense of self (identity), what one chooses is unavoidably a matter of personal concern.

Narrative's attention to the historical dimension of human lives allows us to see how selves are formed/transformed along the course of life. The actions we perform contribute to our being shaped in one way rather than another. Hauerwas argues that we need to be formed/transformed as selves *in order to* come to see the world as it really is. Our proper discernment of the moral world is not a brute fact about us. It requires training. Our ability to see correctly what is before us depends on our proper formation in a community.

To complete his account of the narrative basis of the moral life Hauerwas turns to the Christian story: to the ur-story of life's meaning in the Christian community (creation/sin). Here the reason for the terminology I have been using "formation/transformation" becomes clearer. Because sin and redemption through Christ lie at the heart of the Christian story, formation in Christian virtue is in its depths transformation.

The purpose of the doctrine of sin is to help Christians understand the nature of their own self-deception. In Christian terms, the requirement that selves be transformed implies that there is something in us that resists facing the fundamental truth about ourselves and the world. This fundamental truth is equally articulated in the doctrine of creation, which says we are radically dependent gifts of God. Through the doctrines of sin and creation Christians learn that the basic form of their self-deception, and therefore the starting point of their moral training, is the failure to acknowledge that they are the creatures of a God who created them and their world freely and gratuitously. Narrative is a superior way to do Christian ethics, then, because it expresses conceptually a key Christian belief about how the world is. Narrative helps us to see the structure of Christian views on self, world, and God.[27]

If the Christian story as the ultimate structure of one's personal story implies that the moral life requires transformation, the virtues are the qualities of character a Christian seeks to attain and embody. A virtue is a disposition of the agent—a "readiness" in him or her—to perform particular kinds of action. The significance of speaking of virtue in moral theory is that it assumes that the agent's character plays an important role in how his or her moral life—a life comprised of actions—unfolds.[28]

Virtue represents an important alternative to foundationalist theories because it implies that the agent's emotions are implicated in the moral life, and thus signals a socially embodied philosophical anthropology. Furthermore, virtue implies a distinct moral epistemology on whose account the agent's habits and cultivation play a role in her or his ability to identify and deliberate about moral problems.

Hauerwas's emphasis on virtue follows from his embrace of narrative as the form of the moral life. We are historical agents and our moral lives depend upon how we are formed. This formation, moreover, is contingent upon the conceptions of Christian life handed down by those formed by the story in the past—it occurs in an ongoing tradition. Even more than a person's disposition, for Hauerwas "virtue" is a concept that addresses the ability to *see* certain aspects of the world as salient for the moral life, and thus refers to the ability of discernment. Aquinas's name for the virtue that renders practical reason skillful is of course "prudence." Hauerwas's preference for the virtues presupposes that living truthfully in many situations will require skill and imagination because the created world is full of surprises.[29]

---

27. Hauerwas further defends this formal match by pointing out that narrative is the form of the Gospels, and of the Scriptures themselves when taken as the embodiment of the story of God's relationship with his people. See, *Peaceable Kingdom*, 75ff.

28. This quick sketch of the character of virtue theory is not meant to be exhaustive. For a fuller treatment see, for example, Porter *Recovery of Virtue*.

29. For a fuller account of the difference Christian convictions make to the virtues, see Pinches and Hauerwas, *Christians Among the Virtues*.

Freedom as Agency

> [O]ur ability to "have character" does not require the positing of a transcendental freedom.[30]

Having taken the narrative turn, Hauerwas addresses the problem of a moral psychology that recognizes embodiment (particularity) and is thus appropriate to a Christian ethics.[31] Wanting to ground this psychology in the life of action, he begins with the notion of "agency." The concept of agency is his attempt to respond to the moral psychological questions concerning "freedom" or the "first person point of view" in the light of sin.

In Hauerwas's account, the philosophical analysis of agency is contextualized by a scripturally-rooted Christian doctrine of sin. The doctrine of sin complements a focus on agency, just as the latter helps explicate what the doctrine entails. "Agency" describes what it means to be moral actors—that is, to be in some degree "free"—in tune with the claim that we are historical beings and subject to sin. We are "historical" in the sense that we are the creatures of a God who wills us to be and who has given us a law of life from which we have fallen away. To explicate agency requires treating not only the concepts of freedom and "character," but also the doctrines of creation and sin.

In Reinhold Niebuhr's terms, man lies at the frontier of the spiritual and the material. To be a self implies being an agent, an originator of motion, a "free" being. Yet we are also finite, and limited by our bodily experience. An account of freedom, then, is a response to this basic problem of the tension between man's embodiment and his capacity for transcendence. Hauerwas employs the concept of agency to cope with the paradox of human freedom without succumbing to a dichotomy between freedom and social determination.

Foundationalists locate the center of moral freedom and responsibility in decision. Because of their penchant for abstraction, such theories tend to place emphasis on the agent's awareness. That is, maximal awareness provides the condition under which the agent can be said to *decide* as freely as possible—free, so far as possible, from the contingencies of the world. As an alternative, Hauerwas suggests that our freedom as agents consists in the ability to "claim our actions as our

---

30. Hauerwas, *Peaceable Kingdom*, 43.
31. See chapter 3 of Hauerwas, *Peaceable Kingdom*.

own."[32] To be free is to have a history. "Having a history," moreover, is not merely to have been causally involved in a series of prior actions. One writes one's history by making what one has done an answer to the question of who one is—or at least the clearest sense one can have of "what one has done." The agent's freedom lies in identifying with its actions (claiming them as *my* actions) through making them a part of a personal and communal history.[33] We have free selves to the extent that we can be one—at peace—with what we do.

Rather than emphasize awareness as a capacity whose exercise provides a condition for freedom, in sync with his emphasis on history Hauerwas points to our descriptive abilities. The power of description provides the condition for freedom by enabling us to incorporate what we do, and what happens to us, as a part of our stories (or narratives). Thus, the power of description allows us to *appropriate* our actions. The agent's descriptive abilities constitute the condition for the possibility of identifying with its actions, and thus becoming a historical, or storied, self. Freedom consists in the set of skills that allows us "to make a virtue of necessity."[34]

To be an agent, moreover, requires membership in a community. Our descriptive skills are habits cultivated in us through participation in communities. Such skills could neither be acquired nor sustained outside of the context of a community with a common language. More than this, descriptions are themselves the property of a community. For Hauerwas, then, "our freedom is literally carried by a community."[35]

To test the agency view of freedom, which ties our freedom inextricably to our histories within a particular community, Hauerwas takes up an argument set forth by fellow religious ethicist Gene Outka.[36] Outka argues that it is finally impossible to distinguish between the passive and self-ruling aspects of a human being—that is, between what one has suffered and how one now lives. When we fully take account of

32. Ibid., 36.
33. Ibid., 37.
34. Ibid., 38.
35. "For 'description,' while often verbal, is just as importantly a matter of habit—indeed most verbal skills are also habits. That is why our freedom is literally carried by a community that sustains us in the habits of self-possession—not the least of which is learning to depend on and trust in others" (ibid., 42–43).
36. See Outka, "Character, Vision and Narrative," 110–18, and Hauerwas, *Peaceable Kingdom*, 39–43.

the influence of our surroundings, perhaps even the freedom to claim our lives as ours is threatened; selves are too wounded and confused to achieve self-rule.

In reply to this, Hauerwas asserts that agency, or the ability to be who we are and what we have done, must be in some sense God's gift to us. It is only in response to God's saving presence, which calls us out of our fragmented selves, that we are able to find our life as actors. This presence takes the form of an invitation to be part of a life and a story beyond our own, the story of Jesus' invitation to be part of a kingdom whose defining characteristic is service to the neighbor in need.[37] In this new life of participation in Jesus' agency through the church we will find the wholeness necessary for freedom.

Hauerwas encapsulates the point in the notion of "freedom as the presence of the other."[38] Yet to find our agency through Jesus' call to self-giving service to the other is not another kind of "midair" freedom. The fragmentation that disables our historical selves is traded in for participation in another history and not for an ahistorical heaven. It is the history of God's relation to a chosen people (Israel and the Church) through which he has chosen to make known to the world his self-giving love which enables us to accept and live with our brokenness.

The freedom that comes from accepting the invitation to be part of God's life requires growth in character. "Sin," as we have seen, is for Hauerwas the doctrine by which Christians learn to see themselves as God's creatures, for it exposes their tendency to conceive themselves as the sole authors of their stories. The inability to accept the truth of our messy, historical selves that leads to foundationalism is not only dishonesty; it is *self*-deception. Hauerwas argues that our fear of giving up the unity of self bought through manipulation prevents us from accept-

---

37. "... [I]t is the Christian claim that no one is so completely determined that he or she lacks all means to respond to the story of the story of God and thus find some means to make his life his own. Such a claim is not based on optimistic assumptions about our goodness or our innate ability. Rather it is an affirmation of God's unrelenting desire to have each of us serve in the kingdom. The call to such service we find only in the presence of another, whose need is often the very occasion of our freedom. For it is through the need of another that the greatest hindrance to my freedom, namely my own self-absorption, is finally not so much overcome as simply rendered irrelevant. It is through the other that I am finally able to make peace with myself and thus have the power to make my life my own" (Hauerwas, *Peaceable Kingdom*, 44).

38. Ibid.

ing real peace.[39] Remembering the doctrine of sin in the discussion of agency highlights the point that to understand ourselves as creatures—and thus to become free—is not itself a given but requires *learning*.

Hauerwas's description of human beings as both historical and free thus brings together the narrative conception of human beings and his confession of his Christianity. It is the community that confesses and follows Jesus Christ as he who saves us from sin that gave Hauerwas the language in which to be free. For Hauerwas the Christian this freedom consists in participating in an adventure of self-giving service to the neighbor. This form of living is fitting for the one who realizes he must receive his life as a gift.

Reason and Christian Ethics

> *If theological convictions are meant to construe the world—that is, if they have the character of practical discourse—then ethics is involved in the beginning, not the end, of theology.*[40]

In light of the foregoing, how ought Christian ethics to be done? Now Hauerwas turns from arguments with philosophical foundationalism to address those that make up the community of Christian thinkers. The task he sets out to accomplish is that of making fundamental Christian beliefs and tradition into an account of a rational moral life for followers of Jesus. To do this he is required to work in two stages. The first is a theologically geared analysis about how to formally articulate Christian convictions. The second examines how we may rationally bind ourselves to a particular tradition through considering the reason/revelation theme. In both of these stages, Hauerwas employs narrative as a conception of rationality that bridges, rather than divides, our reflective lives and our practical lives. In this account of the form of Christian ethics, Hauerwas is showing how practical reason can be particular and embodied, and no less rational for that.

---

39. "The recognition that we are most free when we are formed by a story that helps us live appropriate to the reality that our life is a gift is also the context for rightly understanding what it means to be a sinner. Earlier I suggested that sin is not a natural category; that we have to be taught we are sinners. Moreover sin is not just an error or the doing of certain prohibited actions, but sin is the positive attempt to overreach our power as creatures. It is manifested in our pride and sensuality, but its fundamental form is self-deception" (ibid., 46).

40. Hauerwas, *Peaceable Kingdom*, 54.

Scriptural Background of Natural Law

Hauerwas begins with a criticism of the ethical method of Christian "natural law." This method holds that the ethical teachings of the church are rationally grounded in laws of nature that are open to confirmation by the faculty of reason possessed by all human beings. While *prima facie* the point of the natural law approach is to achieve a basic grounding for Christian norms in human nature, Hauerwas argues that this approach ultimately makes Christian moral norms appear arbitrary and imperious. It does this by the problematic claim that the reasons for what Christians are to do are not to be found in what is particular to Christian tradition.

But the point to be noted here is that there is a theological move that precedes and accounts for the separating out of particular Christian convictions from the ground of ethical argument: namely the theological approach that abstracts nature and grace, as theological attributes of the world, from the narrative context of Scripture. Because nature is removed from the narrative setting in which we first recognized it, it can be made into a foundational basis for moral arguments, or the basis of an "ethic for anyone."

The approach to the theological articulation of Christian beliefs, then, is of primary importance—how one does this will shape the way one does Christian ethics. When the method of articulation tends toward excessive abstraction, the result is an unhealthy division between Christians' descriptions of the world and the way they live out these convictions morally. Because the process of abstraction makes Christian convictions about the world—convictions that guide Christians' actions in that world—into freestanding norms, we lose sight of the way these convictions require embodiment in a historical community. The unhealthy effect that foundationalism can have on moral psychology—the "midair" point of view—can be reproduced within Christian theological and moral reflection.

Another result of the theological abstraction of nature from its narrative context is that we come to see the role of Christian convictions to center on the "inner" or "motivational" dimension of moral action. In particular, Christian belief is relegated to emotion and motivation because of the understanding that the epistemological bases of moral action are taken care of by a "natural" rationality—i.e., a rationality that draws on no particular traditions. This too, moreover, promotes a problematic conception of agency that fails to recognize the inseparable connection between agent and action.[41]

The consequences of separating particular Christian convictions from the rational ground of what Christians are to do are not only theoretical vagueness but a certain division in the self's experience as well. If our deepest beliefs as Christians are not to be lived out, we cannot but experience our relation to such beliefs as "alienated." And even the instrumental relation of beliefs and practices described by "motivation" will foster such alienation. We can only be whole persons when our beliefs about the world are embodied in what we do and strive for.

Thus one question this section seeks to answer concerns how Hauerwas approaches the theological task—the articulation of Christian convictions—in such a way as to re-unite the truth-value of Christian beliefs with their practical force, and thus make whole selves. Put simply, Hauerwas's theological ethics inquires as to how to make Christian convictions in their particularity practical, and what kind of method (rationality) is suitable for this task.

We may begin to conceptualize such an alternative to the abstraction of nature and grace from their theological context by considering the ways that we most naturally learn the significance of the convictions that the world is created and redeemed. Is it by asking after the meaning of these beliefs considered discretely, or in terms of their logical properties that we first encounter the truths of Christian faith? This might be so for beings other than we are, perhaps angelic beings who are purely mind. As non-angels, it seems likely that we come to know these Christian truths by identifying our own stories with the story of God's re-creative and redemptive life that Scripture and the church unfold. That is, we come know these truths in the same way we come to a sense of who we are: namely, by claiming ownership (authorship) of our actions by writing them into a personal and communal story.

This historical context in which we know ourselves may be compared to the Scriptures as the context or home in which Christian convictions become accessible. The Scriptures contain the history or narrative in which Christian convictions are at home. To speak of a narrative epistemology is to say that things are known to us in and through the home in which we discover them.

---

41. See the first chapter of this book.

Narrative—including its use as a method of reading Scripture—then constitutes an alternative approach to Christian theology for Hauerwas. How does it work in wedding Christian truth claims and their ethical embodiment? In just the way that our self-knowledge comes from reflection on and appropriation of our own actions, we learn Christian convictions through the church-centered practices that recount the Christian story. The form of these practices consists in learning to understand our own actions by placing them within the story of the Creator's own actions. The form of Scripture is paradigmatic in that it recounts the histories of God's people struggling to live into his story. Thus, for Hauerwas narrative as a theological method is appropriate for the task of Christian ethics, for it facilitates the embodiment of Christian convictions. To adopt the Christian story requires a "qualification," or transformation, of the self and its history.

Reasoning in Revelation

> *The word "revelation" is not a qualifier of the epistemic status of a kind of knowledge.*[42]

Granted the above, the issue for Hauerwas becomes the reconciliation of the narrative method with current conceptions of reason and revelation. He shows here how a narrative reading of the Scriptures enables us to reflectively bind ourselves to the particular history and tradition embodied in the Scriptures—how, that is, narrative brings together epistemological and practical dimensions in the life of a historical community.

He examines what he takes to be a typical contemporary natural lawyer's account of revelation and its relation to reason as sources of authority in morals. This method, he suggests, inevitably leads to a separation of Christian ethical convictions and reality. Richard McCormick argues that to base morality solely on the particular scriptures of Christianity is inherently limiting. More than that, it is self-contradictory for Christians to do so. For the God Christians know in Scripture is creator and Lord of the universe. How then, he asks, could moral knowledge be accessible to those outside the Christian community—i.e., those who presumably do not have access to the knowledge revealed in what are particularly Christian documents? For Christians

---

42. Hauerwas, *Peaceable Kingdom*, 66.

to argue that their morality is particular is in contradiction to what they believe. Furthermore, to insist that Christian morality is particular amounts to imagining God in such a way as to be one who contravenes our very being (nature). Morality only becomes intelligible insofar as it coheres with our nature. To deny this amounts theologically to a kind of voluntarism. Yet the profile of the loving Creator Christians find in revelation does not seem to match the one portrayed by voluntarism.

Hauerwas uses McCormick here to illustrate the ambivalence inherent in this brand of Christian ethics. In attempting to establish a universal ground for moral principles, even ostensibly Christian ones, McCormick argues that to base morality solely on the particular tradition that is Christianity would be un-Christian.

Hauerwas points out, moreover, that McCormick's use of the term "revelation" harbors a certain equivocation. The concept is forced to play the dual and perhaps contradictory roles of referring to what we know of God and of denominating a certain category of knowledge.[43] He seems, that is, determined to give revelation a modest epistemological status because of a prior commitment not to base his ethics on particular and contingent grounds. The political dimension of McCormick's position emerges when he states that moralities rooted in Scripture (read: particular traditions) are by nature "obediential."[44]

Hauerwas argues that revelation is not made distinct by how we know it, but by what it is about—i.e., its subject matter. Revelation tells of God's activity in creating the world and of his will to redeem his creation after the fall. Revelational knowledge indeed refers to happenings in the universe and makes claims about nature. Its proclamations about the world make claims to knowledge-worthiness like any other such

---

43. Of course, as Hauerwas here recounts, such modes of interpreting Scripture abound. For example, it is said that the truths of Scripture do not consist in the reporting of happenings, but in meaningful events of God's self-disclosure that do not take place in ordinary time. Yet what this of course may lead to is the tendency to of human interpreters to propose their meanings before the Scriptures are consulted or attended to.

44. ". . . If Christian faith and revelation add material content to what is knowable in principle by reason, then the churches conceivably could teach moral positions and conclusions independently of the reasons and analyses that recommend these conclusions. This could lend great support to a highly juridical and obediential notion of Christian morality." McCormick, "Does Faith Add to Ethical Perception?" 157. Quoted in Hauerwas, *Peaceable Kingdom*, 64.

statements. Yet these claims have a home—the Scripture as a whole—and it is within the narrative context Scripture provides that revelational claims become meaningful for Christians. Moral claims, like the Ten Commandments, state what appear to be clear and self-sufficient guidelines for moral behavior, but their full significance only becomes apparent when they are placed in the context of God's efforts to create a people after his likeness.[45]

What Hauerwas has done here is to articulate through narrative an alternate view of rationality for the one that dichotomizes reason and revelation. On the basis of the narrative methodology there is no need to negate (abstract from) the particular and history-like character of scriptural revelation in order to make it rational. Rather, abstractions like "nature" should be considered short-hand reminders that help us retell the story of how and why God created the universe—they are, that is, pragmatic tools that help the community reconstitute the larger narrative. Abstract concepts like "nature" and "grace," by their nature, "require narrative display for their intelligibility." The narrative approach to the claims of revelation has the notion of an interpretive community built in.

Of course, by articulating a narrative epistemology, Hauerwas is also pointing again to a kind of knowledge that is knowledge *for us*—that is, accessible to our finite and embodied communities. Revelational statements in fact require communal practices of re-telling and re-enactment in order to be meaningful. The community is not sustained by knowing in abstraction.

In sum, through using narrative as a methodological alternative to the employing of abstract and general concepts, Hauerwas shows how the rationality of Christian beliefs is closely tied to their practical embodiment—his Christian ethics. Learning these beliefs, furthermore, requires a transformation of the self to embody the story of its community. Hauerwas thus exemplifies practical reasoning grounded in social form of life.

---

45. E.g., Lev 19:1–4, "And the Lord said to Moses, 'Say to all the congregation of the people of Israel, You shall be holy; for I the Lord your God am holy. Every one of you shall revere his mother and his father, an you shall keep my Sabbaths: I am the Lord your God. Do not turn or make for yourselves molten gods. I am the Lord your God.'"

RECAP

The question Hauerwas began with was, "What is the task of Christian ethics?" In pursuing the question, he re-defines it so that "Christian ethics" is no longer thought distinct from Christian theology, or "Christian reflection." The task of Christian ethics, according to Hauerwas, is to help make the claims about reality that constitute Christian tradition manifest in the embodied lives of Christians. The approach to theology that abstracts theological truths from their "home" in Christian Scripture and tradition leads to the current *status quo* where Christian truth claims, on the one hand, and the norms that guide Christian lives, on the other, are alienated from one another.

Hauerwas responds to this problem by pointing up a distinct methodology, namely narrative. Narrative methodology treats Christian beliefs as concrete claims about the world that gain their intelligibility in the context of the history of a people and their God. Yet a narrative construal of Christian truth claims does not require a separate discipline that explains how such truth claims shape the lives of Christians. Rather, as we will see in the next section on the church's practices, the Christian believer makes these claims a part of her or his embodied life by actions—that is, by those actions that constitute placing herself or himself within the story within which these claims become intelligible. To borrow from the terms established earlier where we discussed Hauerwas's view of the relation of agency and identity, the claim here is that the agent is able to make the narrative hers or his.

Jesus and the Kingdom

> *You, therefore, must be perfect, as your heavenly Father is perfect.*
> *(Matt 5:48)*

If Christian practical reasoning involves a people learning to weave its story into God's story, they need a tradition and a scripture that provides *examples* of how this is done. Taking up this theme, Hauerwas points out that the Hebrew and Christian Scriptures enjoin the people Israel and the followers of Jesus to become *like* their God. The Christian moral life is well-described as *Imitatio Dei*.

Jesus is of central significance for the Christian life. Yet Jesus' example requires narrative display in the Scriptures. This narrative will show also how those who first encountered him *responded* to him, and thus it provides an image of discipleship. Jesus' message was less about himself than about the kingdom he came to initiate.

There is a tradition of viewing the moral life as a matter of following God's example that pre-dates the arrival of Jesus. Hauerwas notes that the people of Israel believed that certain events whereby God impressed himself into her history revealed the character of God and his intentions for humankind. Therefore Israel's most important religious observance involves remembering God's action within his relationship with her. "Remembering" here implies not merely recalling something whose actuality has come and gone, but keeping the formative past alive by embodying God's past actions within her own present ones. As portrayed in the Scriptures, Israel's imitation of God is enacted in its key institutions: the prophet, the king and the priest. For Yahweh calls the people to a special task and adventure, serves them through leadership, and sacrifices himself for them. Those who occupied these roles were judged by how well they reflected Yahweh's character for the people to follow.[46] Thus Israel strives to make God's character her own (*imitatio Dei*). Hauerwas further notes because God's character is made known through his actions, Israel has no alternative but to enact God's intentions.

For the early church, Hauerwas says, Jesus' life was understood as re-capitulating God's history with Israel, making this history, and thus God's character, freshly visible. In this regard, he directs our attention to the way that the temptation narratives in the Gospels represent this re-capitulation. Like Israel, Jesus' example is displayed for us here in the particular manner he chooses to witness to his own relationship to God. The narratives display this manner by contrasting it with other possibilities. The devil tempts him to manifest his power as God's son by banishing all material want, claiming ultimate dominion and making himself "the sacrifice that God cannot refuse."[47] But Jesus has another agenda. For him God's action cannot be equated with the satisfaction of merely physical needs, coercive political force or hubristic heroism. His witness, Hauerwas observes, consists in giving himself up to his father's will.[48]

---

46. See Hauerwas, *Peaceable Kingdom*, 77–78. Hauerwas is here drawing substantially on Tinsley, *Imitation of God in Christ*.

47. Hauerwas, *Peaceable Kingdom*, 79.

48. Ibid., 79.

Christians are thus to follow Jesus' example by striving to respond to God's action through service to others, imitating his actions. As Hauerwas writes, "In this way of service, we learn of the kind of God we are to love and to whom we are called to obedience. For Jesus' life is the life of God insofar as he serves others as God serves us."[49] The cross reveals that God's love persists in spite of human rejections to the extent of being willing to be crucified by those who reject him.

The life of Jesus continues to reflect God's character as displayed in the story of the Israelites, but there are also innovations. Christians believe Jesus makes possible a way of living in the world even the Israelites thought impossible. Jesus announces an unprecedented form for a community following God to take upon itself: a community that rejects using violence in the service of its ends—ushering in a new age. He thus makes it possible for his followers to witness to God's nature in a new way. The name for this new form, of course, is "the Kingdom of God." Jesus' life discloses that form, revealing yet more determinately how God rules the cosmos by self-giving love. This "eschatological" dimension of Jesus' message implies that he also empowers his followers to be transformed toward the example he offers them. Jesus' life is then both a sign of God's coming kingdom and its (heightened) presence: its announcement and its beginning.

Yet the way of the kingdom is hard to learn. As for the Israelites before them, the example of Jesus comes to light in the drama of God's initiatory actions and the disciples' responses recorded in the Scriptures. Israel, in Hauerwas's rendering, comes to know the pattern of her Lord's way, the path she is to follow, through the story of her failures to be obedient to her God, to identify her will with his. Remembering the history of her idolatry in response to God's faithful love reminds her of how she is to follow God. So for Christians, "the very demands Jesus placed on his followers means that he cannot be known abstracted from the disciples' response."[50] The recording of how the disciples stumble is integral to the example provided in the Christian gospels.

---

49. Ibid., 80.
50. Ibid., 73.

The Church's Sociality

> *The church does not have a social ethic. It is a social ethic.*[51]

Learning the way of the kingdom leads Hauerwas to the question of the Christian community. Narrative as method and epistemology implies that (human) knowing takes place in communities. The (ethical) knowing whereby I integrate events into the story of who I am is inescapably the process of integrating them into the story of who *we* are. While this claim is a methodological one for secular thought, for Hauerwas it is a substantive and material claim. For the significance of Jesus' life—in particular its eschatological *telos*—requires a political community to manifest it. It is manifested, finally, by the ability of individuals to live with one another peaceably.

Christian community does not simply happen; it must be built. Part of that building is the work of Christian ethics. The specific role of Christian ethics is to help the church in the present day to make the stories of Jesus and the people of Israel its own—that is, to practice their re-telling. Thereby, the communal nature of narrative knowing is carried out in the church's self-constituting practice.

The tendency of contemporary Christian ethicists is to consider the social ethic of the church in terms of what the church does for the world outside its walls. Christian "social ethics" therefore comes to concern itself with what is *not* church. This conception of social ethics stems from the assumption that the first task of Christian social ethics is to secure some grounds of cooperation with the society at large. This it must do by seeking common ground. Consequently, its primary task comes to be that of constructing a foundation, a common ground, upon which all parties can operate together.

Ultimately, Hauerwas agrees that the church must consider the world outside its boundaries when pondering its purpose and its moral responsibilities. Yet he expresses the fear that when a social ethic is limited to this external reference, we easily forget that community also points to a constitutive aspect of human knowing as such, so that a social ethic cannot merely be about the "world outside." Hauerwas therefore calls upon Christian ethicist to recognize that the church is essential to their work.

---

51. Ibid., 99.

Christian ethics concerns not the actions of individual Christians but how the Christian people learn to live together. Because Jesus calls those who would follow him to a new *political* reality (i.e., "the kingdom"), the church is required as a necessary condition for Christian convictions to inform the life of practice. It is the arena in which Christians learn to transform their beliefs about God into skills for living. Christian ethical reflection, therefore, must be addressed first to the church, those seeking to form their lives on the example of Jesus.

It is a mistake for such ethics to begin by trying to find common ground with the society at large. When Christian reflection turns first to the world as its audience it neglects the task of formation, and ultimately does the world a disservice. It does so by not being willing to be itself, or acknowledging the value of being itself. For the calling of the church is to embody truthful justice, mercy, and peace.

The question is how the church—aided by Christian ethical reflection—may be constituted as the bearer of Jesus' significance. First the church is constituted by being called by God to serve his purposes. Yet the self-constituting activities within the church also contribute to how it realizes its larger mission. The virtues that mark the church are not ends in themselves. The priority of the church's self-constitution in Hauerwas's project is only preparatory. The church, aided by the Christian ethicist, is to make the justice and truthfulness it embodies visible. Hauerwas argues that God uses the church to make his ways known to the world. The church is finally the "servant community," but to help it realize this role Christian ethics must itself begin in service to the church.

There is a sense in which for the church to be the church requires a recognition of its own separateness. The church is the church over and against "the world." These "relational concepts" do not mark an ontological distinction, but a distinction of agencies: the church represents the people who uniquely confess the ultimate character of the world as the kingdom of God.[52] The political reality of the church is "eschatological": it depends on the belief that God's kingdom both arrived in Jesus' life

---

52. Following Yoder, Hauerwas explains that the difference between church and world is a difference of "agencies." He writes, "the distinction between church and world is not between realms of reality, between orders of creation and redemption, between nature and supernature, but 'rather between the basic personal postures of men, some of whom confess and others of whom do not confess that Jesus is Lord'" (ibid., 101). The quotation is from Yoder, *The Original Revolution*, 116.

and is also still to come. That its own political reality is both "present" and "yet to come" means that the church is a political community that alternately participates, and refuses to participate, in worldly politics. What distinguishes the church in this is its sense of history. Its vision of the unfolding redemption of history implies that it is a community living "in between the times," which is to say "on the way." Its obligation is to make known to the world the political kingdom that is in fact its destiny. It does this by utilizing its agency to witness to the possibilities revealed in the pattern of Jesus' life.

The church is further constituted as a unique witness to the kingdom by the cultivation of the virtues necessary to be a people "on the way." Because virtues are characteristics that help a community sustain itself over time, they must be a part of any community that maintains itself as a viable polity. Yet these virtues are qualified by the stories that political communities tell of the end to which they are destined. In this light, the purpose of Christian ethics, then, is to help us see the ways in which Christian virtues are qualified by the Christian vision of the kingdom of God.

Like other communities, the church relies on the virtues of faith, hope and love. For Hauerwas, however, the special role it attributes to patience marks the distinctive character of the church. Patience is an especially important virtue for a people who believe in a kingdom of peace that is both already and not yet. The role of patience as a virtue that marks off the church can be seen in the manner in which it shapes the way Christians seek justice. Christian longing for justice is intensified by the hope Christians have in Jesus. Yet the glaring injustices they see in the world around them may tempt them to take justice into their own hands. To become a violent people would betray the very character of the kingdom for which they hope, since their sovereign rules in the form of a suffering servant. "God," he writes, "does not rule creation through coercion, but through a cross."[53] The church as polis, then, must learn to suffer with their longing for a just world—to patiently hope for it—for they believe such justice will not be brought about through their impatient efforts to secure it. Not by force, but by the activity of the God of love and mercy, which they are to imitate, will justice be brought about.

---

53. Hauerwas, *Peaceable Kingdom*, 104.

Christian patience is also expressed in a willingness to let others wield the power and control of social institutions, come to them what may. To "live out of control" provides the church with perspective necessary to witness to the coming kingdom. This perspective sustains the hope that "God will use our faithfulness to make his kingdom a reality in the world."[54]

Reframing Decisions: Casuistry and Narrative Method

Christians live in their contemporary world formed and continuously transformed by their communally carried narrative. They still must face and resolve the ethical issues of their time and place. How will they do this?

In answer, Hauerwas turns to a popular method of ethical reasoning according to which a community uses past experiences as paradigms for guiding them through present decisions—i.e., casuistry. He is careful to stipulate *how* Christian ethics exemplifies such use of settled judgments from the past to provide guidance in the face of present dilemmas, for there is a foundationalist casuistry he seeks to avoid. Thus, he finds it necessary to proceed treating the form and content of Christian casuistry together. This means grounding casuistic method in the narrative self-understanding of Christian tradition. In order to show how this can be done—how casuistry can be embodied in a community—Hauerwas describes how casuistic method functions within Christians' attempts to live their lives in a manner that is faithful to their formative story. But he also demonstrates that Christian convictions make a real difference in how one deliberates and acts (and allows God to act) in concrete situations.

In general, casuistry signifies a method of ethical reasoning consisting in case-like descriptions of present moral dilemmas, more general or "settled" cases called "paradigms," and general action-guiding principles. In justifying a certain way of resolving the case at hand one appeals to the example provided by a paradigm case—here used as a more general guideline—whose form offers a way of interpreting the current case and implies a direction for practical resolution. General moral "principles" abstracted from paradigm cases may provide still wider perspective on the paradigms themselves.

54. Ibid., 105.

Casuistry has sometimes been appropriated by the foundationalist tradition of ethical reasoning. For our purposes here, the salient characteristic of this use of it is that in looking for an account of action-guiding norms, it turns in the direction of greater abstraction, and away from the communal context where the rule was first observed.

Such a casuistry, further, emphasizes decision-making. The task of the moral deliberator is to come up with a justifiable resolution, and method of resolution, for the dilemma with which a person is confronted. The method of resolution ought to follow a rational form in being consistent with other such deliberations and employing publicly accessible criteria.

As noted above, foundationalist approaches imply that the kind of agent one is has little to do with the kinds of moral problems one faces, and consequently such agents as there are in these accounts are rendered in a certain and significant sense passive. We note further that the emphasis on consistency and public criteria suggest the salient characteristics of the agent are precisely those he or she shares with everyone else. The moral agent acts primarily as an individual and not as a member of a particular community.

A narrative mode of moral reflection, by contrast, proposes that paradigm cases serve as guides to re-telling a formative story that tells people *who* they are. Consequently, rules that stem from those cases are to be explained by reference to a story formative of self-understanding. They are expressions of the story insofar as they mark out practical norms for living in accordance with the self-knowledge that the story provides. Particular prohibitions can be read as markers of the limits of this self-knowledge: If one goes beyond such limits, it is no longer clear that they are the same kind of people they had been formerly—i.e., they will have to tell their stories differently. Hauerwas reminds us that the question "what ought I to be?" comes prior to the question "what ought I to do?"[55]

Hauerwas's narrative-grounded casuistry is a kind of practical reasoning that must take place within a particular, identity-conferring, tradition. His is a *Christian* casuistry in the sense that the paradigm examples to which present dilemmas are referred are shaped by the narrative through which Christian agents constitute their self-under-

---

55. See ibid., 19ff.

standing.[56] Both the paradigm examples and the agents who refer to them receive the qualifier "Christian." Christians' use of casuistry, then, can be characterized as an activity in which they try on practical interpretations and test them in terms of story of Jesus, which they seek to make their own through discipleship. The great potential for error in the moral life shows up the importance of "sin," or falling off the path, as an intrinsic part of the journey of following Jesus.

To illustrate this method, we may turn to a brief story based on one of Hauerwas's own examples.[57] A friend was on his way back from a trade conference on a plane when one of his colleagues, whom he had always found attractive, suggested that they might go out for a drink upon landing and perhaps spend the night together. Something reflexive caused him to nervously decline the offer and he later confessed that the first thought to occur to him in the moment was not "Is it right?" but "how would I explain to my family why I was late?" The "decision," in other words, stemmed from the identity-conferring story he had been living and his unwillingness to change that story. The agent refers the case confronting him to standards or paradigms by imagining how he would have to change the story in order to live in a consistent manner—that is, a manner consistent with his proposed choice. Deliberation here involves employing the imagination to see how the possibilities we are confronted with can be made to cohere, or not, with the story that sustains the lives we call our own.

So the rule "do not commit adultery" emerges from the pattern of lived life—lived socially in the context of significant others—within the life story of the man. The family story of marriage and children is normally thought incompatible with one-night affairs. To neglect the rule would be to propose an alternative concept of the family and of its roles of "spouse," "parent," etc.

We have spoken of a narrative casuistry in a way that may give too individualistic an impression. The story from which individuals form their own stories is essentially the product of a *community's* narrating

---

56. "What I mean by casuistry, then, is not just the attempt to adjudicate difficult cases of conscience within a system of moral principles, but is the process by which a tradition tests whether its practices are consistent (that is, truthful) or inconsistent in the light of its basic habits and convictions or whether these convictions require new practices and behavior" (ibid, 120).

57. See ibid., 129–30.

activity—i.e., the church. It is the church that for Hauerwas is the fundamental bearer of the Christian story.

The meaning of "church" in this context is more like an "ongoing conversation."[58] The "conversation," furthermore, is not necessarily a formal one, though such discussions are no doubt part of the church's life. Perhaps more fundamentally this conversation consists in individuals learning from the examples of others how to live the story better than they had been living it before. In this sense, casuistry is about honing the virtues, or skills, required by the story that forms one's identity.

Envisioning Possibilities for Action

So far we have described Christian casuistry in terms of an activity of narrating the Christian story in the context of the church. But what difference does this story actually make to how one acts in the moral life? When it comes to the ultimate moment of making a *decision* to follow course A versus course B, does the formative story of Christianity really matter?

The role of any identity-conferring story is to form persons who see the morally salient dimensions of their lives in a particular way and make moral decisions accordingly. The model of moral reasoning that attempts to abstract guiding principles from the context in which they are at home also tends to shine a spotlight on moments of decision-making. Yet such models neglect the preparation required in order to formulate the "dilemma" the agent confronts. Hauerwas's response to the decision-centered casuist involves, in effect, taking the discussion a step back to consider the conditions for identifying dilemmas as dilemmas. Self-constituting narratives provides the resources necessary for giving recognizable shape to the material of the moral problems we must negotiate—i.e., the competing goods of a dilemma themselves. Better put, self-constituting narratives provide the resources on which agents draw in learning to describe what holds importance in their lives.

The question, "What difference does the Christian story make for moral decision-making?" can be re-phrased as, "how do Christians see the world?" Unlike those who imply that decisions simply confront us, Hauerwas insists that the kind of problems we face is conditioned by how we see. Vision matters.

58. See ibid., 98.

Still, the moral life is also a life of action and includes both deliberation and choice of an end. How do the convictions supplied by the Christian story inform moral deliberation about life and death matters, such as the case where one must decide whether to violently restrain, and possibly kill, an assailant in order to save the life of a victim, a third party, when the death of that person is what the assailant intends?

How could one fail to do what one can to protect an innocent person? This case, Hauerwas implies, seems to permit of only one resolution. The decision—to kill if necessary in order to protect the innocent—is in a sense "forced" upon us. There therefore must be some circumstances in which violence is permitted.

Yet Hauerwas behooves us to resist accepting this conclusion so quickly. "What presuppositions undergird it?" he would have us ask. The conclusion, "I ought to kill the assailant," seems in fact to draw from an identity-conferring narrative that teaches us to describe the situation, and my role in it, in a particular way. For instance, my role as the would-be intervening actor who kills the attacker assumes that I am the master of the situation who gets to determine the outcome, relegating the two others with me to a peripheral role. I am the free agent; their roles are pre-determined and fixed.

The conclusion that I ought to kill the aggressor flows also from the assumption that individual human life, in this dispensation, is an end in itself. According to this vision of human life, and its corresponding ethics, the intention to kill another is the paradigmatically immoral act. It takes away the life, and thereby the liberty, of the other. Because the aggressor's intended act amounts to the ultimate insult against the institution of morality, just about any means of preventing him may be justified. Thus, this vision of human life and morality dovetails with the interventionist conclusion.

To show how the Christian story may make a difference in how agents deliberate and, ultimately, act, Hauerwas follows the lead of his mentor John Howard Yoder in challenging the premises that force the conclusion—i.e., "I ought to kill the aggressor."[59] For Yoder, the acceptance of violence as the proper or just must imply a narrative crucially different from the one Christians are called to tell. He claims further that the narrative just outlined limits possible answers to the question,

---

59. Ibid., 123–27.

"What would you do in such circumstances . . . ?" by failing to imagine the potential for transformation in the "you" making the decision.[60]

In addition to the possibilities 1) that the agent kills the aggressor and saves the life of the victim and; 2) the related possibility of his trying to do so, but failing, Yoder adds the possibility that the agent; 3) does something natural to emotionally disarm the attacker and avoid violence, or; 4) that the agent allows himself to be killed in place of the victim, or finally; 5) that the agent allows the tragic result that the aggressor succeeds in taking the life of his innocent victim to occur, assuming that he cannot offer himself instead.[61]

These additional possibilities (3, 4, 5) are "made possible" by the distinctive resources the Christian story provides for imagining the situation. For instance, option 5 of letting the action take its course after having exhausted non-violent means to prevent it may express the Christian's belief in "providence": the conviction that God's loving care orders human lives in a way that behooves Christians to recognize limits on their own power. This description of God's agency cannot permit the belief that human beings are "masters" of their circumstances. Acknowledging God's provision in history rather suggests that Christians strive in their actions to faithfully respond to God's gifts.

Option 3 is made possible by the Christian understanding that all persons, including "enemies," are susceptible of a change of heart. In fact, the peace that Christ brings to their lives also calls upon Christians to be stimulants of changes of heart and reconciliation to God in their neighbors.

A Christian may allow himself to be killed (4) because his story teaches him to look to a life beyond this one. In the tradition of the martyrs—those who in giving up their lives contributed to the upbuilding of the kingdom through their witness—Christians learn to see the reality of the kingdom that transcends worldly goods, even life. For the idea of martyrdom implies that the good for our lives, rather than in their preservation at all costs, consists in the way they contribute to the upbuilding of God's kingdom in the world. Martyrdom can be seen as intensifying the claim of providence that God acts and is the ultimate master.

---

60. See Yoder, "What Would You Do If . . . ?" 82–83.
61. Hauerwas, *Peaceable Kingdom*, 125–26.

In these examples, then, we see how Christian descriptions open up new possibilities for how a situation is construed, and consequently how moral decisions are made and lived out. Each option draws on descriptions which are made intelligible by the self-constituting story of Christians. Beyond this, Hauerwas has argued that the practical deliberation that draws from the descriptive resources of the Christian story is richer than that which too quickly accepts the necessity of violent response. How is this so?

According to Hauerwas, those moral theories that focus on decisions and the abstract norms that justify them tend not to recognize the identity-conferring stories that all moral agents carry. In fact, he implies, their failure to recognize these stories may be a consequence of inarticulacy concerning the story-dependency of their theories. In light of this lack in self-understanding, such theories in fact display a rigid manner of moving from principle to situation. The characterization their theories provide of situations seems predictable and fixed. The move from theory to dilemma is in fact under-explored. We can understand the motive behind this. To talk about the underlying story would be to open to view, and thus to put in play, the way that our basic self-understandings function in the formation of practical imperatives. By drawing attention to situations that seem to forecast their own (decision-) resolutions, the decision-focused theorist manages to avoid the difficult task of inquiring what our story requires of us. For such inquiry often leads to a feeling of indeterminacy, as our stories do not always offer clear solutions.[62] The Christian story, on the other hand, according to Hauerwas gains its imaginative power by embracing the possibility of transformation of the agent, and thus of the kinds of decisions one must "of necessity" make.

We might do well here to recall Iris Murdoch's description of the moral task as essentially one of overcoming the distortions of illusion and fantasy and seeing clearly. Choice arrives late on the scene, when much of the truly moral work is accomplished. We only know we have a dilemma on our hands when the whole background of evaluations is in place, and has so characterized our situation. Hauerwas has shown how Christian convictions shape the agent's vision of a situation and give a particular description of what is morally required of him or her.

62. For a much fuller discussion of his views on the relation of moral concepts to moral experience, see Hauerwas's "Situation Ethics." See also footnote 3 of this chapter.

Conclusion

Anscombe argued that practical reasoning was different from theoretical reasoning in its very form. She illustrated this formal difference by examining Aristotle's practical syllogisms, the kind of reasoning that goes on within an agent. Basically, in these syllogisms the conclusion does not follow from the premises by way of entailment. This implies, she concluded, that premises of the practical syllogism only lead to the conclusion when "said" by someone who wants what is stated in the first premise, a description of some good attainable by action. The inferential logic of such syllogisms only works in a particular sort of context: the context of agency.

Saying only this, however, might tempt us to see practical reasoning highly subjective. This is not so, and to see why we need to pause a moment on typical first premises in Aristotle's syllogisms. "Jersey cows are suitable for Idaho farmers . . . ," and "Dry food suits human beings," are examples of such first premises. Formally, these premises name some good, which is a good specifically in relation to a trait of the being, or kind of being, who is to go through the steps. In other words, the first premises of practical syllogisms refer to an agent in some specified aspect (as a farmer, or as a human being). These aspects contribute intelligibility to the good to be attained by action, the conclusion of the syllogism.

This is to say, the goods named in the first premises of practical syllogisms are not random; they are not goods simply because they are the objects of desire. Rather, they are *objects* of the agent's desire because they are "under the description" of goods. Practical reasoning, by its very form, makes concrete both the agent and the purpose of his action. But what is it to say that the agent desires what is named in the first premise under the description of something good for him? It means that the desiring involved here has a reason behind it, and reasons are bound up with language, the power of description.

As we saw in chapter 1, the descriptions under which the agent takes his ends are not his own property as an individual subject. Rather, they are carried by a community, and more specifically its form of life. The agent, we must presume, learns to employ these descriptions as he learns to become a part of the form of life that sustains them. He thereby learns to reason practically. It is part of the very form of practical reasoning, then, to be political.

Taylor draws the connection between practical reasoning and the agent in his work. In particular, he fights vigorously against social theory's proclivity to undo the agent's descriptions of the good in order to explain its behavior according to a pre-ordained calculus. Yet Taylor never names a community whose politics would shape agents and provide them with their description of the good. This allows Taylor to conceive of practical reasoning in a way open to changing conceptions of the good when they are provided by better theoretical explanations of human being and action. Unfortunately, Taylor's practical reasoning thereby loses its political base, separating the subject from any concrete context of ends. Taylor's self is finally disembodied.

My argument is that Hauerwas answers Anscombe's challenge more successfully than Charles Taylor because Hauerwas fully expresses the way the political is integral to the very form of practical reasoning. Hauerwas's practical reasoning is structurally political in that his theological ethics is a making-practical the story of a particular polis—the church. There is an integration of ethical reflection and description as to how Christian convictions about the world shape Christian people. That is why the primary language of his ethical reflection is that of the virtues, and why one cannot fully describe the methodology to be used in Christian ethics without specifying the material convictions carried by the Christian community. The church is central to his practical reasoning.[63] I have tried to argue for this claim here by first showing how Hauerwas moves forward from the critique of the metaphor of

---

63. The following passage from the Introduction to *A Community of Character* is revealing of Hauerwas's overall project in this regard. He writes, "The justification for calling this book 'social ethics' is that I wish to show why any consideration of the truth of Christian convictions cannot be divorced from the kind of community the church is and should be. Though much of the book involves a running critique of liberal political and ethical theory, my primary interest is to challenge the church to regain a sense of the significance of the polity that derives from convictions peculiar to Christians. In particular, I have tried to show why, if the church is to serve our liberal society or any society, it is crucial for Christians to regain an appropriate sense of separateness from that society.... Though seldom noticed, the reductionistic tendencies of modern theology are as much due to the loss of a sense of the political significance of the Gospel as to the more strictly 'intellectual' challenges engendered by the Enlightenment. The proponents of 'political theology' are therefore right to claim that the meaning and truth of Christian convictions cannot be separated from their political implications. They are wrong, however, to associate 'politics' only with questions of social change. Rather, the 'political' question crucial to the church is what kind of community the church must be to be faithful to the narratives central to Christian convictions" (2).

"agent as decision maker" in much moral philosophy toward a commitment to specifying the background, or world, in which Christian self-understanding operates. Secondly, I argued for it by tracing the example of Hauerwasian practical reasoning found in *The Peaceable Kingdom*. Here I emphasized the way that the various aspects of his practical reasoning—methodological and doctrinal—hang together. The central metaphor that unifies the parts is that of the church, whose task is to balance the various material convictions that give it its unique form. Hauerwas emphasizes that the ethical task of the church is "to be the church" because the church is the common body which sustains the descriptions essential to the work of Christian ethics. Hauerwas names this ethics (politically) as the church's witness to peace. The obligation to be the church is a linguistic and political task—through memory and the cultivation of particular virtues the church maintains the skills to retell the story of God's ruling of creation. In telling this story faithfully, they become a people who live to provide a foretaste of the peace made real in Jesus Christ.

CHAPTER 4

Practical Reason, Justice, and Liberation

Gloria Albrecht and Jeffrey Stout have both offered thorough critiques of Hauerwas's work.[1] Both critiques target Hauerwas's articulation of the function of the church as a political body integrally related to Christian character and his treatment of the question of how such a church stands to make an impact on the world. Indeed, these two aspects belong together. Furthermore, both use the concept of justice in their analysis and criticisms of him.

In this chapter I am looking at the politics of practical reason in a way distinct from, but intimately related to, the approach tied to the three concepts of human agency, practical reason, and politics. I am using two authors' use of justice as a way into their presuppositions about moral formation within a tradition. I hope the reader will see how these two—moral formation and tradition—are inextricably bound up with politics in the sense I have been developing.

This chapter engages the aforementioned critiques philosophically, assuming their authors share with Hauerwas an interest in the concepts of which I have been speaking: practical reason in relation to accounts of human agency and politics. It questions whether their conceptions of justice are adequate by examining whether they account for the political character of practical reason. In other words, I read Albrecht and Stout as though they were attempting to respond to Anscombe's challenge.

---

1. The texts of theirs to which I will be referring in what follows are Stout, *Democracy and Tradition* and Albrecht, *Character of Our Communities*.

Let's begin by noting the differences between Albrecht and Stout. Stout is a philosopher and student of religions. He also locates himself in a particular political and intellectual tradition. He is an American pragmatist in the tradition of Emerson, Dewey, and Whitman. Like them, his interest lies in the health of American democracy, and since Christians abound in America he cares deeply about how Christians participate. With this in mind, he climbs inside of Christian theological ethics in order to dialogue with Hauerwas in his own terms; he performs "immanent criticism" while remaining a visitor to a strange land.

Gloria Albrecht, on the other hand, writes about Hauerwas as a fellow Christian. The battle between her and Hauerwas is familial, representing a disagreement among Christians as to how best to articulate the way forward for the church. The standards, then, for arbitrating in this debate would naturally come from the craft of theological ethics itself. Yet, I will claim that in this case the philosophical matters of how practical reason and justice are to be related need to be addressed first. This will allow me to tie her and Stout together in my treatment of them.

Albrecht and Stout are of a piece in that they put their criticism by saying that Hauerwas has neglected justice as one of the Christian virtues. I will try to show that beneath this charge lies the fact that both critics stumble over, or perhaps actively resist, Hauerwas's assumption that theological ethics is a discipline of the church.

Saying that Hauerwas is lacking in the justice department might lead one to assume that he has ignored it. But this is not entirely true. Although when Stout refers to Hauerwas's discussion of justice in *After Christendom*, it is mainly to draw attention to the unfortunate ring of the title—"Why Justice is a Bad Idea for Christians"—Hauerwas rigorously grapples with justice language and its usage here. Granted, his approach to justice here is negative as he sets out to uncover why talk of "justice" is a temptation for Christians. He wants to debunk, that is, the idea that having a theory of justice may save the church from the complexities of its relation to the world in a post-establishment age. In other words, Christians hope that discovering a theory of justice will tell us exactly what we need to offer to the world and what to take from it. But theories of justice are profoundly informed by the character of the people that comes up with them. Hauerwas thinks John Rawls' theory, for example, is tailored to wealthy and technologically advanced nation states. He argues that Christians should beware lest we give up any resource we might have to resist such an identity.[2] Thus, if Hauerwas thinks justice a "bad idea" for Christians, it is because our very high hopes make us insufficiently discriminatory in regard to conceptions of justice on offer.

But more than this, Hauerwas's concern is to recall how "justice" works within the framework of a politics of practical reasoning. A few substantive guidelines for how speaking about justice in moral philosophy or in Christian ethics can be gleaned from his treatment. The first is that we should beware of the use of justice as a kind of universal tool for delivering ethical recommendations for a variety of societies. He simply does not believe justice works this way. One of the tricky characteristics of modern theories of justice is that they tend to present themselves as offering an account of justice for anyone anywhere. This perhaps accounts for Christians' failure to be discriminatory.[3] From his criticisms of contemporary justice theories such as those of Rawls and Nozick, we might also glean that justice must be situated in relationship to a shared conception of the good. As MacIntyre has shown, the importance of the good also implies that discussions of justice be related to the practically wise person (*phronimos*), or someone who displays the virtue of practical reasoning in an exemplary manner.[4]

Insisting, as Hauerwas does, that justice be applied in contexts wherein a shared understanding of good is named means that our use of justice is always contingent and historical. To speak of justice as though it was anyone's justice is to place a burden on the concept it cannot bear. It also leads to self-deception.

Important for this chapter is the claim that speaking of justice presupposes a political setting. That justice is a virtue—that is, a qualification of human agency—and must be situated with respect to a set of virtues to be embodied in a practically wise person means that to speak of justice presupposes such a setting. Here I will try to show that to say that justice is political further implies that anyone speaking of the virtue of justice ought to have an account of how the standards of

---

2. Although he recognizes that those Christians (i.e., himself) that live in such societies are inevitably deeply shaped by them.

3. It should be noted that, though this chapter on justice is largely in the form of a warning, Hauerwas does not say that Christians are free from what justice demands.

4. This theme of *Whose Justice? Which Rationality?* is developed in many parts of the book.

justice are sustained over time, and how the young are brought to the point of being able to see such standards and put them into practice: that is, of authority and moral formation. Such terms as agency, good, formation, tradition and authority—variants of the three I have been using all along— are the terms around which I will interrogate the use of justice by Stout and Albrecht.

It can perhaps be put simply. To use justice in a way untethered to a community that forms persons to recognize shared goods implies an inability to understand why Hauerwas claims that for Christians to be just presupposes the church. For justice to be of use in criticizing social norms, those who seek justice must lean on their having been formed to recognize shared goods.

Moral Formation and Justice: Stout's Critique of Hauerwas

Anscombe's challenge was to find a more adequate philosophical psychology upon which to ground moral philosophy. What distinguishes Stanley Hauerwas's account of practical reasoning from those of other moralists like Charles Taylor who answer that challenge is found in his description of the church and its person-transforming practices. Hauerwas's psychology and account of practical reasoning are grounded in a polity. Many might claim with good reason that extensive comparison of Stout and Hauerwas is unlikely to reveal much, aside from the obvious fact that Stout is interested mainly in democracy while Hauerwas with the God of Jesus Christ and his church.[5] While I appreciate this criticism, I believe the comparison may help my purpose of making us better readers of Hauerwas, or at least avoid a particular misreading. Further, the criticism neglects some of the common ground between them.[6] Still, it can be difficult to name the substantive differences between Stout and

---

5. Those who think that is all that can be usefully said about their difference will find this section somewhat tiresome. I am including it because I believe that it can help us learn something about Hauerwas, as well as Stout, and lead the way to better readings of him.

6. However, it is my contention that examining Stout and Hauerwas, or Stout and *his* Hauerwas, in terms of the logic of ethical concepts both of them rely upon will throw some light upon how Hauerwas is often heard, or mis-heard. One reason for this is that Stout is by and large a skillful reader of Hauerwas. The fact that he doesn't fall into some of the pitfalls that come of a poor understanding of ethical concepts like narrative and tradition allow us to see more clearly what Hauerwas is up to.

Hauerwas. This is in part due to Stout's indirect manner of leveling criticisms at Hauerwas—his "immanent criticism." This forces one to try and distinguish between what Stout thinks of Hauerwas and his explanation of why others criticize Hauerwas as they do. His overriding purpose is to show why Hauerwas and those influenced by him ought to identify more strongly with the larger political association called American democracy. Indeed, at the same time that Stout criticizes Hauerwas, he is constructing his picture of the polity, with its attendant social practices, that he wants us to join. In order to engage critically with Stout's criticisms of Hauerwas, then, also requires carrying out two tasks at the same time. That is, it requires examining whether Stout's portrayal of Hauerwas is accurate, and more importantly it requires that one must ask whether the polity Stout describes is worth joining.[7]

The engagement between Stout and Hauerwas—from which MacIntyre, for that matter, cannot be excluded—is part of an ongoing conversation between them. And the story of this conversation contains mutual influence as well as significant difference. More importantly, *Democracy and Tradition* ought to be seen as in part a response to the key criticism Hauerwas, following MacIntyre, has issued to modern moral discourse, particularly "liberalism." Namely, that we find in such discourse a tradition that is unable to account for itself as a tradition. Stout, as the title suggests, has attempted to show that the American democratic instantiation of liberalism can so account for itself, and that therefore this criticism fails.

My critique of Stout is an immanent criticism. I will present him in dialogue with Hauerwas, and attempt to get inside his own sense of things. In so doing, I will in effect be drawing more on *Democracy and Tradition* than his criticism of Hauerwas on justice. The reader may also note that I am comparing Stout's account with my own sense, derived from sympathies with the Christian commitments of Hauerwas and MacIntyre. I begin with the themes of moral imagination and moral formation. I then turn to the issue of authority with special attention to its function in forming the moral imagination. This leads me to the theme of tradition as it relates to authority. I then turn to justice it-

---

7. My analysis here will not be exhaustive and some of the more important themes will be treated at greater length in the following chapter that juxtaposes Stout's and MacIntyre's conceptions of practical reasoning. The purpose of the analysis of these moral tools is to bring to light the features of Hauerwas's work most responsible for his many mis-readings.

self, and its relation to politics. After an interlude on a challenge posed to Stout by philosopher Sabina Lovibond, I conclude by considering Stout's justice and the ultimate good. In the following chapter, I focus on his account of practical reason. My aim in all this is to ask whether Stout's conception of tradition is sufficiently historical, and how this conception informs his reading of Hauerwas.

Moral Imagination and Moral Formation: After Quandary Ethics

Moral imagination, or the formation of the individual in virtue, takes on a different hue in Stout and in Hauerwas. Neither likes the systematic aspiration of quandary ethics. The problem with such methods is that they are insufficiently reflective—their portrait of the moral life is too thin. The examples are controlled by the doctrine or point that the author wants to make. They make the moral life seem too easy—too simple and straightforward. For Stout, the moral imagination is embodied in the activity of reading essays where the mind is taken back and forth between examples (details) and a broad point that is illustrated by the examples. Not only must the point ("doctrine") not attempt to control or take over the example, but the example should do some of the dictating. That's to say, the point should remain open to change (or, perhaps, "re-formulation"). Part of the whole process is that the reader learns how to question whether the example truly serves the point or not.[8] If the example does not serve the point the author intends, perhaps it serves another point? By learning to question in this way the reader acquires (and practices) an important moral skill: what Stout calls "responsibility."[9]

Stout's discussion of the essay is meant to clarify where he and Hauerwas significantly differ on the issue of moral imagination and formation when it comes to the method they ultimately adopt. It is

---

8. There is a potential confusion here, which should be avoided. For instance, what does it mean to ask the question, "Did the author choose her examples well?" On a certain reading of Stout's point, this question would not make sense. For it seems to imply that there is a criterion for choosing examples, and it is how well it matches the point one is trying to make. If Stout were saying that one . . . the issue is what stretch of time you are looking at. If you take a long-term view, then of course the point may be revisable in light of the examples.

9. It is not clear whether Stout believes that a person who is responsible in this way is also a "just" person. Yet he seems to imply that this is the case.

therefore worth dwelling on the question of what point Stout is trying to make through his discussion of the essay. This I believe can be done by meditating for a while on a word (or, concept) that Stout takes somewhat for granted in his use of it here—namely, the word "doctrine." Most often "doctrine" here is being used as a synonym for "point" or even "abstract idea" or "theme" to be fleshed out with cases or exempli. But, as I am confident Stout would agree, it is also possible to consider doctrine as naming a social practice—i.e. the practice of teaching and learning. By looking at it this way I believe we will be able to trace the relationship of doctrine to other moral notions that belong to the same family (and are, in a sense, interdependent)—such as "authority" and "tradition." But I begin with the common ground under Hauerwas and Stout, found in their shared narrative of the failures of modern moral theory.

Modern moral theory held the ambition to form a comprehensive system of ethical reasoning. The system was bi-level. The lower level—the level that touched the ground of human decision making an action—was to be composed of cases describing moral situations. The higher level was to consist in moral principles under which the cases could be subsumed. In other words, the moral principles shed light on what ought to be done in the cases, and the cases were handy ways of illustrating what the moral principles were. Taken as a whole, the principles were claimed to give a comprehensive account of morality and a sure-fire way of understanding what to do in our practical lives. The name for this approach to ethical theory, given belatedly by those who found it inadequate, is "quandary ethics."[10] The main problem with such ethics is the agents in the cases are assumed to be "anyone." There is no accounting for why some persons might see the decision as having a moral import while others do not.

Because the problem with this ethics lies in its preference for "thin" accounts at the low level of moral situations, the solution requires thicker descriptions. What can provide more detail, especially the kind of detail that allows us to discern the "who"—the agent/person who is coping with the moral dilemma at hand? The answer is "narrative." Through a narrative approach to understanding morality one comes to see the point, or what is at stake, in a given situation for the persons who must resolve it. It does so by allowing us to see the agent as a character in a story whose ending is a matter of the frustration or

---

10. See Pincoffs, *Quandaries and Virtues*.

realization or perhaps reformulation of its purposes. We see also how the agent's virtues and vices inform the purposes it holds.

While it might seem that introducing narrative is a way of supplementing what is going on in quandary ethics by focusing more on the construction of cases, this would be misleading. Yet this I think could be misleading in its desire to ameliorate the debate. The turn to narrative attempts to remedy the shortcomings of quandary ethics by displacing it for a different paradigm. It is not clear, that is, that the role of principles in the quandaries model can exercise a recognizably similar function in the narrative mode.[11] As Hauerwas and Burrell put it in their seminal essay, "From System to Story," "the point need not be detachable from the narrative itself; in fact, we think a story better that does not issue in a determinate *moral*."[12]

Where then does the point come from, or how is it illustrated? Stout asserts that it depends on the kind of stories one favors. He remarks that for Hauerwas and Burrell the stories they like are oriented around "exemplary instances" of the quality of character in question. Stories like Augustine's *Confessions*. The next step is that a person of faith is essentially one who takes some such stories to be canonical, or to have the authority of a standard.

More will be said below about stories that display "exemplary instances."[13] But now we must go on to consider the limits of their agreement.

To begin to understand where the two part ways, we must attend to Stout's characterization of Hauerwas's mature position, or how Hauerwas has developed the narrative impulse. It is the nature of narrative to involve us in the life of the character making choices. But for Hauerwas, says Stout, the way narratives do their moral work is by displaying "exemplary instances" of certain character traits or virtues. This

11. The role of principles in relation to cases has been given a sophisticated formulation in recent editions of Beauchamp and Childress' *Principles of Biomedical Ethics*.

12. Hauerwas and Burrell, "From System to Story," 28. Quoted in *Democracy and Tradition*, 143 (emphasis original).

13. It ought further to be noted that Hauerwas's position, as articulated in "Casuistry in Context: The Need for Tradition," is that case-based reasoning has its place, once it is put in the context of the kinds of narrative described above (169–84). It would be interesting to explore whether Hauerwas's mature position on the debate about quandary ethics, which I believe is displayed in the kind of reasoning I discussed at the close of the previous chapter, and which incorporates a kind of casuistry in it, would challenge somewhat Stout's characterization.

point is closely connected to the claim that some narratives themselves possess the significance and weight that demand our special attention to them. This is what is meant by the notion "canonical."

The canonical weight of certain narratives expresses something about moral imagination and moral formation. A student must establish a certain relationship to these stories and their characters in order to be well formed, or to gain the necessary virtues. The structure of this relationship, at least at first, tends to be submissive or based on obedience. It is by trusting in the characters who have this authority that we learn to go on.

What does this look like in Hauerwas? Stout answers this when he says that Hauerwas favors the kind of narrative found in "the classic life." This genre has its roots in the Greco-Roman culture of *"paideia,"* where individuals formed themselves morally by imitating particular persons identified as exemplary. The lives of these exemplary persons were then established as classics or canonical representatives within a particular tradition. Along with this, a kind of hierarchy comes to characterize the social landscape; there are ethical "aristocrats" and ethical novices.

The way moral formation happens is through close and personal contact between students and teachers. One has to be around such people in order to learn from them.

Hauerwas's adaptation of this moral genre consists in identifying exemplary Christian lives, such as those of saints, as well as of course attending to the story of Jesus incorporated in the gospels. In *The Peaceable Kingdom*, as we noted in the previous chapter, he claims that we come to see the significance of the Scriptures in those Christians who through experience have incorporated them into their lives. What's more, the direct "contact" required for the transmission of learning happens in church, the "essential role" of which "is to put us in contact with those ethical aristocrats who are good at living the Christian faith."[14]

Stout's point is that the kind of relationship between reader and text (novice and aristocrat) made necessary by paideia tends to give rise to a rhetoric in important ways similar to that of quandary ethics, with its principles and thinned out cases. In the same way that quandary ethics feels a pressure to thin-out the case descriptions it uses so that they

---

14. Hauerwas and Willimon, *Resident Aliens: Life in the Christian Colony*, 182. Quoted in *Democracy and Tradition*, 167.

clearly point to a moral generality, the aspiration to have a clear moral to be displayed for the student in the classic life leads to a reductive simplicity; narratives with complex implications are reduced to readily graspable points. Stout's main example is Hauerwas's reading of the Gospels, the life of Jesus, as exemplifying God's non-violence.

Before addressing the way in which Stout develops the narrative impulse, we must say a word or two about Stout's appraisal of the way MacIntyre has shaped Hauerwas's work. For a great deal of Stout's argument depends upon Hauerwas's (MacIntyre-inspired) characterization of "modernity." Stout alleges that Hauerwas, perhaps without being conscious of doing so, has created a rhetoric in which modernity names the culture produced by the currents of thought manifest in reductive ethical systems like quandary ethics and reductive political theories like social contract theory and libertarianism. In fact, it is Hauerwas's failure to distinguish modern political theories from modern culture— an inability also characteristic of Milbank, says Stout—that underlies the problem. The influence of MacIntyre's rhetoric of historical decline is primarily responsible, but the synthesis of MacIntyre's view of the modern world with Yoder's "dualistic" view of the church in relation to the world adds reinforcement.[15]

As we saw, Stout shares Hauerwas's dissatisfaction with modern ethical theory. He objects, however, when Hauerwas strictly identifies the ethical discourse moderns employ with modern moral theory. MacIntyre's ideology-driven account of modernity generates a caricature that in fact banishes from view its many moral resources. Stout here seeks to recover some of these in order to challenge the identification with modern ethical theory. He finds evidence for distinguishing the two—modernity and modern moral theory—first of all, in the fact that modern audiences are frequently repulsed when they hear philosophers trying to capture their moral lives systematically in a set of principles. This skepticism towards theory, he argues, gave rise (and form) to alternative, yet still characteristically *modern*, modes of moral reflection in new literary genres.

For Stout the most important of these genres is the essay. Its *raison d'etre* is the suspicion that moral philosophy indulges "a temptation to

---

15. For Stout's full discussion of the effects of Hauerwas's combining MacIntyre and Yoder, see *Democracy and Tradition*, 147–49.

engage in presumptuously dogmatic and excessively abstract thought."[16] He believes that the essay can be used to complicate Hauerwas's account of the ethics of example. Like the ethics of example, the essay favors stories exploring exemplary lives to the establishment of a system of principles, yet the kind of reflection on these lives inspired by the essay is distinct in kind.

In the essay moral reflection takes the form of a continuous movement between richly described examples and general ideas. Stout emphasizes that direction of influence is not predetermined: sometimes the particular details support the general idea, and sometimes they render it problematic. This characteristic of the essay leads Stout to describe its form as "conversational." It inspires critical thought because its very form resists closure. The reader is called upon to respond by entering into the exploration being conducted.

Borrowing the description offered by Robert Musil, Stout states that the essay as a genre of moral reflection "stands between example and doctrine."[17] While the essay uses examples in order to illustrate general notions, its inconclusiveness invites a reader to think things through for oneself. His description of the essay furthermore makes the nature of its contrast with moral philosophy clear. The latter is so tied to "doctrinal" concerns—the concern to provide a coherent system—that it refuses all but the most congenial examples.

Thus, for Stout the relation of modern moral theory to the moral culture of modernity is tenuous.[18] It is highly misleading, he believes, to reduce the latter to the former, for modern culture has deep resources for moral imagination and formation to equip modern individuals to live their times. His account of the essay and the moral work it does is summed up in the claim that the essay places the reader between doctrine and example causing her to think things through for herself. Now we can see that for Stout the essay also stands in contrast to the classic life, and its culture of paideia, and for similar reasons. With perhaps distinct ultimate aims, the classic life also puts the doctrine in the driver's seat, and thus fails to capture this back and forth movement. Stout obviously believes that the essay represents a more fruitful way to

16. Ibid., 164.
17. Musil, *The Man Without Qualities*.
18. Compare MacIntyre's claim in *After Virtue* that modern moral theory is a response to, and expression of, social realities in modern Europe

develop the narrative impulse in ethics than a return to the classic life and the culture of paideia.

Stout argues that the essay oversees a distinctively modern form of moral formation. While the essay and paideia are different, it would be churlish to write off the former as an anti-culture, the mere "acids of individualism." The essay is one important expression of a modern culture that goes deeper than modern moral theory and is responsible for shaping the character of modern people. Hauerwas is himself indebted to the modernity of the essay, Stout points out. What frustrates Stout most is that Hauerwas goes on writing essays and reading novels (another modern literary genre) while claiming that modernity contains no resources of value to the theological ethicist. "Hypocrite!" cries Stout.

Stout is surely correct to point out that Hauerwas is indebted to such modern resources as the essay. But let us now look closer at the kind of moral formation Stout associates with this modern genre. With the picture of the individual becoming responsible for evaluating moral doctrines in relation to examples meant to illustrate them, we have begun to glimpse this model of moral formation. I believe we can come to a fuller grasp by focusing on the concept of authority in his work.

I propose here to understand authority as playing a role within the practice of teaching and learning. For the learner to come to grasp, and appropriate to himself, what the teacher has already mastered, the learner must attribute a certain authority to the teacher and the teacher must accept that authority. I believe Stout and Hauerwas would accept this. Yet Stout and Hauerwas seem to have a disagreement about the nature of authority. How is this so?

It would be easy to overstate the differences of the two on this issue of authority in relation to moral formation. There are times when Stout writes as though his main contention with Hauerwas is the latter's sloppiness in the way he uses the terms "liberal" and "modern." Nevertheless, pursuing the question may shed some light on what more is at stake.[19]

For Stout Hauerwas's conception of authority has two sources: the model of moral education of paideia (the cult of the Saints, for Hauerwas) and the place of the church in Christian life and Christian

---

19 For instance, it is not clear how Stout's account of the essay fits together with his claim that democracies, to be communities of virtue, also need "ethical aristocracies." Are these two moments in the development of his position regarding moral formation? If so, how do they complement one another? Or, as I suspect, are they simply two different angles from which to try to show up the problems in Hauerwas's position?

ethics. There are people who can be said to live out the story of the Gospel in an exemplary way, and the place you find the memorials of such people is the church—an established institution. The first source implies that our reliance upon others for formation is concrete and embodied. We might say, we need to see, touch and smell our teachers, not just to read them. The second implies that proper moral formation is bound up with an established set of teachings and rites about whose canonization we were not consulted. We are simply to trust that these institutions were founded to keep us from going astray.

What bothers Stout about this conception of authority? We get an answer to this by attending to his discussion of the essay. The key point is that essays instruct, and form us as learners, by calling upon us to actively participate in the learning process itself. That learning process is perhaps best understood in terms of conversation between two at least potentially equal partners in cooperation. The learner might be thought of here as a proto-equal partner, already learning the role of conversation partner. The goal of the learning is what Stout calls "responsibility." Here this means being accountable for one's attributions of authority to those from whom one learns. Someone with democratic formation should always anticipate being called upon to give an account for where, and in whom, they have placed their trust.

What this means is that, for Stout, the model of churchly paideia is problematic on two counts. First, being close to and spending time with exemplary people (saints) represents to him an overly passive form of trust in authorities, our teachers. Second, naming the church as the place where such exemplars are to be found is overly restrictive, and bound to exclude true authority which might arise anywhere. Here Stout refers to the consensus between Orthodox Protestants and Emersonian perfectionists at the time of our nation's founding with regard to the importance of freedom of speech.[20] The reason for this protection is that we would not wish to suppress those voices that might prove inspired. We need to learn not to be overly deferent to authority, so that we will have the benefit of those who have something truly important to say to us.

---

20. Behind the protection of free speech, Stout emphasizes, was a "substantive moral concern." Stout writes, "I agree with Hauerwas's claim that an ethical aristocracy is essential to the maintenance of a virtuous community, assuming that 'aristocracy' is here being used metaphorically . . ." Stout, *Democracy and Tradition*, 167.

Stout, furthermore, clearly sees something afoul in the conception of authority that Hauerwas draws upon. To attribute authority in the way modeled by church-paideia is to betray an important gain within modern society. This is to do with the ways we allow power to be exercised by some over others. One can see this when one realizes that Stout sees something of the imperiousness that drives modern moral theory—an imperiousness motivated by the desire to establish order over the particularities and contingencies of modern societies—within Hauerwas's promotion of deference to the established church.

Who is correct? If authority's role is to be located in the practice of teaching and learning, does Stout or Hauerwas give the better account of its place in moral formation? I wish to tease this out further at the abstract level of logic—that is, the logic of the practice implicit in the use of the term "doctrine"—by examining the connection of authority to another concept within the same family of moral notions. As hinted above, I believe answering this question requires drawing on a further term within the lexicon of this debate—namely, that of *tradition*. How does the notion of tradition help to clarify the disagreement between Stout and Hauerwas, and perhaps even to pick a side?

Let us return to doctrine understood in terms of the social practice of teaching and learning. I claimed above that this practice must involve in some way the idea of authority; the student has to attribute authority in order to learn, and (perhaps) the teacher has to claim it in order to teach. The issue of the relation of doctrine and example in moral rhetoric can be understood in this context. Putting it into this context for a moment might help clarify why understanding the role of authority within moral formation requires the notion of a tradition.

Stout has claimed that modern discourses like the ones he champions have complicated somewhat the relationship of doctrines and examples. Still, I would imagine that Stout is not dispensing with what I take to be the basic logic of examples within rhetoric—namely, that examples are chosen by a teacher or speaker in order clarify the point she or he wants to get across. (That is why we can say of someone that he chose an example "well" or "poorly.") This implies that if the example chosen by the author does not do a good job of helping the audience understand the broader point, it has not done what it was intended to do, and a different one should be adopted next time. Perhaps also it signifies that the speaker is not, or not yet, a skillful rhetorician.

When Stout argues that the essay complicates the relationship between example and doctrine, and thus challenges and reforms premodern conceptions of the role of authority in moral education, I do not think he means to negate this basic outline of how examples help one make a point. Instead, I imagine that what Stout has in mind is how, given a longer time frame, we must assume that our finitude will show its effects on our teaching. We must be aware that we inevitably will "get it wrong" and need to revise and recast. But is this adequately accounted for in Stout's re-formulation of moral formation—namely, the transition he proposes from paideia to the model based on conversation between (proto-) equal partners and on responsibility? I claim, and perhaps Stout would agree, that to deal with this problem we need also the notion of a moral tradition.

Why is tradition indispensable here? First, tradition acknowledges the basic finitude of human moral reflection and proclaims that our moral wisdom is by nature time-bound. Each new generation must decide whether and how to take up what has been handed down to it. But that assumes that something has been successfully handed down. Thus, the second reason why tradition is indispensable is because it takes account of the fact that moral learning is something that must be in some way passed on to a succeeding generation. It is tradition, we might say, that makes possible moral reflection and, we hope, enables it to serve future generations.

What influence does the claim that tradition is necessary exercise on how authority rightly functions? One key point, it seems to me, is that tradition forces our focus onto the moral education of children. By doing so, it reminds us that authority requires a more direct application in proportion to the youth of a child. It requires, we might say, a greater proximity—and demand for obedience—in children who are only proto-discursive and for whom the world is encountered largely in terms of tactile information and emotional intentions. More mature forms of human agency, we ought to recall, is built upon the child's immediate engagement with the world. One might assume that example and doctrine are closely tied together in the child's world.

Furthermore, tradition helps us see that moral formation must be seen in the context of a whole human life. The question of how we start off is to be related to that of our destination, or what we are meant to be. In his account of the essay, Stout implicitly claims that the student receives formation that would make her "like" the essay-writer. The skill of the essay-writer at issue here is the ability to move back and forth between details or examples and general points, in such a way that embodies critical questioning. Now, perhaps that is merely a skill, and not the kind of thing that counts toward moral (or, character) formation. This would depend, I suppose, on whether it is seen in an isolated way, as a classroom exercise say, or as something which shapes the student's life as a whole. Does it shape her or his desires and the kind of action she or he takes pleasure in? The kind of practices that contribute to moral formation, that is, must be connected up with a series of other practices. Taken as a whole, we can assume, these practices will constitute what is necessary for human beings to live the sort of lives that is proper to them. By tying authority and formation to whole lives, tradition recovers some a motive that led to the turn from system (quandary ethics) to story (narrative)—namely the ability to attend to particular lives. Further, if we add that humans are the sort of creature that don't spring up from the get-go ready to take on the activities of a fully mature member of the species, the practices in question will have to be passed down, and it is here that the argument for "tradition" comes full circle.

This seems to me the locus of the strongest challenge to put to Stout's account of moral formation—its implied account of how moral wisdom is passed on between generations. The challenge raises the question of whether Stout takes adequate account of the embodied (or, animal) nature of human moral learning. In recognizing our animality we come to see that formation entails the shaping of desire and what we find pleasurable or painful as much as (and before) it implies rational discourse, or conversation.

It is not clear that we can understand authority in Stout's democratic tradition from just this account of moral formation and the essay. But this close examination of it has led us to suspect that Stout's authority does not adequately account for its connection to tradition. That is to say, I have suggested that the concern that Stout seeks to address through his discussion of the essay—namely, that over-attachment to the doctrine side of the example-doctrine dialectic—is best understood when we consider why tradition plays an important role in moral discourse. Yet I have also claimed that tradition leads us to take seriously precisely the kind of moral authority that Stout decries in Hauerwas.

Perhaps it is misleading to single out authority and tradition as though they could exist independently of the political setting of which they are a part. For Hauerwas authority and tradition become intelligible in the context of the church. It is in the church that authority and tradition serve trans-generational moral formation of a particular kind. The church, in other words, is the political context—requiring display in story and not system—that makes possible formation in Christian character. Stout, I have been suggesting, has not adequately accounted for the politics of moral formation.

I must now leave behind this examination of differences between Stout and Hauerwas on moral formation in order to consider Stout's use of justice in his criticisms of Hauerwas.

Justice and the Political Nature of Practical Reason

Stout believes that much that is wrong, or at least excessive, in Hauerwas's rhetoric could be corrected if Hauerwas were to re-incorporate the language of justice into his work. But rather than responding to this claim, this section will be devoted to getting clear on what Stout means by "justice." I want to discern whether justice is a political virtue for Stout, and if so what kind of a political virtue it is. In explaining why the charge that Hauerwas has failed to take account of his own social location is sustainable, Stout introduces an example that suggests what justice might mean from a democratic point of view. The example is meant to encapsulate the debate between a Christian feminist like Albrecht, from whom the example comes, and a Christian traditionalist like Hauerwas. Stout's more ultimate objective is to display the relation of freedom and justice within democratic tradition. En route he seeks to recover freedom from a usage that absurdly pretends we can live without any social constraints whatsoever. Here is the contrast: While "liberationists" are concerned with freedom from social constraints that are "oppressive," traditionalists emphasize the need for discipline and the apprentice-master relationship as what makes free human practices possible, and subsequently the achievement of high standards. Stout writes:

> If a young woman is going to become an excellent jazz musician, she will have to deal with standards of competence and excellence and strive to constrain her musical performances accordingly. She will be well served by apprenticing herself to

someone more experienced and accomplished than herself and, up to a certain point in her development, by imitating models of excellence. But a prerequisite for becoming free to play jazz well is the freedom to play at all. Another is access to competent teachers who care about helping her get better and offer her encouragement.[21]

Stout's example provides a clear illustration of the relation of freedom and "constraint by norms" and also displays the tie of justice and freedom. On the one hand, freedom is enabled by the discipline of a particular practice like Jazz. This is freedom for excellence. On the other hand, social constraints may be such that they inhibit freedom. In this case freedom is not freedom within, or made possible by, such constraints but freedom *from* them, or "liberation." It is in this latter case that justice arises as a means of questioning and one hopes of changing the social constraints at issue.

Nevertheless it begs a question: on what grounds are we to judge access to a particular practice just?

A potential problem here is that Stout almost gives the impression that justice becomes important only in the latter case, where the relevant social constraints need to be changed. In truth, justice is operative in both arenas of freedom. Justice operates in the first case, where a student is seeking to become a jazz musician with the requisite conditions in place, insofar as the student and teacher, and the tradition itself, each get their due respect, obedience, etc. The distribution of praise within the practice is just, we may presume, when it is proportionate to merit in the relevant skills of jazz-playing. Justice also of course operates in the latter case when the social constraints that unfairly exclude girls from the freedom of opportunity, and the freedom of resources, needed to become a jazz musician are called into question.

What grounds the reference to justice in explicating the freedoms at play in both these contexts? That is, what unites the use of the word "justice" in both cases? To begin with, we might say, the term justice is used in both cases in order to name the relationship between individuals and what is due them. This is to say, justice refers to how goods are distributed. And yet this brings to light the equivocal use of freedom in Stout's parlance. In the first case, freedom qualifies the activity of the

---

21. Stout, *Democracy and Tradition*, 151.

student who is becoming a jazz musician. It is a teleological conception of freedom insofar as it becomes increasingly real as the student approximates her goal defined in terms of the mature state of an excellent musician. One cannot really comprehend the freedom—here meaning "playing Jazz well"—apart from the telos. Justice is one of the virtues that sustains the social practice whereby individuals can pursue this course of becoming excellent jazz musicians. In the second case, freedom is a little more complicated. Most basically, justice makes us free insofar as it makes it possible for us to question, and have a part in authorizing, the norms by which we are constrained. Whether Stout wishes those norms to be identified as the norms of a "society" or the norms of a particular practice is an important question to be answered in the course of things. When we speak of the "exclusion" of certain groups from a particular practice, it seems to be "society" we have in mind as the object of justice. Yet, this begs the question "what *is* society?" if it is not simply a collection of practices like jazz. This is important because the norms that exclude a particular group from certain roles may be directly related to their required participation in others. Forgetting this, we might naively believe that one can change social norms in one area in a way that leaves others unaltered.

    Let us say that to speak of justice in relation to freedom in this sense means that justice is to be applied first to society's norms, and as a result the norms of particular practices will change. So, if we dismantle some aspect of "patriarchy" (a description of social norms that does not tie itself immediately to a particular practice), we can so fix things that girls have the conditions in place to become jazz musicians. (We thus get both levels of concern into our account.) This still begs the question: on what grounds are we to decide that a particular distribution of freedoms at the level of society is just? (Or, that a particular society's distribution of freedoms is just in an exemplary way?)

    Stout has developed a way of answering such questions. It is through his claim that justice understood as questioning the normative constraints under which we live is itself a practice. He writes:

> One thing women need to be liberated to participate in, I would argue, is the democratic practice in which we try to take responsibility, as a people, for the activities and institutions that constitute our common life together. The institutions in question include the family, the firm, the market, the university, and

the church. The practices include nurturing the young, the production and distribution of goods, the pursuit of learning, and worship.[22]

Is democracy just another practice, like Jazz, or is it a "meta" or "hyper" practice? If the former, what links it up with the other practices? Or, to put the question another way, "what kind of people does democracy produce?" and "what kind of justice do they practice?" To pursue these questions, I turn to an exchange between Stout and the philosopher Sabina Lovibond. Lovibond, I believe, pursues these very questions with respect to Stout.

Justice as Conversation and Normative Modernity: Lovibond on Stout

By modeling the public deliberations he envisions for America, chapter 3 of *Democracy and Tradition*, entitled "Religious Reasons in Political Argument," makes clear that the polity Stout has in mind has, as its constitutive activity, conversation. In Stout's democracy, conversation is understood as a social practice and therefore is guided by norms toward certain goods. There are, furthermore, certain virtues required to carry out the practice, and sustain it. Like social practices generally, the goods to be achieved cannot be described fully without considering the virtues needed to achieve them. For instance, one of the goods to be distributed in a democratic society are freedoms to have a voice. But the exercise of this freedom presupposes the cultivation of certain dispositions—i.e. civility, courage, sincerity. Stout's conception of justice is to be located in the context of this practice of conversation: the living out of certain democratic freedoms.

In Stout's description of the basis of proper manners of public deliberation, which are undergirded by the set of proper dispositions or character traits, he discusses the issue of epistemic justification. His account of the social practice of democratic conversation is grounded in his views about how we are justified in believing something, and this in turn shapes his vision of public reasoning. It is circular. Epistemic justification is important, he believes, first because one needs some understanding of how people arrive at their rational beliefs in order to know the rules for exchanging such beliefs in public discourse. Stout's

---

22. Ibid., 152.

account is permissive in this regard. Drawing on the romanticist notion of "expressive rationality," Stout wants to celebrate ordinary life (*sittlichkeit*) for its role in generating ways of believing—later to be put to the test. His account trades upon a distinction between being justified in believing something, and drawing on one's beliefs when one reasons in public by expressing one's views, and being able to justify what one believes to one's audience.

Second, epistemic justification is important because a proper account of it provides a ground for one set of these rules of conversation, those to do with civility. Insofar as we understand how particular are the contexts in which people form beliefs, we are less likely to condemn them a priori for having beliefs unlike our own.[23] Above all, Stout's account of epistemic justification is important because it facilitates learning more about the people who are our interlocutors. Since in the conversation of democracy we are bound to one another in ways we cannot escape—and this itself perhaps makes it somewhat distinct from other conversations—it is in our interest to know why our fellow citizens believe and act as they do. Democracy thrives on the resources of the languages of belief of different communities.

What does justice have to do with epistemic justification in the context of Stout's account of democratic conversation? Since Stout's account of epistemic justification provides the underlying rationale for such conversation, and the freedom to participate in that conversation is one of the goods of this conversation understood as a social practice, justice and epistemic justification are allied. Stout's account of epistemic justification tells us what that freedom amounts to. It helps us thus to understand what is our due, and why.

The link between epistemic justification and justice requires us to name another democratic virtue: civility. When we understand epistemic justification properly we know what civility means in the context of public deliberation—that is, we know how to treat others qua fellow citizens. From civility we see that justice, as it informs the conversation, also derives from this account. For, as just mentioned, in the social practice of democracy, an important shared good is the freedom to participate. Since uncivil treatment of a participant in the

23. Taken as a whole, as he makes plain in chapter 3, taking the context of belief formation into account represents a more anthropological approach than the one whereby Rawlsians form their conception of public reason and its rules.

conversation does damage to the good of freedom for that participant, it also an instance of injustice toward him or her.

In her response to *Democracy and Tradition* appearing in the *Journal of Religious Ethics*, entitled "Religion and Modernity: Living in the Hypercontext,"[24] Sabina Lovibond is struck by Stout's account of epistemic justification. She sees and affirms that this can be said to undergird civility, as a constitutive virtue for the social practice of democratic conversation. However, she also finds it problematic as part of an account of practical reason. It is hampered because it does not take sufficient care to preserve the "unity" of practical reason found in Kant, and presumably in other significant moral philosophers. (In the end, so to speak, what is missing from Stout's account of practical reason is a strong enough role for truth, here seen as the *telos* practical reasoning strives toward.) It therefore comes too close to the doctrines of "descriptivism" or "relativism." Lovibond performs what I believe can be called an immanent critique of Stout's account of epistemic justification—she seeks, that is, to amend his account in a friendly way, drawing upon several of Stout's own assumptions. Moreover, she does so in a way that is useful to my purpose of examining that nature of the polity in which justice, and Stout's other democratic virtues, function.

Stout, as we noted, describes justification in terms of what an individual does with his or her situation, including what he or she is acculturated to believe and presumably her own creative configuration of her cultural inheritance. For contrast, Lovibond quotes John McDowell, claiming that "A justified belief is one that rests on *good* reasons; and a good reason must be one that will not lead you astray if you base your thought and action upon it; otherwise it would not be good, but *pro tanto* faulty."[25]

The context of this quote is a contrast McDowell draws between "justification" and mere "exculpation" of a belief. Lovibond draws on McDowell to begin to explain her hesitancy about Stout's account of what it means to be justified in believing something. The first symptom of her discomfort is that "Stout's discussion feels so deferential toward religious belief, or more accurately, toward those who are reluctant to cultivate any inhibitions about insisting on such belief in the presence of

---

24. Lovibond, "Religion and Modernity," 617–31

25. McDowell, *Mind and World*, 13. Quoted in Lovibond, "Religion and Modernity," 620.

those who do not share it." But the point cuts both ways, since neither should atheists hope that their atheism provides any special reason for their view to persuade its audience. Lovibond's hesitancy is based on the notion that an overly permissive account of justification releases our interlocutors from accountability to be reasonable in what they believe.

She recognizes that Stout's account, stressing the situational character of belief formation and justification, is not without criteria for assessing the rationality of an individual's beliefs. That assessment looks to the activity of the individual in making proper use of the resources of his or her epistemic horizon. This includes that the agent has duly considered the relevant reasons for doubting the beliefs it holds, and/or that it may be guilty of a culpable neglect of evidence. To be justified, in this sense, is to have done our duty as "inquiring minds," and to be free therefore from blame in holding our beliefs. Lovibond admits that one of the virtues of this approach lies in the concreteness of such criteria of evaluation.

But this is not the only legitimate use of the term "justification," according to Lovibond. A distinct usage is hinted at in McDowell's placement of the adjective "good" in front of "reasons" (for belief), and concerns the issue of whether the beliefs held by someone are "true," in the sense that in trusting in them you will not be led astray. Though perhaps more difficult to grasp than the above description of intellectual competence, truth understood this way nevertheless provides a criterion for evaluating someone's beliefs.

To help us see better what is at stake, Lovibond asks us to distinguish two senses of justification, corresponding to Richard Foley's observation of two "different projects for epistemologies to pursue."[26] (This distinction was prefigured in her reference to McDowell.) "One project," Foley writes, "is to explore what is required for us to put your own intellectual house in order. Another is to explore what is required for us to stand in a relation of knowledge to our environment." Following Foley, I presume, Lovibond refers to "internalist" (how Stout leans) versus "externalist" (how McDowell leans) modes of justification. The concerns of the externalist account might be said to correspond with her emphasis on "realism" in her earlier work.[27] There she showed how undercutting

26. Foley, "Justification, Epistemic," 157–65.

27. For a full account of Lovibond's position, see her *Realism and Imagination in Ethics*.

an arbitrary separation between "facts" and "values"—the product of the problematic epistemology of foundationalism—puts moral claims back into the category of truth claims. Once there we can use an "externalist" standard for them like other kinds of belief, asking "do they adequately correspond to our best grasp of the way thing are?"

Lovibond shows what is at stake in the difference between these two senses of justification, and at the same time offers a friendly reconstruction of Stout's account. She, in effect, splits the difference between internalist and externalist views. The advantage of the internalist account of justification is to be found in the aid it provides to the ethos of democratic conversation, as Stout makes clear in his description of civility as a virtue necessary for democratic conversation. It allows us to deal with the case where we want to say of someone, "his belief is justified, though false," and to do so in a manner that does not blame them or write them off as suffering from a rationality deficit. We begin, that is, by asking "how far (if at all) [their] beliefs really deviate from 'what any reasonable person would believe situated in exactly the same way they are.'" However, as Lovibond points out, Stout cannot mean that this *prima facie* trust is to be "combined with the (conversation-stopping) determinist assumption that any individual person, reasonable or otherwise, is bound to think exactly as they do if situated exactly as they are." "Instead," she says—and here she is reconfiguring Stout's view by placing it in a broader practical context—"it is meant to prompt some critical reflection, informed by the evaluative content of our idea of reasonableness, on the merits of what fellow citizen X or Y has accomplished in the way of intellectual processing of his or her social experience, which will presumably overlap to a greater or lesser degree with one's own." Placing it in this broader practical context—which may be understood in terms of the unity of practical reason aforementioned—the "internalist" sense of justification foregrounded by Stout comes to be seen as a starting point in a longer process of reflection. We begin, in other words, by reflecting on how well our interlocutor is keeping house intellectually. But to get to the full sense of justification requires a further step that calls for reflection on whether the interlocutor's beliefs need more development still. The full measure of this process is to be understood by seeing reason as teleologically oriented to "truth." In other words, we trust that an individual's beliefs are justified by the situation in which they went about informing them, but we also evaluate what they have done in this regard on a basis that is not reducible to that situation. Our "idea of reasonableness" has, or should have, "a residual critical content" that allows us to ask whether or our interlocutor's beliefs are adequate as they stand, or need to be amended.

This "residual critical content" of reasonableness, it seems to me, implies movement from the internalist account of justification to the externalist one. For Lovibond, I believe, it implies that the "inquiring mind" whose actions are a standard on the internalist account must possess the trait of openness to reality. This openness, I think further, cannot be reduced to the virtues that help constitute the practice of democratic conversation, such as civility or tolerance. (It requires introducing a new virtue, truthfulness.) Just as on the externalist account, justification cannot be based solely on the consent, or lack of consent, of the other members of one's dialogue situation. The correctness of the doctrine proclaiming that our access to truth is always mediated does not entail there is not some truth which nobody happens to now know. If this is so, and if Stout is committed to both senses of justification, he too must recognize that practical rationality has a standard besides merely dialogical competency. One cannot substitute "tolerance" for this standard, which is truth. Truth stands in a teleological relationship to such reasoning.

Lovibond makes this point about justification in relation to rationality ("good" reasons) in a further way by re-picturing the dialogue situation with an emphasis on the first person point of view. How, she asks, would *I* respond if someone told me that one of my fundamental moral beliefs were justified only in "my context" (implying that the next question would be, "But what is that to me?")? If she were in the hot seat, she says, she hopes she would not take refuge in her entitlement to her belief, backed by something like the internalist account of justification. To do so, in other words, would be to diminish reason's claims upon her.

This leads into her point that when we recognize that justificatory reasoning always takes place in a context, we must also see such contexts as by nature open to one another *and* as oriented toward a standard of reason not-reducible to any given context—truth.[28] Lovibond

---

28. "The critical theorist may, however, still feel that Stout leans too far in the direction of relativism. Isn't there a logical gap, he or she may ask, between the pragmatist's (correct) observation that justification is an activity, and as such takes place in a determinate intellectual and practical context; and on the other hand the idea that

suggests that the point can be put in another way, by stating that the context of justification, for our purposes today, can only be the context that spreads out over all actual (and possible) interlocutors. Following Stout, she names this the "hypercontext, modernity."[29] Truth, whose justificatory corollary is full rationality, is defined as the epistemic situation of modernity. To put it succinctly, to act with the proper competence of a rational inquirer is to act as though one's epistemic context were the hypercontext.

It is certainly of importance here, however, that in the naming of this ultimate context of epistemic justification, Lovibond slips into the mode of narrative. This becomes apparent when she says that "modernity" is the "destiny" for all human beings. The narrative account of epistemology on which she is drawing attempts to show how the pluralism of the premodern world, under particular historical conditions, leads to a "disenchanted world" through the repeated fusing of local horizons. But her narrative is given fuller illustration when she endeavors to tell the story of religion within the larger story of progress toward disenchantment, with the aid of Kant's *Religion within the Limits of Reason Alone*, whose story is as follows. In the pre-modern epoch, people needed the ritual forms of religious expression to provide a buttress for moral behavior. But the ultimate source of moral behavior is not the religious forms but the demands of rational nature. It is this rational nature that has made use of religions as a vehicle for helping everyone to understand its practical demands. The progress toward modernity permits of the releasing of the spirit of morality from its bodily trappings; the telos of reason is a universality, which cannot ultimately do with particular forms, and the purpose of particularity has been to help carry reason to its teleological destination. Lovibond claims the result of all this, which we have been calling the hypercontext, to be much like the kind of secularity Stout describes in *Democracy and Tradition*. Stout's description of the secular nature of public discourse stems from the notion that a religious believer entering a public discussion can no longer assume that the particular religious underpinning of her claims are justified, in the sense of being commonly acknowledge

---

reasons themselves are the property of particular groups of people . . . ?" Lovibond, "Religion and Modernity," 621.

29. This comes up in Stout's discussion of the work of critical theorist Seyla Benhabib. *Democracy and Tradition*, 176–78.

by the members of her audience. Her justification for drawing on these beliefs in the public square, then, pertains to the claim that everyone's beliefs must stem from some acculturation or other.[30] Lovibond claims that this is a condition in which historical religions have become more and more like window-dressing as far as public discourse is concerned, nice to look at but without any real force. While historical religions will not have gone away, they are unlikely to be the cause of uncivil disagreement in public discourse. For such arguments are bound to be over differences in historical particulars (e.g. the character of God as understood in different traditions), and everyone assumes because of the secular consensus that such quarrels cannot be in the spirit of any religion. This is because religion's purpose is to serve morality.

Does justification, particularly its externalist use—and here I am supposing Lovibond to have successfully re-constructed Stout's view—necessarily presuppose the hypercontext, modernity, which itself presupposes this narrative? Stout will want to challenge this, and in fact has already done so in his discussion of critical theorist Seyla Benhabib in *Democracy and Tradition*. He begins by tracing the development of Benhabib's thought as she interprets the tradition of critical theory from Marx to Habermas. The trend she highlights is the movement away from foundationalist toward social communicative practices. Her own distinction comes when she criticizes Habermas for founding his model on communication with a "generalized other"; in a way reminiscent of Hauerwas's critique of quandary ethics, Benhabib believes that critical theory must make the particular life the center of ethical reflection. But curiously for Stout, this turn toward the particular is somehow combined with an assertion of the Kantian idea, preserved by the precursors of Habermas, of a moral point of view characterized by universality and secularity. This is perhaps partly explained by the fact that Benhabib also upholds a description of modernity predicated on the Weberian thesis of "disenchantment." This thesis is both normative and historical/descriptive. For the first, it holds that to be modern consists in a certain disposition, characterized by a sense of alienation from what Hegel called *sittlichkeit*. Second, it includes an historical account of what led to this worldview and made it necessary. Stout's immanent criticism of Benhabib points to a tension between the concern that led her to part with Habermas' use of a generalized other in his account of

---

30. See Stout, *Democracy and Tradition*, chapter 4.

discourse and her embracing nevertheless the universal moral point of view, together with its historical narrative.

This immanent critique of Benhabib shows how Stout will resist a position like that which Lovibond has articulated about religion, and in what respects. He resists, first, their tying of practical rationality to a universal (and disenchanted, i.e., non-religious) point of view. Second, he resists the narrative explanation which reinforces this account of moral rationality, and underwrites the dismissal of religion. (He does so by simply pointing out that, if sociological theories are to be judged by how well they predict outcomes, this one has the difficult task of accounting for the widespread religiosity characteristic of modern nations like the United States.) He must therefore also resist Lovibond's implied assertion that something like this very story—developed through Kant's critique of religion—underwrites his own account of public discourse in a democracy.

What is at stake can perhaps be outlined in the following conditional statements. If Lovibond's generous re-presentation of Stout's account of epistemic justification is correct[31]—and here I mean particularly where she shows that Stout's, and in fact any adequate account of justification, presupposes a combination of internalist and externalist components—then Stout will have to show why his account of democracy isn't relevantly similar to the epistemic context she refers to as "the hypercontext, modernity." For we have shown that there is a connection between accounts of justification and descriptions of polities and their practices of public discourse. And if it turns out to be the case that Stout's democracy is substantially similar to Lovibond's modernity, Stout will then have the burden of showing why he doesn't need something like her (or Benhabib's) narrative about modernity.

What might this mean for Stout's virtues, particularly justice? We have seen how Stout's account of the virtues is enmeshed in his description of the practice of democratic conversation and therefore also on his account of justification. The central role of civility makes sense in the context of a public discursive practice whose quality depends upon its

31. Stout himself may not agree with the description of Lovibond's constructive commentary on his account of justification. In his response to her in the same issue of the *Journal of Religious Ethics*, he resists Lovibond's suggestion that his account of justification might be too permissive, and he implies that the stronger sense she derives from McDowell's distinction makes him uncomfortable. See Stout, "Comments on Six Responses," 710–16.

being hospitable to diverse voices, or individual's whose acculturation entitles them to incommensurable beliefs about the ultimate good.

How might these matters look different if Lovibond's immanent critique of Stout's account of justification in relation to public discourse succeeds? First, how would the description of democratic conversation as a discursive practice be altered? I suggest it would do so by adding a new task for the participants of such discussion. If justification is to due justice to the externalist concerns—the residual critical content of the notion of reasonableness that remains after assessing the competency of our interlocutors—public discourse requires arguing about the ultimate good to be brought about through their polity, and includes the narrative that makes its striving intelligible. The virtues espoused as excellent will include those that are directly related to this additional task of comprehending the ultimate good. Thus, truthfulness might become a key political virtue, or perhaps the proper name for this virtue is "wisdom." The virtues now at the fore—civility, candor—would not of course go away, since they are essential to this and other significant social practices. But they would come to be seen as derivative.

Justice too would need to be reconceived. On Stout's view justice primarily serves the purposes of conversation understood as its own end. The primary good for justice to distribute is freedom of participation. But if the conversation is also to be about the ultimate good—and the narrative that makes it intelligible—than freedom itself will have to be more explicitly teleological: the better we approximate the ultimate good, the more free we are. Justice, then, will need to take account of the ultimate purpose of freedom.

Justice, Politics, and the Good: Some Final Questions and a Promissory Note

Is democracy just another practice, like Jazz, or is it a "meta" or "hyper" practice? If the former, what links it up with the other practices? This was the question we had asked before beginning our digression on Stout and Lovibond.

In the introduction to this chapter I mentioned that, in his chapter on justice in *After Christendom*, Hauerwas does not seek to suppress justice talk so much as to offer a warning about what all comes with the "justice package." The dominant modern theories of justice are intertwined with a politics one of whose peculiar characteristics is an unwillingness (or, hesitation) to name the goods that provide justice talk with its material substance. This characteristic most certainly influences the way that justice is actually practiced in said society, and this actuality may not be one Christians can get behind. What's more, the temptation of contemporary theories of justice, when indulged, lead to a distorted understanding of how justice operates. For we come to believe that justice names a kind of universal tool that can be applied to societies independently of their ability to name and argue over what goods really matter for it. As I remarked previously, Hauerwas's objection to the talk of justice by Albrecht and Stout amounts to their thinking justice can do things that he believes it cannot do.

From the MacIntyre/Hauerwas perspective, which I share, the problem with Stout's account of the practice of democracy is not that it refers to "our common life together" without naming any shared goods of this life, or referring to the virtues required to achieve them. It does, and Stout's account in this sense responds to the concerns articulated by Hauerwas and MacIntyre. Nevertheless, he sometimes uses justice language in ways that presume it can be detached from such shared understandings. In addition to his general assertion that Hauerwas's adoption of justice talk would provide a bridge between the concerns of the church and those of the world, his uses of Albrecht to criticize Hauerwas and Susan Okin to criticize MacIntyre imply belief in a context-free justice. For in doing so he assumes that they and Hauerwas inhabit the same politics of justice.

This suggests that Stout's account of democratic society has not adequately spelled out the material conditions that make the argument over justice intelligible. What are we to make of the fact that Stout willfully remains taciturn about the question of the ultimate good? The new traditionalists' critique of liberalism famously points out that such theories make the lack of consensus on the ultimate good into a normative foundation for its brand of politics. "Pluralism" is the name often given to this politics. Does this creep into Stout's view when he paradoxically insinuates that the absence of a shared conception of the ultimate good makes the need to support the "common life" of American democracy all the more urgent? But can practical reason accomplish the task of making judgments of just and unjust without the ultimate good? I take up this question in the context of the dialogue between Stout and MacIntyre in the next chapter.

We can also put this challenge to Stout by returning to the issue of narrative. Does Stout's preference for the essay lead him to be overly reticent about the story's "end." I believe that Stout's reticence about the end, or eschaton, of his narrative leads to the kinds of (mis)readings of him represented by Lovibond.

Hauerwas the Man: Justice and the Politics of Liberation

This section turns to Gloria Albrecht's critique of Hauerwas in *The Character of Our Communities*. Albrecht also worries that Hauerwas is too little concerned with justice. Like Stout's, her critique functions at the level of an account of human agency, or practical reason, and a conception of politics. That is, she recognizes the crucial relation between these concepts, as a vision of politics provides the background within which human agency becomes intelligible. Also like Stout's, Albrecht's account of these concepts is expressed in her talk of justice.

Does Hauerwas fail to adequately understand himself? Does he take account of his social location when he writes about Christians for Christians and as a Christian? These questions come forth prominently in Gloria Albrecht's biting critique. She argues in her book that, because Hauerwas has allowed influences to do with his social position to shape his work without his awareness, the Christian ethics he performs does not contribute to a church that is just toward women and other marginalized people. In other words, Hauerwas's ecclesiology cannot comprehend justice as liberation for oppressed groups. But in Albrecht's book these questions and this challenge veil an underlying set of questions and assumptions. Her critique of Hauerwas depends upon her own arguments for a particular way of seeing human agency, practical reason, and politics leading toward an account of Christian ethics. It is no accident that Albrecht's criticisms take the reader on a complex trail, with forays into the philosophy of language and sociology of culture.

In this section, I first consider Albrecht and Hauerwas in terms of human agency in relation to narrative. Both Hauerwas and Albrecht believe that narrative rightly leads us to recognize the historical character of human agency. But Albrecht has a further ambition for the narrative in regard to human agents, and this can only be understood with reference to her politics. I then follow her into her account of the sources of that politics in post-structuralist and feminist conceptions of language and identity. This politics, whose name is "liberation," is intimately tied to justice, its main virtue. In the next section, I question whether Albrecht's account of narrative and of politics can sustain her use of justice. Put differently, I ask how her justice provides hope for the possibility of such a politics. In other terms, this section asks whether in focusing on liberation Albrecht has named a good capable of training us to have just desires. If not, I point out, her use of justice will be in tension with her affirmation of the historical character of human agency. Next, I return to Albrecht's questioning of the embodied character of Hauerwas's church, suggesting how it might be so embodied. Finally, I consider whether and how the church conceived as a story-formed polity might hold out hope to make Christians just.

Human Agency and Narrative in Hauerwas and Albrecht

Running through Albrecht's critique is the concept of human agency. As we have seen, this term can easily be related to practical reason since human agency provides the context in which practical reason is to be understood, and practical reason is a component of an account of the human agent. Albrecht treats agency in relation to narrative, truth, or knowledge ("epistemology"), politics, and justice. The turn to narrative, as we have seen, was taken by some philosophers and theologians as a therapy for a kind of abstraction to which modern moral theories are prone. But does Albrecht's appropriation of narrative become overly determined by some kind of theory?

Albrecht and Hauerwas agree that, by making norms the first concern, modern moral thought produced a distorted conception of the human agent. They further agree that agents only come to see and make use of norms through the stories of their lives. Albrecht believes, however, that Hauerwas has not fully escaped the totalizing tendencies of the modern agency, and so has reproduced it in his work. Borrowing terms from Lints, she argues that postliberals like Hauerwas are guilty of "dragging a foot" in modernity's faith in reason and truth.[32] Postliberals, broadly speaking, simply reject the moves of earlier theologians to ground their convictions in universal reason, but instead emphasize the narrative nature of all truth. They apply this to their own context by suggesting that it is only by learning to appropriate the biblical story that Christians learn to tell truth from falsity.

32. Lints, *Fabric of Theology*.

In other words, the postliberal agent gains coherence not from universal reason but by making the narrative of a particular historical community its own. The truth of a narrative is located in the people who are formed in relation to it and who keep it alive by passing it on.

Albrecht seems to see postliberalism as a new kind of foundationalism. For in each case, the agent gains a sense of unity and certainty about himself.[33] Albrecht would grant, however, that to see how Hauerwas ends up a modernist—or, as I think she means, something just as bad—requires displaying a few of the moves in his theological ethics proper, or his appropriation of the Christian narrative.

Hauerwas has written about his identity as a Texan as a way of illustrating that human agents are shaped by narrative and that our narratives will largely determine our moral vision. Therefore, our ability to go on from where we started has to do not with a kind of emancipation from our particular past, but with the resources in our heritage for being honest about our own limitations. Remembering his story as a Texan, therefore, helps him to oppose the liberal pretension that we invent ourselves.

Albrecht however sees in Hauerwas's story something quite different—namely the roots of a kind of totalitarian violence that mirrors liberalism. For her, encoded in this story is an explanation of why Hauerwas is unable to see himself truthfully, and as a result unable to envision what justice toward others demands. More unfortunately still, he has reproduced the limitations of this story in his vision of the church.

The salient aspects of Hauerwas's personal story for Albrecht are these:[34] 1) Hauerwas's identity as a Texan includes racist and sexist elements; 2) that to have an identity one must have a set of particular loyalties, and to name some as "other"; 3) that the loyalties are transmitted diachronically, and that the fathers are privileged in transmitting the stories that matter; and 4) that violence will be necessary to protect one's story from others and their stories. The story of Hauerwas the Texan, according to Albrecht, is not significantly changed in the story

---

33. She does not ask, as I think she should, about what *kind* of unity in the self postliberals affirm. For I believe they would offer an account of unity importantly different from that assumed by foundationalism.

34. The very neatness in Albrecht's transposition of Hauerwas's Texan narrative onto his rendition of the Christian story as a theological ethicist, however, makes one suspicious that Albrecht has reduced "narrative" to an abstraction.

of Hauerwas the Texan-become-a-follower-of-Christ, but instead the latter reproduces the former in a new vocabulary. This, she claims, is displayed in his ecclesial practical reasoning. For her, Hauerwas's theological ethics, in particular his explication of sin as violence and of God as non-violent Redeemer, grows directly out of the soil of his Texan identity. In truth, his account of theological non-violence is little more than a dressed-up version of the story of a (violent) Texan; it will serve to buttress the socially invulnerable postliberal self. She writes:

> From his description of being raised Texan and his adoption of a Texan epistemology, Hauerwas moves to a series of important assumptions for ethics. He will describe human subjectivity, the relationship between individuals and society, and the narrative nature of knowledge. The result, I will argue, is the reassertion of a theory of essential human nature which serves to tie all of his assumptions together.[35]

What we will see is that Albrecht's critique is political. We should expect this because of the aforementioned connection of human agency and politics.

Justice and the Politics of Liberation

A useful way to begin to elucidate the postmodern self is by paying attention to how she summarizes her criticisms of Hauerwas. She begins chapter 5 in the following way:

> In response to the postpositivistic crisis in epistemology, both Welch's feminist theology of liberation and Hauerwas's ethics of character turn for verification to the evidence, in history and in community, that our truth claims do what they claim is truth. It has been my argument in the last chapter that Hauerwas's proposal for a church of resident aliens fails to accomplish his intended goal of forming people able to live peaceably. By failing to follow through with the radical implications of our complete historicism, Hauerwas repeats the error of universalizing a perspective that arises out of a historically particular and socially located position.[36]

---

35. Albrecht, *Character of our Communities*, 31.
36. Ibid., 138.

Since Hauerwas wants Christian lives to be the test of Christian truth claims, her charge is aimed to hit Hauerwas where it will hurt, but what are the "radical implications of our complete historicism" and how will following through with them help us to be peaceable? To begin with, "complete historicism" is Albrecht's description of human agency. The rejection of the Enlightenment's universal reasoner should be pushed to its limit so that "historical" becomes the primary adjective for what humans are. The problem with Hauerwas is that he does not carry out his rejection of the disengaged subject rigorously and thoroughly enough, and "the unfortunate result is not the formation of nonviolent people but the maintenance of social privilege for dominant white society generally, and for dominant white males particularly."The urgency of her challenge to fellow white feminists is made intelligible by her belief that justice is at stake here. For the "recognition of our fully historical consciousness and analysis of the humanly constructed discourses that compete for our embodiment lead to the conclusion that justice is integral to truth."[37]

Just as she analyzed Hauerwas in terms of his story, Albrecht begins her account of moral agency/epistemology with her own story. Albrecht's story displays that her need to go beyond liberalism is an emancipatory one. It is a story of an identity that moves from identification as oppressed to oppressor. As a woman in a patriarchal society, Albrecht's first move toward liberation involved her embracing liberal feminism. Liberal feminism had a point in revealing that the rights attributed universally to human beings by the champions of classical liberalism must be extended in practice and principle from males only to males and females. But this freedom and universality of rights, used by feminists for the first stage of liberation, would become a stumbling block as things went on. Albrecht confesses that the allegiance to freedom among feminists quickly became a means of domination as it allowed the white middle class to dominate men and women of color and of the working class. The commitment to emancipation therefore ironically required the giving up of "freedom," at least in its liberal guise. An approach scrupulously attentive to historical contingencies was required. The "radical implications" she is after would seem to

37. Ibid. In a complementary image, used in summoning her fellow white feminists to practice self-vigilance, she refers to this account of human agency by "embodied reason" grounded in "embodied experiences."

be a politics that does not liberate one group while at the same time tightening the bonds of others. Her next question is where to find such approach in recent philosophy and theology.

Because all discourses of identity are essentially human constructions, for Albrecht "justice" is the name for an on-going struggle for the power to shape those discourses (to our own advantage). The positive side of this struggle is its underdetermined character. Because these discourses are merely human, it is possible for those placed at the margins to contest the self-descriptions that flow out of the dominant stance of the privileged. More than this, however, the malleable nature of human discourse, identity, and truth means that those with good will, and who are attentive to this malleability, can continuously critique the grammar and practices that inevitably harden into sediment. One picks up the scent of critical theory here. To be a just person on Albrecht's account begins with being one who does not suppress (or shy away from) the process, or struggle, through which identity is constructed.

Albrecht offers a somewhat different account of justice in another place where she states that justice points to "rightly ordered relationships of mutuality within the total web of our social relations," which, she says, may also be called "the reign of God." Justice, she says, can be seen as "the virtue that directs and empowers one to act on behalf of human well-being." In the section of criticisms that follow I will argue that the language of "rightly ordered relationships" and "human well-being" cannot be sustained within either Albrecht's post-structuralist account of language and identity or by the conception of the "reign of God" she claims is held out by postmodern Christianity. At present, I simply wish to show how her conception of justice hangs together with her conceptions of the self and the politics of liberation.

To begin, as mentioned, Albrecht ties the issue of truth to that of what is right (ethics). This is necessary because all moral thinking is tied to political interest. "The first step toward objectivity," she writes, "is to acknowledge that my standpoint, my descriptions, and my method of moral thinking are inherently political; they express and defend some group's interests and my loyalty to that group."[38]

Next, after tying one's identity to one's interest group, she offers a description of what social orders composed of such groups are neces-

---

38. I believe this to be a characteristic move for thinkers in this camp, particularly those who cite for authority Foucault's insight about knowledge and power.

sarily like, coupled with a claim about how goodness and truth can cause some degree of change. Social injustice is the basic characteristic of society. Our self-identification is a function of where and how we stand in society, oppressor or oppressed. As she puts it:

> The second step is to acknowledge that social injustice means that our groups are interrelated in systems of domination and exploitation. Using poststructuralist theory and discourse analysis, a feminist ethics of liberation connects the crisis of knowledge (what is truth) and the crisis of ethics (what is good). We can then judge truth by where, and with whom, it leads us to stand. We can participate in the transformation of church and society because "we can choose between different accounts of reality on the basis of their social implications."[39]

The description of social orders as by nature exploitative makes intelligible the notion that comprehending that order and working to change it—"stand up to the man" or "fight the power," you might say—must go hand in hand.

Liberation, then, is the name of a politics. Within it, injustice—the dichotomy of oppressor and oppressed—does work both descriptively and normatively. Its relative permanency perhaps shows her to be drawing on a biblical conception of sin. Its effect and manifestation is that some groups are dominating others—a sort of domination which does "violence" to its victim's spirits, or sense of self, as much as to their bodies.[40] Further, that "we can participate" in such changes is central for Albrecht. Yet to lay claim to such participation requires that our identities also include an awareness of the governing dynamic of the politics of injustice, to be provided by the discourse of liberation (from the Bible or elsewhere). Here we see the similarity of Albrecht's position to the critical theory approach. Then, in the context of a self-aware understanding of politics, "participation" names an important social good within the just society Albrecht is envisioning. (She later refers to it as "creativity" and "co-creativity.") I will comment below on the way that Albrecht uses concepts (e.g., sin and creation) culled from the Bible.

---

39. Albrecht, *Character of our Communities*, 95.

40. "Violence names the experience of being defined by dominant discourses that are embedded in the structures of our institutions, in the material practices of our social, political and economic systems, as well as in the theories and stories that give them plausibility." Albrecht, *Character of our Communities*, 96.

This self-aware or liberated agency is reflected in Albrecht's elaboration of what it means to be just. What enables us to describe ourselves truthfully is itself justice. Just practices are rooted in an "experience" of injustice, where some are dominating and others dominated. "Having experienced the distortions produced by dominant narratives," she writes, "this feminist ethic of liberation looks for an emancipatory epistemology, a knowledge seeking that is 'for, not just about, that majority of the members of our species who have fragmented selves and oppositional consciousness (i.e. women & minorities).'"[41] Further, she explains that "choosing to encounter the marginalized 'other' at their sites of empowered resistance, choosing to be open to their histories and traditions, exposes the strengths and weaknesses of my own social location" such that "objectivity . . . is an ongoing social process" and "how 'truthful' objectivity will be is fully dependent on the *justice* of the social process that produces it" (my emphasis).

Justice then requires that the privileged take the "risk" of becoming vulnerable before the oppressed, since their identity is predicated upon the suffering of the oppressed. Justice, in the liberation framework, points to a process of vulnerability and disorientation. Since Albrecht earlier tied identity to language, we would expect justice to be about a transformation of how we talk as well.

This account becomes more intelligible when placed in the context of Albrecht's own biography. That "freedom" (liberal) which liberated white women from male oppression became a means of dominating marginalized others. The account of justice displayed here seeks emancipation from the old cure.

Can the politics of liberation sustain justice? That is, can such a politics make us just?

Justice and Politics: How to Hold Justice and Liberation Together?

Albrecht's couching of her account of human agency in her own story as a woman seeking liberation would seem to fit well with her assertion that human agency is historical in character. But having seen more of her accounts of the true, the good, and the just, the question arises whether these are adequate to sustain that account of human agency, an

---

41. Albrecht, *Character of our Communities*, 95–96. For the texts quoted here by Albrecht, see Welch, *A Feminist Ethic of Risk*.

account we recall that requires the formation of a person's desires. We have just seen how her conception of agency, which becomes intelligible through the story of women's liberation, is situated within the politics of liberation. It is this politics that must be the source of just people. But just as any politics gains its particular character from its conception of the good, or the orienting direction of its story, we must ask whether the politics of liberation can transform us toward becoming just. My own suspicion is that the story in which liberation is the telos does not adequately specify the good toward which we are to train our desires.

It must be said that there is an ambivalence within Albrecht's account of justice in relation to the good. Some of her language—particularly that drawn from a difference feminism such as Carol Gilligan's[42]—suggests she has taken the route of what Taylor calls substantive justice. For example, she writes:

> Therefore, justice, understood as the virtue that directs and empowers one to act on behalf of human well-being, is essential to salvation. Such a justice is not merely procedural, but is the very substance of social relations. And, such a justice must be extended to include all women and the entirety of our social relations . . . The goal of this feminist ethics of liberation . . . is, therefore to expose and transform the violence of marginalization and disempowerment by choosing . . . to call into being practices of interdependence aimed toward equality of participation in the social construction of meaning.[43]

We have seen that Albrecht's account of justice emphasizes her willingness to resist the temptation to shy away from the struggle of working out the norms by which we will be governed. Justice, in her rendering, sometimes sounds a lot like the virtue of courage. This may go with Albrecht's insistence on the historical nature of human agency, with our identity in relation to what we value always revisable by further argument. She also states that justice means that which "empowers one to act on behalf of human well-being." This suggests that she supposes an account of human nature and what makes it good ("well-being") and perhaps complements her emphasis on "mutuality" as defining "rightly ordered relationships." Human beings, we may surmise, are on her account social or political beings.

---

42. Gilligan, *In a Different Voice*.
43. Albrecht, *Character of our Communities*, 97–98.

But if justice names a historically situated struggle, what is the end or goal that gives this story its unity and point? That is, how does the story of striving for justice lead to human flourishing? The assertion that justice names a historically situated struggle is her most basic point, and this casts a certain shadow over her use of the terms "well-being" and "rightly ordered relationships of mutuality." The telos or ultimate good whose achievement fuels the historical struggle for justice is called "liberation." Is liberation, so defined, good enough to sustain Albrecht's defining of justice as a virtue that sustains human well-being and rightly ordered relationships?

As Hauerwas and others have pointed out with respect to liberation theology, liberation itself cannot be the criteria by which we evaluate a given set of historical circumstances as "rightly ordered."[44] Liberty is not its own justification, in other words. It rather works in the reverse. The results of particular processes of liberation can only be evaluated by deciding whether or not they are just. And the concept of justice here must be a substantive one, grounded in a thicker conception of the good than "liberation" as liberty.

As Aristotle pointed out, there is a formal justice that simply states (arithmetically, as he puts it) that equals ought to receive the same treatment.[45] Or, negatively, to treat two subjects differently who are equal in the relevant respects constitutes an injustice. But then the interesting questions arise when we inquire, "what are the relevant aspects according to which these two are 'equals'?" The individuals in question must be in some particular way identified and categorized before we can apply the norm of formal justice to them. To call two subjects "equals" seems always to raise the question, "equal how?," or presuppose that we have already in some way answered the question. Liberation thought, rightly noting the totalizing tendencies of narratives such as liberalism, highlights the fact of discursive difference and especially the subaltern.[46] Yet ultimately our response to this question requires specifying the goods of practices. Aristotle's intention, I believe, implies that we must also seek to describe the ultimate good (the telos), of human lives. So we are back at the question of the telos.

---

44. See Hauerwas *After Christendom*, 50–58.
45. See Pakaluk, *Aristotle's Nicomachean Ethics*, 181–205.
46. For a good account of these matters, see Long, *Divine Economy*, 83–87.

The diversity of meanings may explain why, in Book V of the *Nichomachean Ethics*, Aristotle assumes that in speaking of justice one must specify the context about which one is speaking. There is complete justice, or "lawfulness," which refers to having all the virtues necessary to be good. The notion that such justice implies conformity to law indicates Aristotle's belief that virtues that pertain to human beings have the polis as their necessary setting.[47] Then there is particular justice whose opposite is activity we might call self-aggrandizement. Particular justice looks at the exchanges between individuals and takes both distributive and commutative forms. This justice is not purely egalitarian but proportional, and considers roles and excellences. Still, underlying these instances is the presumed vision of the good in a polis, and thus the question of the telos is crucial.

This shows why MacIntyre points out that justice is no more autonomous, in the sense of a principle whose means of application can be made explicit outside of time, than any other virtue.[48] Like all virtues, he claims, the performance of justice depends upon practical wisdom (phronesis), so that it is not possible fully to possess one virtue without the others.

But what is the activity of phronesis? MacIntyre points out that phronesis is the combination of vision and deliberation that discerns both the ultimate good and its relation to the goods achievable through my actions here and now. In this sense, he brings us around to the connections between justice, the ultimate good, and the political.

That liberation is the ultimate good in relation to which justice is defined for Albrecht can perhaps be seen in her description of the politics that provides the setting for the seeking of this good. It is a politics in which human action (creativity) is understood as a rhetorical power to construct laws over against the rhetorical powers of others, or of those serving a different set of interests. That is to say, the powers at play are structured in terms of dominant agencies and oppressed agencies. In Albrecht's version, the rhetoric of women's interests represents the agency whose goal is justice, since women in our time experience oppression. As she notes, following Sheilia Davaney, "some experiences do more truth than others."[49]

---

47. Aristotle *Nichomachean Ethics* 1129b, 10–1130a, 1.
48. See chapter 7 of *Whose Justice? Which Rationality?*
49. Albrecht, *Character of our Communities*, 95.

I share Albrecht's belief that our society in many respects reflects male-domination. But there is a danger in reducing politics to a contest between oppressed and oppressor. Politics understood as the arena of conflict between individuals with private interests is not a politics of the human good. Such a conflictual politics naturally gives rise to a procedural account of justice. Because a procedural justice primarily intends to arbitrate between incommensurable private interests, it cannot adequately account for the need for formation in the virtues within a community. Procedural accounts, furthermore, reject their historicity, pretending to float free of such particularity. Albrecht would want to avoid this, but she cannot do so without a different politics of justice.

Where might such a politics be found? All I have really been saying is that Albrecht's account of justice is "procedural" and not substantive in the sense of presupposing a shared love of the good amongst the people it is to regulate. This can be taken to indicate both that Albrecht is deeply influenced by modernity's dominant conceptions of justice, themselves indebted to an individualist notion of freedom, and that it does not pay sufficient regard to the formation that makes us just people. My critique then has consisted in comparing her account of justice to that of ancient Greek wisdom. Equally valid, however, would be to critique her account of justice theologically. Here we could single out her account of "liberation" and ask whether her accounts of Jesus and his body, the church, are sufficient to make us people who liberate the poor and the oppressed. While this might be worthwhile, I will not attempt it here.[50] For one of the most salient characteristics of Albrecht's accounts of justice and liberation is that she does not allow them to be formed by the confessions and practices of the church. I will rather go on to the modest task of attempting to shed light on why she neglects the resources of the church as a politics that make intelligible the life of striving for liberation.

Can the Church Form Witnesses to Justice?

This section queries Albrecht as a theologian, and in particularly her reticences. It seems she refuses to give the church a chance when it comes to forming just people, and instead places trust in feminist theory.

---

50. For an account of how liberation specifies justice within a theologically substantive account of the good, see Bell, "Justice and Liberation," 182–95.

We have labored in the preceding sections to show the connections between human agency, practical reason, and politics. We have seen how both Albrecht and Hauerwas show a concern for how we picture the human agent, and that for both to grasp the historical embeddedness of human agency is crucial. This raises the concern of how to situate the agent historically. Albrecht argued that Hauerwas's way of re-telling his own story failed to adequately account for the historical contingency of his identity and therefore was not truthful. Specifically, he fails to see how sexism and racism have shaped him. Not only has his Texan story failed to help him see this, but neither has the Christian story.

But how does one narrate oneself truthfully? Where does one find the resources to produce the story that adequately captures one's life? Returning to our questions above, we may say that any account of the resources necessary for a truthful narrative about one's identity as an agent must include the political setting. So far have we come. We have rehearsed what Albrecht finds to be off about Hauerwas's church. With what would she have us replace it? Her criticisms of Hauerwas allow us indirectly to begin to formulate her answer. Hauerwas fails to narrate himself truthfully because he fails finally to make his origins as a male, white Texan into an object of critical reflection. Or, perhaps it is more accurate to say, he fails to make them such in the right way.

Hauerwas's attention to his formation does not disclose his influences adequately because the details of his life are not placed in the framework of that theory which would bring out their true significance. Hauerwas speaks of his being male in terms of the particular loyalties, preferences, fears, relationships, and awkwardnesses that go along with masculinity in his time and place. He speaks of his whiteness in similar ways, including even the kinds of prejudices that were part of the very air he breathed, and thus shaped him. What he does not do is understand himself as white, male, and heterosexual in terms of the theoretical "-isms" (feminism, classism, heterosexism, racism) that reveal these categories as crucial in setting up the structures of power that instantiate the control of the dominant over the marginalized and abnormal—a control that takes both explicit legal forms and implicit or "cultural" forms through categories like "normal" and "abnormal" (the -isms, that is, of liberation). This is not to say that Hauerwas must deny that such theories allow us to make truthful observations. For Albrecht, these clearly are the crucial categories for self-understanding. What makes them privileged is that they not only reveal the real nature of our understanding and relationships, they at the same time tell us what we should do about it. Such theories are not simply in the business of description but also of producing the norms for social reform.

What is worse, Hauerwas's neglect of the -isms that constitute the narrative of liberation implies that he reinforces the presence of worldly injustices that already infect the church. His account of sin, in relation to non-violence, serves to hide the church's own oppression of its women and its non-white members. Hauerwas's church champions family values that are not costly to its (male) members, and does so in a way that leaves institutionalized violence within the patriarchal families of its members unmolested.

Albrecht's driving concern in her critique of Hauerwas is that the church, contaminated by injustice, may reproduce worldly forms of oppression. But could it be that Albrecht's narrative of liberation does not so much aid the church toward becoming just as replace it with a different story? Could it be that an overestimation of the power of such theories as poststructuralist feminism makes her impatient with the imperfect and contingent plodding of the church? Perhaps her suspicion of the church's perversion runs so deep that she is overly cautious about naming and putting to use the graces God still works through it?

Samuel Wells and Debra Dean Murphy have both pointed out that Albrecht bypasses the church itself when it comes to marshalling resources to fight injustice both within and without the church. Murphy provides a path that shows how Albrecht's own feminist commitments could lead her to make the church more significant in her work.[51] She argues that anyone who wishes to appreciate the embodied nature of life and of our challenges as moral agents—as feminists certainly do—must recognize our dependence on the wisdom handed down to us, however imperfect. The only alternative is the kind of foundation dreamed up by the Enlightenment, a myth that feminists like Albrecht have rejected. Murphy therefore points out how Albrecht's neglect of the authority embodied in the visible church has propelled her to locate authority erroneously in an essentialized notion of "women's experience." For a Christian, the existence of the practices that embody church authority, then, can be received as a gift that helps us avoid self-

---

51. Dean Murphy, "Community, Character, and Gender," 338–55.

deception. Murphy, therefore, also urges that turning to the practices of the church as a source for the changes that feminists rightly seek is as reasonable a move for someone concerned with the effects of sexism as any we may conceivably make.

Furthermore, Wells argues rightly that Albrecht's use of feminist theory that includes an "essentialzed women's experience" has caused her to misunderstand the role of the church in Hauerwas. As we have seen, Albrecht alleges that Hauerwas's conception of the church results from a problematic epistemology. But as Wells rightly notes, for Hauerwas the church is not a result of his epistemology, it simply is his epistemology. The test of truthfulness for his ethical reasonings, then, is not to be gleaned from his theory of, or theory-leading-up-to, the church. Rather, the proving ground consists in those practices—celebrating the Lord's Supper, peace-making—that make the church the church. Albrecht has intimated that these practices are so deeply corrupted by the culture surrounding them that they have already proved themselves unable to supply the critical force we need. For example, she points to the habit of church in Sneem, Ireland, of dressing up girls in white as brides of Christ to receive their first communion. While Hauerwas might see such practices as one of the ways that the church embodies God in the world, Albrecht claims that such practices "embody a long Christian history of men's domination of women." This is because "dressing little girls in white as brides in a church where only males represent Christ is a traditioned practice that sustains sexist hegemonic power and betrays the sacred."[52]

Wells, looking at the selfsame practice, finds in it a resource that forms Christians to resist such hegemonic power, sometimes in the face of grave risk. He recounts the story that involves this practice, a story dating back to the sixth century, that links this practice of dress with an effect quite different from the fortifying of worldly prejudice. The story is set in the time just before the Muslim ascendancy of Arabia when Monophysite Christianity and Judaism were vying for dominance in Arabia. At that time, there was a Christian widow, named Ruhayma, whose King, having decided in favor of Judaism, commanded her to renounce Christ or face death. In preparation for the giving of her reply,

---

52. Albrecht, "Review, *In Good Company*," 219–27. Quoted in Wells, *Transforming Fate into Destiny*, 72–73.

or perhaps part of the reply itself, Ruhayma dressed herself and her daughters in their communion gowns. She spoke the following words to those gathered in the marketplace:

> Look at me, for twice you have seen my face: at my first wedding, and now at this second one also. With unveiled face before all of you I went over to my first spouse, and now again with unveiled face I am going to Christ my Lord and my God .... just as he came to us .... If I denied Christ, I should die, but if I did not deny Christ, I should live .... Behold how with unveiled face I am going out of your city in which I have lived as if in a temporary dwelling, so that I may journey, I and my daughters, to the other city, because it is to that place that I have betrothed them.[53]

Ruhayma then told the king of her decision, and he executed her for it. Yet, ironically says Wells, it is her own name, associated with faithfulness and courage, that has lived on in memory, and not that of the king who killed her.

Wells's response to Albrecht's conclusion, then: Maybe, let's look and see. In so responding he unveils an *a priori* certainty that infuses Albrecht's condemnation of Hauerwas. This certainty, we may now say, comes from Albrecht's failure to recognize the normative nature of her critical tools. She fails, that is, to see that her confrontation with Hauerwas is one based on political vision.

Wells's deeper points are that the practices of the church allow it to be constituted as a distinctive polis, and that Albrecht has overlooked this. One enters into that polis through baptism, which signifies a true change of political loyalties for one. This is the "other city" where belonging to God and one another is covenantal. The politics of this city, the church, we might say, can sustain the story that makes intelligible the life of striving for liberation as a life of true human goodness.

---

53. Shahid, *Martyrs of Najran*, 54–60. Quoted in Wells, *Transforming Fate into Destiny*, 72–73.

CHAPTER 5

Alasdair MacIntryre and Jeffrey Stout: Practical Reason as Traditioned

INTRODUCTION

In the first part of the preceding chapter, I engaged Stout's criticisms of Hauerwas around the concept of justice in relation to Christian engagement in the world. I found that the notion of justice was best unpacked by reference to the notions of tradition, moral formation, and politics. These notions already bring us into the territory I wish to explore in this chapter by examining Stout in relationship to MacIntyre. I promised there that I would go on to examine more closely practical reasoning in Stout and here I attempt to do this.

To state my thesis succinctly, I will argue here that Stout's account of democratic practical reasoning renders incoherent his claim to have integrated the ethics of character into his defense of the modern democratic form of life. Using Alasdair MacIntyre's "core account of the virtues" from *After Virtue*, I will try to highlight what I judge to be missing from Stout's account.[1]

---

[1]. My purpose here is not merely to criticize Stout's account of democratic moral reasoning, but to help those interested in the return to virtue in moral philosophy and theological ethics in the latter half of the twentieth century understand and evaluate its place within that history. By analyzing Stout's account of the virtues in *Democracy and Tradition* and that of Alasdair MacIntyre in *After Virtue* comparatively, I will argue on philosophical grounds for a reading of Stout's book that places it in a strained relation to the movement called "the return to virtue."

In the first part of the chapter, therefore, I will endeavor to give an outline of the kind of practical reason Stout develops in the book. For the purpose of comparison, I go on to sketch the account provided by MacIntyre in *After Virtue*. I then use this comparison to draw out in what respects I find Stout's account deficient.

All this, of course, is meant to be of service to the larger purpose of the book—namely, to highlight that practical reason is political in character, or assumes a community that seeks to discern the good by becoming good people. It is yet another way of highlighting the connection of the three key concepts of human agency, practical reason, and politics.

Stout's Account of Practical Reason

The purpose of *Democracy and Tradition* is to articulate the practical reasoning implicit in the life of American democracy. One of Stout's ways of pointing us in the right direction is negative. He argues that this kind of moral discourse must not be confused with the one that has been upheld in many of America's philosophy departments as the political theory of democratic politics. More particularly, Stout finds the notion of "public reason" in theories inspired by Rawls far too abstract, and restricted in the kinds of argument it would allow, to properly characterize our modern democratic discourse. Discomfort with such abstraction leads Stout beyond philosophy alone in *Democracy and Tradition*, and into the poetic resources within American and European letters in order to paint a portrait of how we reason practically. In fact, he supports this choice philosophically by arguing that reason itself should be conceived as expressive of our rational practices, rather than as a disembodied referee, placing a priori limits to what we can think and then say. His preference for a Hegelian logic that begins in *sitlich* cultural life over a Kantian *a priori* practical reason is an underlying theme of the book.

In this section of the chapter I will present Stout's account of democratic practical reasoning in three stages. I begin with his account of how democracy as a tradition specifies certain virtues of character and in particular a certain form of "piety." Stout further develops his view of practical reasoning through a genealogical argument concerning the passage from medieval to modern genres of moral instruction. This transition moves from morality plays to essays, and illustrates the phenomenon of "excess" as a point of change within the "ethics of example." Finally, I turn to chapter 9 in the third part of *Democracy and Tradition*, where Stout gives a more precise description of practical reasoning in a more abstract and theoretical mode. I believe it is here that we can most clearly see the structure of his thought.

In order to get a feel for how Democratic practical discourse works, I now turn to the first of these three exemplifications of *Democracy and Tradition*'s account of practical reasoning.

Stout's Account of Piety as Traditioned Democratic Moral Psychology

Part I of *Democracy and Tradition* is devoted to articulating the tradition of democratic character and virtue. While attempting to make plain the dependence of character on tradition, and thus make common ground with religious critics of democracy, Stout engages a discussion of "piety." Piety is defined as "a just acknowledgment of the sources of one's existence and continuance through life."

Piety serves a central purpose here because all accounts of virtue rely upon a living tradition. This includes training of the young by their elders, who in effect hand on the conversation about what virtues are and why they matter.

Stout here leads the reader to believe he is making common cause with proponents of the return to virtue, and particularly those of a religious bent. And, to a point, he is. But his other motive is to show how one does not need to give the topic of virtue entirely over to its "traditionalist" defenders—that is, those who see modernity in terms of a threat to virtue—and that instead one can "re-conceive" it in a democratic mode. As we will see, Stout wishes to re-conceive piety such that the way it defers to authority will be in harmony with democratic ideals.

Stout follows Emerson and Whitman in constructing an image of the democratically pious person as one who is self-responsible for imagining the "sources of [her or his] existence." In this, he wishes to split the difference between a character who arrogantly claims ownership of her or his accomplishments and one who has an overly deferential stance to the past that deadens her or his poetic capability to express reverence through ever renewed images. Recognizing the individual's role in imagining the sources of its existence opens such images to the discursive interchange characteristic of modern democracies. When the self-reliantly pious person defers to authority, he also "seeks to take responsibility for this commitment by making it explicit, poetically or philosophically, in the form of a claim—as something for which reasons can be requested."[2]

This conception of democratic piety, furthermore, has its ground in an emerging democratic culture, which, in contradistinction to the privileging of aristocracy found in earlier cultures, holds up ordinary citizens as exemplary. And it is the human being as individual (or *individuated*) that comes into focus here. This idea of democratic piety finds fuller expression in Stout's particular rendering of "gratitude." He claims that the self-reliantly pious person is grateful to others in a manner that is limited by her refusal of "masochistic self-abasement." For, he writes, "it does not belong to the virtue of justice for me to do more than I could possibly do to make the account square."[3] We see here how two virtues, justice and pious gratitude, qualify one another and thus fit together within Stout's account of the democratic virtues.

Charles Pinches has pointed out, however, that Stout's account of piety as a virtue seems to neglect the material instantiations that make piety part of a way of life. Piety, he notes, as a virtue grounded in gratitude for what has come before us, has much to do with memory. But memory, Pinches argues, and particular public memory, must be located in specific types of personal relations, which are themselves set within particular social settings.[4] It is about "how gifts are given and received within [such relations] in such specific settings as a family meal." Stout's account of piety, he notes, fails to ground piety in such concrete settings, and seems mostly concerned with the rejection of an "older" piety characteristic of "hierarchical" societies. But this begs the question of whether Stout is using piety mainly for the rhetorical

---

2. Stout, *Democracy and Tradition*, 31.

3. Stout here quotes the following passage from Emerson's essay *Experience*: "When I receive a gift, I do not macerate my body to make the account square, for, if I should die, I could not make the account square. The benefit overran the merit the first day, and has overran the merit ever since. The merit itself, so-called, I reckon part of the receiving." Emerson, *Emerson: Essays and Lectures*, 491. Quoted in Stout, *Democracy and Tradition*, 38.

4. Pinches, "Stout, Hauerwas and the Body of America," 9–31. Pinches points out that the fatal flaw of Stout's account of piety is its abstract and impersonal character, whereas gratitude by its nature must have a concrete object and particular forms of expression. See also Pinches, *Gathering of Memories*.

purpose of contrasting democracy to other kinds of society which get only a caricature-like description.

"Between Example and Doctrine" as a Mode of Reasoning in "Community" (Tradition)

The second example of what Stout has in mind by democratic practical reasoning comes in Part II of the book, during Stout's thorough-going criticism of Hauerwas. The topic under discussion is "quandary ethics," and while Stout sympathizes with Hauerwas's preference for an "ethics of example" grounded in narrative accounts of self in relation to world, he wishes to point up important differences in their uses of narrative and example.[5]

Stout argues that Hauerwas is not the only one to see the faults in doing moral philosophy through the analysis of quandaries.[6] In fact, the skepticism of many readers to this sort of approach has given rise to alternative, yet still characteristically *modern*, modes of moral reflection in other literary genres. For Stout the most important of these modern genres is the essay, which he says grew out of the suspicion that moral philosophy indulges "a temptation to engage in presumptuously dogmatic and excessively abstract thought."[7] Like the ethics of example, the essay favors stories exploring exemplary lives over the establishment of a system of principles, yet the kind of reflection on these lives inspired by the essay is distinct in kind.

In the essay moral reflection takes the form of a continuous movement between richly described examples and general ideas. Stout emphasizes that direction of influence is not predetermined. Sometimes the particular details support the general idea, and sometimes they

---

5. Readers who have read my discussion of Stout in the previous chapter—particularly the comparison between Stout and Hauerwas on the relation of examples and doctrines—will recognize that I am going over familiar territory. I have a slightly different emphasis here. If these issues are already quite familiar, you may want to skip to section 4, entitled "democratic authority and states of emergency."

6. Stout claims that Hauerwas has too quickly identified modern moral discourse with quandary ethics and thus overlooked resources in the former not limited to moral theory. Stout here seeks to recover some of modernity's overlooked resources in order to challenge its identification with the modern ethical theory described above. He notes that modern readers have often been skeptical of philosophy's theoretical analyses of moral quandaries.

7. Stout, *Democracy and Tradition*, 164.

render it problematic. This characteristic of the essay leads Stout to describe its form as "conversational." It inspires critical thought because its very form resists closure. The reader is called upon to respond by entering into the exploration being conducted.

Borrowing the description offered by Robert Musil, Stout states that the essay as a genre of moral reflection "stands between example and doctrine."[8] While the essay uses examples in order to illustrate general notions, its inconclusiveness invites a reader to think things through for oneself. His description of the essay furthermore makes the nature of its contrast with moral philosophy clear. The latter is so concerned to provide a logically coherent system, that it refuses all but the most congenial examples.

With this in mind, Stout turns to Hauerwas. While Hauerwas also rejects modern moral philosophy's ambitions to provide moral justification with a system, and commonly writes essays, Stout asserts that his favored kind of ethics of example is "the classic life." This genre has its roots in the Greco-Roman culture of "*paideia*," where individuals formed themselves morally by imitating particular persons identified as exemplary. The lives of these exemplary persons were then established as classics or canonical representatives within a particular tradition.

To spell out what distinguishes the classic life and the essay along the same lines, Stout turns to John Lyons' book *Exemplum*, a study of the transition undergone by the trope of example from the period of medieval morality plays and fables to more modern works such as the *Heptameron* of Marguerite of Navarre and the essays of Montaigne.[9] Lyons argues that the fundamental relationship between the example and the more general points it illuminates comes under strain in the transition from the medieval to the modern period. The relation is rendered problematic by a new fascination with rich accounts of historical particulars that arises within the culture. As lives are described in greater detail, it becomes difficult for authors to connect them with the doctrines they are meant exemplify. Lyons refers to this new phenomenon concerning the relation of examples to general ideas by the term "excess."[10] The examples outgrow the ideas they are meant to exemplify.

---

8. Musil, *Man Without Qualities*, 273. Quoted in Stout, *Democracy and Tradition*, 165.

9. Lyons, *Exemplum*, xi.

10. Stout, *Democracy and Tradition*, 169.

Stout observes that this phenomenon of excess is precisely what disrupted the "culture of *paideia*," or the formation of persons around exemplary lives. The latter relied on a stable connection between concrete examples and the general moral notions to which they point.

The essay (Montaigne, Navarre), in turn, created audiences who embodied the *ethos* of the new democratic spirit. Readers were moved by the ideal of taking individual responsibility for one's values and those governing one's society. This further implied a social structure that would not block an individual's expression, and gave rise to the democratic ideal of "equal voice," whose "premise is that society must take care not to block the expression of thoughts that might prove to be inspired."[11] Thus, political democracy is underwritten by this ethos of intellectual responsibility.

Recap

Stout narrates a kind of individualism based on the transition into modernity and the kind of rhetorical transformations that occasioned the transition. The latter are seen in the literary transition from hagiographic portraits of exemplary human beings to the essay, with its penchant for positioning the reader as an individual between various examples and the moral truths or doctrines they are meant to exemplify. Stemming from this transition there comes also a re-conception of authoritative figures as being inherently questionable, and therefore accountable to the individual who ultimately invests them with authority. One can say that authority, for Stout, is a concept which fundamentally depends on the companion concept of "responsibility"—that is, the responsibility of the one acknowledging a figure's authority to hold them accountable for exercising it properly. This is against the *paideia* account where Stout implies (misleadingly) we mimic our exemplars. While responsibility is not itself a virtue, but rather the structure of moral discourse in democracies, for Stout it is closely related to justice. For the just person is one who grants authority to persons and truth-claims on an ad hoc basis, but never transfers to them his own right and responsibility to be

---

11. Ibid., 167. Stout notes that Emerson's and Whitman's suspicion of institutional arrangements that might quash "true prophecy" before it is heard was based on a "substantive spiritual concern."

an authority. Questioning the authority of authors is a common activity of a just person within a democratic account of justice.[12]

This account of justice reinforces the Stoutian account of piety as "self-reliant" in the previous section. There, Stout attempted to portray the virtue of being aware of our debts to others and to nature in a way that stops short of violating the individual's integrity. The "integrity" of an individual for Stout, we may now say, consists in his or her ability to take responsibility for him or herself.

Whether in terms of an Emersonian re-conception of piety or a literary/cultural transition from saints' lives to the essay, what Stout has done is to outline a conception of the human agent in the terms of individualism. The human agent is definitively a reasoner who takes responsibility for what he or she believes. Naturally, this responsibility is carried out in discursive exchange with other members of our communities, and even, with piety, in terms of our relations to others long gone from this world. But ultimately we are all responsible for ourselves. Perhaps something Stout says about gratitude is salient here. The limits on gratitude stem from the notion of bodily integrity. I should not consider it my duty to abase myself in order to show that I acknowledge my debt to you.

Worth observing here is that Stout's individualism produces a view of human agency that emphasizes the intellectual. Our common work is not so much the domestic kind such as goes into raising children, but engaging in public-style debates. Is this an adequate picture of human agency and our lives as practical reasoners? As we proceed in the next section to consider Stout's more philosophical account of democratic practical reason, we will have this question in mind.

Democratic Authority and States of Emergency

In chapter 8, "Democratic Norms in the Age of Terrorism," Stout provides a formal account of practical reasoning, answering the question: What is special about democratic practical reasoning? There are two salient characteristics: 1) democratic reasoning is capable of generating norms that are universal in scope; and 2) it stems from the activity of

---

12. If we had more time, we might look to Stout's discussion of justice for confirmation. He argues that a just person is one who patrols the border where he defers to the authority of others rather than explicitly questioning that authority.

making explicit the norms that shape our characteristic moral practices. Stout hopes that this form of universal reasoning will not be confused with Kantian "pure practical reason." The latter assumes a culture-free point of view, whereas for Stout universal reasoning is sustained by a way of life (*sittlickheit,* in the Hegelian sense). Stout therefore also attempts here to connect the form of democratic practical reasoning to the practices of those who enact it. I will argue here, however, that the result of Stout's analysis is a portrait of practical reason that disassociates it from human action.

Following Brandom, Stout divides practical reason into three types. The first is represented by the statement: "Going to the store is my only way to get milk, so I shall go to the store." If we treat this kind of inference as materially good, Stout claims, then we recognize that there is a form of practical reasoning based on desire. (In other words, the premise that would make this inference complete or valid is, "I want milk.") The second type is represented in the statement: "I am a lifeguard on the job, so I shall keep close watch over the swimmers under my protection." If we were to probe further, we would find that those who accept this as an acceptable bit of practical reasoning ascribe to the speaker a commitment regarding role-based responsibilities of lifeguards. In addition to preferential and role based types, there is third. The statement—"Ridiculing a child for his limp would humiliate him needlessly, so I shall refrain from doing so"—implies for certain reasoners that there are forms of behavior that are universally prohibited. For those who count this type of inference as materially good, the term "cruelty" might provide a general category for such behaviors.

Stout's reason for breaking down practical reasoning this way is precisely to show the differences between kinds of practical inference. It will also allow him to give an account of how democratic culture is unique among cultures. His purposes here are first of all analytic. The three part classification allows him to draw out and focus on the kind of premise each one draws upon for validity. Upon inspection, we see that each of these premises is importantly different in kind, thus establishing the distinction between preferential, role-related and universal practical inferences. Stout is especially interested in the third type—universal—because they are integral to democratic culture. By showing how such obligations are universal in scope, but not necessarily universal in their validity, Stout is able to argue that democracy's unique form of practical reason is not by nature a pretension to a groundless, timeless, pure form of rationality.

Stout has a narrative to accompany this arrangement of practical reasoning. Students of ethics have noted that earlier cultures did not have the sense of unconditional moral "ought" that we have today. Their practical reasoning seems largely to have been embedded in socially recognized roles, as in type two above. Thus, our culture seems to have emerged out of anterior cultures and to have moved beyond them—making it distinct. Hegel saw that conflicts in role-related duties spurred this change, and art forms like the Greek tragedy made possible a new way of life. "Tragedy, Rhetoric . . ." became the "expressive resources" of a culture that recognizes new kinds of practical inferences. These inferences are universal in scope because they are based on a newfound ability to isolate and reflect on the norms that bind us. In this way such norms are not left implicit in our practices, but have been "brought within the sphere of responsibility."[13]

Putting aside the unflattering portrayal of other cultures—not as irrational, but certainly less so than we are—there is another problem. It is that the analysis divides practical reason up so well that it becomes difficult to re-unite the parts. In other words, the unity of practical reason is imperiled. Certainly dividing up practical reason into these three types enables us to see the distinction between reason-giving based on preference and that based on role, but in Stout's account it becomes difficult to move in the other direction: discerning what they share. In trying to highlight why the lifeguard's reasonings are distinct from those of the milk-seeker, Stout claims that the lifeguard's duty to watch over the swimmers under his protection "does not depend on [his] desire to keep a close eye on the swimmers under [his] protection. Nor does it depend on my desire to be, or remain, a lifeguard—to occupy the role that entails the responsibility."[14] Is this true? My response is, "yes and no." It is true that we do not expect a lifeguard to remind himself every minute that being a lifeguard is something desirable to him, but neither is it safe to assume that being a lifeguard forms no part of the kind of life he believes desirable for himself. By adopting a scheme that reduces desire to simple preference, Stout gives up the means to unite the varied types of practical reasoning that compose a single human life.

13. Stout, *Democracy and Tradition*, 194.
14. Ibid., 189.

The problem, I am afraid, is deeper when it comes to the third type of practical inference. Democratic practical reasoning is in part the product of an unplanned development within a particular culture. It is also in part an activity of intellectual reflection aided by discursive reasoning which may be[15] embodied in certain institutions. Stout perhaps hits it right when he says it can be thought of as a kind of role-based reasoning, where the role is that of democratic citizen, and there exists the underlying understanding that one's more particular story neither precludes one from stepping into the role nor affects the role itself. It is a universally available role, in principle at least.

The problem is that Stout does not give any indication why anyone would want to occupy this role (that is, why they would want to be a democratic citizen). To be fair, Stout does suggest that a certain kind of transformation of self is required in order to engage in the activity that constitutes this kind of reason exchange and conversation. Are there reasons we should want to be so formed? Are the activities pleasurable or rewarding in some moral way? In his description the norms that would direct our actions are placed against no background of qualitative distinctions besides the activity (of exchanging reasons) itself. The activity is just something we do.

Yet in my view there is no warrant to call reasoning practical—as opposed to theoretical or discursive—if it does not somehow account for desire: how we are motivated into action and shaped by our histories.

Turning to the question of character, we might ask what kind of people they would be who engage in the kind of practical reasoning Stout has outlined. The picture Stout offers is of people who competently seek the satisfaction of their immediate needs, do their jobs responsibly, and most importantly who question each other a great deal. One might picture a debate society or a group of students learning the art of argumentation: how to question each other's assumptions. Or, with Stout we might picture Stout and his siblings trying to catch a train.[16] In both of these pictures, the kind of people we discover are highly cerebral, or disembodied. Without some means of connecting the democratic reasoner to the former two types, Stout's account of practical reason cannot but lead to the picture of a disembodied self.

15. Or it may not be. See my comments on Stout's conception of a tradition below.
16. See Stout, *Democracy and Tradition*, 210–12.

In the next section I turn to another another conception of practical reasoning—namely, MacIntyre's Aristotelian one. Comparing Stout with Aristotle here might at this point prove illuminating. For Aristotle too speaks of reasons for action that hold for all human beings, though in a distinct way. Aristotle relies on a definition of the human being that gains its intelligibility from the human *telos*: the end or object of all practical reasoning within a human life (namely, "happiness"). Thus is Aristotle's account able to offer the unity of practical reason that makes talk of character intelligible. While Aristotle's practical reasoning is also contingent on certain conditions that are beyond the individual's power, he is as likely to focus on the development of desirable characteristics in a maturing person as on *sittlichkeit*.

Stout would certainly find it unwise in our pluralistic context to rely upon a type of practical reason that assumes a conception of human happiness. Further, Aristotle's conception of the human *telos* fits into a larger set of metaphysical commitments which are far from obvious to us moderns. It threatens, moreover, to cover over the valuable insight that moral norms are contingent upon a people's practices. Is there a way to gain the unity of practical reason provided by something like Aristotle's telos of human nature—a unity which I claim is necessary to make talk of character intelligible—without making Aristotle's assumptions about a metaphysically-grounded human essence? I turn to the MacIntyre of *After Virtue*[17] to find such an account of practical reason.

MacIntyre's Account of the Virtues in *After Virtue*

Alasdair MacIntyre's moral reasoning is reasoning grounded in social practices whose goods require the development of the virtues. These social practices, furthermore, are always embedded in broader social settings. Further, both the practices themselves and their social settings have histories. Human agency is thus embedded in shared goods and shared histories of the pursuit of those goods. I am interested especially in what MacIntyre takes from Aristotle here, since Aristotle represents the kind of substantive account of morality in which practical reasoning is linked to character. By substantive here I mean Aristotle's focus

17. I have chosen to focus on *After Virtue* rather than more recent developments of MacIntyre's position on practical reason in *Dependent Rational Animals*, because I believe the position in *After Virtue* remains closer to Stout's own views. Therefore, the comparison will tend to be more focused.

on the human *telos* and the virtues required to achieve it, along with his concern for the particular kind of social setting, or polis, in which the virtues can be sustained.[18] For MacIntyre to speak of character requires conceiving of a human life as a unity, ordered toward an ultimate end. What MacIntyre's discussion of Aristotle and the virtues in *After Virtue* chapters 12–15 contributes to Aristotelian ethical tradition is a re-description of the *telos* of human life in terms of narrative.

In what follows, then, I will first lead us in reconsidering MacIntyre's relationship to Aristotle in *After Virtue*, chapter 12, and then to a consideration of his own position, for which Aristotle's account serves as the basis but which also incorporates his dissatisfaction with aspects of Aristotle in chapters 13 and 14. Having outlined MacIntyre's view, I will ask which of its dimensions Stout can accept. By so asking, I hope to identify what is missing from Stout's account of the tradition of democratic moral discourse that renders problematic the claim that he has retrieved the notion of character for moral life –namely, the timeful character of practical reason.

MacIntyre on Aristotle

MacIntyre claims that there are certain aspects of Aristotle's account of the virtues which are unacceptable from a contemporary standpoint in general and from his own standpoint in particular. But he nevertheless argues that Aristotle's account forms the basis of a tradition of understanding the place of the virtues in human life that is both usable and affirmable. Aristotle held that the virtues were the characteristics needed by human beings to reach their ultimate end. They consisted in a training of the passions, a kind of training that could only occur in a social body of the right kind, and yet they pointed to a universal standard for human beings.

In the opening lines of the *Nichomachean Ethics*, where he defines the inquiry he will undertake, Aristotle observes that ethics, as a part of philosophy concerned with the goods to be achieved by activity, is a branch of "politics," the master science of the human good.[19] Here,

---

18. Put differently, "substantive" applies to accounts of moral agency that do not simply look to procedure as the condition for the possibility of moral claims that transcend the local. Rather, such an account is "universal" in the sense that it is to be measured by the truthfulness of its understanding of human beings in relation to the world.

19. "Now if there exists an end in the realm of action which we desire for its own

Aristotle first raises his questions about the virtues and the good life by asking, "what do *we* say about the qualities of character that are praiseworthy/blameworthy?" MacIntyre notes that Aristotle is thereby presupposing the Athenian polis as the necessary (and natural) setting for posing the question of the virtues. He envisions the theorizing work to come as a matter of making explicit the assumptions already embedded in Athenian social life. Thus, MacIntyre concludes, for Aristotle the virtues always stem from and presuppose a social setting.

Further, the virtues gain their intelligibility from their function to bring about the human *telos*. Aristotle was a realist about morality who believed that the ultimate good that is sought through human activity was derived from the very nature of the human being. The virtues are not merely a contingent means to this end but their functioning partially constitutes human flourishing.

On the other hand, MacIntyre observes that the socially-situated nature of ethics, on the one hand, and its reliance upon a species-specific definition of the human being, on the other, together constitute a constant tension in Aristotle's ethics.[20]

The virtues, furthermore, require training, for their subject is human actions and passions. The aspect of human nature to which moral education is to be applied is not predetermined by nature, but naturally open to receiving a certain habituation.[21] How the young are trained is thus crucial, and a training in virtue fundamentally teaches them which desires and kinds of actions they ought to desire for their own sake. This training of the desires consists essentially in their being made subject to reason within the orderly soul.

MacIntyre then turns to the relation of obeying rules to the exercise of virtues in Aristotle. In contrast to their strict separation in modern moral discourse, Aristotle's account presents these two activities as

---

sake, an end which determines all our other desires...then obviously this end will be the good, that is, the highest good....This good, one should think, belongs to the most sovereign and most comprehensive master science, and politics clearly fits this description" (Aristotle *Nichomachean Ethics* 1094a, 26).

20. So MacIntyre concludes, "Aristotle thus sets himself the task of giving an account of the good which is at once local and particular—located in and partially defined by the characteristics of the *polis*—and yet also cosmic and universal. The tension between these poles is felt throughout the argument of the Ethics" (MacIntyre, *After Virtue*, 148).

21. See Aristotle *Nichomachean Ethics* 1103a, 20-25.

integrated within a larger vision. What makes this integration intelligible is that both virtues and rules derive their significance from a political setting, i.e. a practice in which individuals join to seek a common good. Virtues are specified in terms of qualities without which the very goods making social cooperation beneficial could not be achieved. Rules, representing absolute prohibitions, single out certain behaviors which, if allowed, would threaten the very life of the community. The purpose of such rules is to convey to the offender and the other community members that by offending them the offender has effectively excluded him or herself from the community. According to MacIntyre, the fact that intellectual virtues like judgment are necessary for the carrying out of moral virtues, like justice, underscores the *comprehensive* nature of Aristotle's ethics.

What is meant by "comprehensive" here? The set of moral virtues, or disciplined sentiments, together with intellectual virtues, like the capacity to judge more or less what a given situation calls for, coalesce in the measure called "character," which is a unitary but complex criteria of evaluation. A person's character denotes the quality of a person as regards her or his excellence as a human being. It is also a claim that essential to human agency is being formed in a community to see and seek after a particular conception of the good. This is why MacIntyre notes that to evaluate our lives using the language of character depends upon our being part of a community with a shared vision of what is good for us, perhaps even wide agreement on this matter.

This conclusion, he recognizes, raises the well-known worry about whether the unity presupposed in the notion of character militates against recognizing the diversity that exists in most historical societies. And if our societies cannot be said to share a common vision of the good, we may wonder whether character distorts human nature as we know it. Yet this assumption of agreement on the good within a society also illumines Aristotle's belief that the basic glue of societies is friendship, a bond constituted by a shared vision of the good, allowing each partner to wish good to the other for her or his own sake.

MacIntyre gives voice to this concern when he questions whether or not Aristotle's view can account for moral conflict. The fact that Aristotle's tendency is to avoid or manage conflict suggests to him that he failed to discern the *historical* nature of the polis as the setting for the virtues.[22] Aristotle's belief that those who do not live in city-states are by nature incapable of political relationships provides further evidence that his account of virtues is ahistorical.[23] In short, while Aristotle rightly assumes that an account of the virtues must be grounded in a social setting, he fails to recognize that all social settings have histories and for this reason are contingent.

This objection, while relevant, is not fatal to Aristotle's concept of character. Merely a small modification—re-describing the unity or telos found therein—will allow it to account for the historical nature of human life in society. The unity of character can coexist with the timeful character of practical reason. Two aspects already present in Aristotle's view contribute to its ability to recover itself. First, his assumption that the virtues require a political context for their intelligibility suggests that the social element itself cannot be separated from the virtues. Second, he shows that the passions we experience depend upon the kind of virtues we have cultivated. This implies that the virtues are connected to culture (insofar as they are connected to a polis), and avoids the kind of naturalism about sentiments we see in the eighteenth century.

MacIntyre's Continuation of the Aristotelian Tradition

MacIntyre's re-description of Aristotelian character culminates in the claim that "narrative" names the form to be discovered in the human moral life. His development of Aristotle—his Aristotelianism, if you will—is found in chapters 14–15 of *After Virtue*, where he outlines his "core account of the virtues." The term "core" here signals that MacIntyre's intention is to highlight what is essential in this virtue tradition.

---

22. An important source of evidence for this claim can be found in Aristotle's reading of the tragedy of Oedipus Rex. He assumes that the key to explaining such crises must be a fatal flaw in the character of one of the protagonists. See MacIntyre, *After Virtue*, 157 and 163.

23. This refers to the controversial topic of "natural slaves." MacIntyre notes also the paradox that Aristotle was a servant of the Macedonian royal power that would destroy the city-state as a free society. "Aristotle did not understand the transience of the *polis* because he had little or no understanding of historicity in general. Thus a whole range of questions cannot arise for him including those which concern the ways in which men might pass from being slaves or barbarians to being citizens of a *polis*. Some men just *are* slaves 'by nature,' on Aristotle's view'" (ibid., 160).

This core account will be framed around three conceptual foundations—namely, 1) social practices; 2) the notion of a unified or whole human life and; 3) narrative—all of these as the context in which human action must be placed in order to make intelligible talk of character and the virtues.[24]

The notion of a social practice seems to derive from the beginning of the *Nichomachean Ethics*, where Aristotle states that all kinds of human activity seem to aim at some good and this good becomes the defining characteristic of the activity in question. Most all of human life can be seen in terms of a hierarchy of such activities, with politics, because its good comprehends those of all the other spheres of activity (medicine, ship-building, strategy, household management), situated at the helm. MacIntyre is not concerned so much to name the ultimate good of human activity, as to identify the structure of a certain kind of human activity, a practice. A *practice* is a kind of human activity in which individuals come together in cooperation to seek a shared good. It is also a kind of human activity for which the aim of the activity is "internal" to the activity itself. This can be distinguished from what we might call "instrumental" action where the action itself is a means, and one of many possible means, to a stated goal. For instrumental action the choice of means "a" or "b–z" could only be evaluated on the basis of how efficiently they bring about the desired result, which is itself indifferent to the means by which it is attained. When speaking of a practice, on the other hand, we must say that means and end are integral to one another, for the action required in order to achieve the end is itself part of the end. This further implies that a person familiar with a practice is uniquely able to recognize the end being sought.

For MacIntyre, "practice" names the account of human action required to make character, or "the virtues," intelligible. Within a practice the individual actions or performances undertaken to achieve a shared good are not indifferent to the good we seek. Our actions must be of a certain quality in order for the good to be realized, which makes it appropriate to speak of acting "well" or "poorly", as opposed to simply "effectively/ineffectively"—that is, to use virtue vocabulary. Thus, the goods that define a particular practice also specify the virtues required to achieve them. Within a practice, conversely, the good is specified in

24. MacIntyre begins his core account of the virtues in chapter 14 of *After Virtue* (186ff) and continues to develop it through chapter 15.

terms of the virtues, and thus the kind of people, needed to achieve it. The character traits of individuals, and not their actions in the abstract, *are themselves the means* toward the end/good.

Yet practice by itself proves inadequate to the task of making character in relation to human action intelligible. The remaining two aspects of the core account are rooted in the Aristotelian idea of an ultimate end, the *telos*, for human activity. The central function of this notion is to allow for adequately specifying the context in which human action—and a human life—becomes intelligible, even beyond the context provided by practices. MacIntyre's assertion that the concept of "the unity of a human life" is necessary stems from the claim that if we end with practices as the context for human actions, the intelligibility we gain for them and for character will be short-lived, and ultimately break down. The goods pursued in our practices will come into conflict. Beyond this, each person participates in more than one practice, and given time these are bound to produce incompatible ends. A superior ordering power will therefore be required.

A single individual will participate in several practices. When the goods pursued in one practice conflict with those in another, the agent might be poised between paralysis and arbitrariness. Take for instance the practice of teaching, with its good of learning and the virtue of patience on the part of teachers with their students. An excellent teacher must show patience with a pupil slow to learn. But what if the pupil is just too slow—that is, so slow that it attending to her compromises the teacher's ability to satisfy other requirements of the practice, such as giving sufficient attention to all one's pupils? To answer this question will require understanding the relation of goods and virtues within a practices. But it also requires relating the goods and virtues of a particular practice to other human commitments. In this sense, to answer the question "Should the teacher give up on the pupil?" requires placing patience inside of a broader context than just the practice of teaching. We have arrived at the cusp of considering a human life as a whole, or as a unity. Only in this way can the agent's life be rescued from arbitrariness. It is the notion of a final and self-sufficient good (*telos*) that allows us to consider human life in this way, as well as to imagine the relations between the goods and corresponding virtues of one practice to the goods and virtues of others.[25] "What kind of life is a good life?"

---

25. This "relating" can take several forms. Primarily we may think of it in terms of

The notion of a unity of a human life presupposes that there are *kinds* of human lives and some more choiceworthy than others.

Thus, the second aspect of MacIntyre's core conception is that it requires the moral life of human beings to possess a certain kind of unity. While there is a sense in which the telos allows for a kind of immediate ordering of goods, we should note that the unity spoken of here does not refer to a physical or spatial integrity so much as a unity in time. That this notion of unity points to the timeful dimension of human activity becomes clear when we consider it in light of its Aristotelian basis—namely, happiness as the good both final and self-sufficient. One chooses and acts in pursuit of this end for its own sake and never as a means to other ends. *Eudaimonia* (happiness), a life lived in such a manner that the one whose life it is can be said to be flourishing, characterizes the human being who is active in precisely those respects that utilize his or her specifically human capacities and uses them well. The whole study of ethics is to help students see what actions and dispositions make up that kind of life. *Eudaimonia*, as many of us teachers emphasize with our students, is not properly defined as a pleasant psycho-physiological state, but as a way of living one's whole life—that is, a way of living that is sustainable, and sustained, over time.[26]

The unity of a human life is made necessary by the fact that each of us participates in several practices and our identities are an attempt to weave these together over time. The notion of unity rests conceptually upon that of an ultimate good for human life (the human telos). And yet, as we saw above, Aristotle's account of the telos pays too little attention to the contingent and historical character of human life. In the section on narrative, MacIntyre attempts to correct this by re-describing selfhood in terms of the model of a character in a literary work, such as a novel. The situation of such a character is bounded by a past which must be affirmed, a present to be lived, and an envisioned future to be anticipated. This is to say that the form of a human life is best modeled on that of a narrative. The character must rely on an interpretation of the past and a vision of the future in order to understand his or

re-describing the virtue as specified in one practice in terms of the context provided by another. Ultimately, this means placing the virtue within another narrative about the final end of a human life.

26. For a very helpful discussion of the temporal character of Aristotle's eudaimonia, see chapter 1, "On Being Temporally Happy," in Hauerwas and Pinches, *Christians Among the Virtues*, 3–16.

her present. MacIntyre has just shown us that where human action is concerned, practices are the ubiquitous context. The third aspect of his core account of the virtues aims to teach us that all practices—in fact all actions and all human lives considered individually—produce and are sustained by, narrative histories as their conceptual contexts. What is more, "narrative" names the kind of unity in human lives which makes possible our talk of character.

MacIntyre begins with actions themselves. Analytic philosophers, he claims, made a fundamental mistake in trying to isolate "actions-in-themselves" as the object of analysis, for the most basic datum is an "intelligible action"—an action that can be explained to others. To give an account of an action will always be to place it within the story, or stories, in which we are characters.

To illustrate the concept of an intelligible action, MacIntyre has us imagine a man outside his house on all fours. What is he doing? The explanation of an action requires some knowledge of the agent's intentions, and making sense of those requires familiarity with social practices and their histories. Perhaps he is "putting the garden in order before winter" or "taking exercise" or "pleasing his wife." To comprehend any of these descriptions—and thus the man's action—requires being able to locate actions in a context—namely, a practice (gardening) or an institution (marriage). Our ability to so locate actions within practices or institution will require some familiarity with the history of such practices and institutions.

MacIntyre observes that in addition to knowing something of the intention-descriptions with which the agent operates, the process by which we comprehend actions frequently requires having a sense of how intentions are ordered temporally within the agent. A single action performed by MacIntyre, for instance, may be alternately described as "writing a sentence," "finishing a book," "trying to get tenure," or "contributing to the debate over the theory of action." The difference lies in how large a time frame into MacIntyre's future one wishes to consider. The intelligibility of all actions requires their being ordered temporally, or in terms of nearness to, or distance from, the present. We cannot fully understand a present action without seeing its relation to a future goal. Nor can the more ultimate descriptions be grasped without seeing how the intermediate ones lead up to them. To understand an action fully is thus to write the history of which it is a part.

In both of these approaches to explaining an action, the form of history or writing a narrative, plays the central role. The essential form of human action is thus a story, or narrative. The human agent is simultaneously author and character in his own life story. Narrative is thus the basic structure through which any piece of behavior becomes an intelligible human action.

Yet to envision ourselves as the authors of our life stories threatens to once again summon up the solipsistic, modern self. Such a self boldly claims, "I can write my story any way I want." It is therefore important to MacIntyre's account that the way we tell our stories is always constrained by the way others describe us. Given the different roles we play in our own and others' stories, we can say that we are both actors and authors in these dramas. We play roles that have been written for us, and at the same time take ownership of these roles as we learn to live them out gracefully. No matter how forced the decision may appear, we are always susceptible of being called upon to account for what we have done. And yet we are never more than co-authors of our lives.

This way in which our stories interweave with those of others means that to be a person is most fundamentally a matter of learning to inhabit the stories of which we find ourselves part. Truthfulness is a mark of good character in that it allows us to acknowledge this dependence on others.

Human actions become intelligible as parts of an actual or possible history. What kind of unity, or order, does this provide for a human life? For could not a storied life take such a turn as to make it difficult to understand the present in light of the past? And would this not make our own visions of the future somewhat irrelevant? (Further, if our own vision of the future has so little determinative force upon the shape our life takes, what reason is there for talk of character?) MacIntyre is willing to go on without finally silencing such questions. Nevertheless, he allows us to see that they are prone to exaggerated claims that give a false impression of our situation. Though the agent's past does not determine the future, neither is its influence so negligible that an arbitrary choice is decisive. Rather, our histories shape us in such a way that certain courses, though they seem like "options" for some, are not possible for us. MacIntyre describes this reciprocal relation between the character we have developed and the goal of life, in terms of life as a "quest." The notion of quest presumes that, though indeed we set out in a certain direction, the character of our destination (*telos*) becomes clearer only as we negotiate the obstacles along our path.[27]

My main point in this discussion of MacIntyre here has been to show that his account of practical reason makes sense of character by incorporating the notion of the unity of a human life as the timeful unity of a narrative.

MacIntyre and Stout: Piety and Justice in Practice

What Stout's account of practical reason lacks, and what distances him from MacIntyre, is the notion of the unity of moral life and of practical reason. While Stout considers reasoning to be a contextual affair, he lacks a concept—that of the *telos*—which would bring these contexts together in a unified human life. In other words, he seems unable to overcome the situation where the goods specified in the various practices in which an agent participates come into conflict. Practical reason, on Stout's account, remains fragmented, but the ethics of character requires a practical reason that strives toward unity. In order to show this in Stout, I will briefly re-examine two of the virtues constitutive of the democratic tradition: piety and justice. What I hope to show is that Stout's democracy is an epi-tradition, or a tradition that relies upon more basic practices that it does not adequately acknowledge.

In naming piety as one of the democratic virtues, Stout claims that democracy, like all substantive traditions, requires historical continuity. This means, or ought to mean, that democratic traditions need to be passed down to the young in order to bridge the span of generations. No doubt for that reason, piety has traditionally been conceived as relating to specific persons, such as one's parents. Yet, as Charles Pinches has noted, Stout's failure to refer to parents or *any* specific object appropriate for piety, causes his account of this virtue to suffer from vagueness.[28] Because, argues Pinches, Stout defines piety in such general terms as

---

27. "It is clear the medieval conception of a quest is not at all that of a search for something already adequately characterized, as miners search for gold or geologists for oil. It is in the course of the quest and only through encountering and coping with the various particular harms, dangers, temptations and distractions which provide any quest with its episodes and incidents that the goal of the quest is finally understood" (MacIntyre, *After Virtue*, 218).

28. For this and the following two quotations, see Pinches, "Democracy, America and the Church," 239-60.

"the sources of one's existence and progress through life," "he does not really give direction about to whom piety binds us, nor about how it governs and directs what is done in our relations with them." For Pinches, Stout's statement that "Gratitude, not loyalty or deference, is, for the tradition of Emersonian perfectionism, the better part of piety,"[29] only intensifies the critical question. "We are grateful," Pinches writes, "for specific gifts given . . . . But what does gratitude offered to these 'sources' mean, concretely? And, moreover, does gratitude or piety offered to these sources bind us communally in any clear way?"[30] Piety, in Pinches' estimation, must be behavior directed toward specific objects within concrete practices. The point of such practices is to gather their participants together through shared understandings. All this points to the conclusion that Stout's democracy hovers above the concrete practices that sustain our lives.

It is an irony of the book that a trademark of Stout's re-conceived virtues is that they foreground the self in the way MacIntyre thought endemic to modern political thought. That is, the modern self is defined in such a way that it is only contingently related to the good, and it is possible to speak of the self and the good independently. This characteristic of Stout's democratic virtues may be hinted at in his "self-reliant" piety, but I believe the central locus is his conception of justice. In the Aristotelian vision, the just person is formed by a polis to see the goods that are to be shared. Yet Stout implies in his section on Hauerwas that justice is a procedural matter. He follows Albrecht in assuming that we already know what the goods are, so that justice discussions can be fundamentally centered on how they are distributed or made accessible. Stout's account of justice is sharp and critical, and even prophetic. It is perhaps the basis of Stout's other virtues insofar as the kinds of conversation and argument it names are at the heart of democracy as a discursive practice. Even piety must be just in order to be self-reliant, avoiding unmerited loyalty or undue deference. Yet it lacks the grounding required for an account of the virtues—and character—to be intelligible in its terms. This is because it places the self or agent (i.e., here, the democratic reasoner) prior to any account of the goods toward which human action ought to be directed. But justice

---

29. Stout, *Democracy and Tradition*, 38
30. Pinches, "Democracy, America and the Church," 246.

is as much about formation as it is about distribution. To use Stout's example, surely it is only through having been blessed with participation in a practice like Jazz that an agent can come to know what justice is.

In sum, Stout's democratic tradition must be integrated with the practices that make us people capable of carrying on the kinds of public conversations he describes in chapter 3 as "immanent criticism." As it stands, the tradition he describes strikes one as cerebral, a disembodied game. Incorporating the notion of the unity of a human life would facilitate this integration and authenticate his use of the ethics of character.

Conclusion: Moral Truth and Transformation, or Why Ethics Should be Life-Changing

I begin this conclusion as I began the chapter by turning to the personal. I can recall a peculiar feeling occurring when I read MacIntyre as a graduate student and came to the part about the unity of a human life. My response was neither merely one of wishing to follow a clever philosophical argument, nor of stumbling on a recapitulation of a quaint epoch in moral philosophy, but rather something like gospel. It was "good news" that seemed at the same time naïve and wonderfully real. I think this is because, like so many young, highly educated people, my perspective likely alternated between an iconoclastic post-modern euphoria and an enlightened, stoical liberal pluralism. Could this idea of a unified human life be possible? Could it be true?

The reader may be worried at this point that the author is about to be captured by a reactionary conservatism that believes all we need to do is finish carving up the universe with the right kind of theological metaphysics. I do not, however, think that what MacIntyre has opened up to us is properly read as an invitation to that kind of reaction. What he has shown, rather, is that accounts of the moral life as whole and human are not by nature irrational. This does not prove that there is *one* such account, or that any particular account of this kind is simply true. Still, MacIntyre may come to be seen as having opened for us a way to be more truthful by acknowledging the real differences between what we take to be true about the self, God, and the world. That his work should have this effect on us depends upon our allowance that accounts of a *human* moral life, or a life as a whole—what I have been calling "substantive" accounts of the moral life—are at least possible.

But perhaps MacIntyre does even more for us in that he helps us to see in a new way what "truth" might mean in regard to an account of the moral life. I would describe it this way. When one claims that an account of the moral life aspires to be true, one implies that if one were to accept it as true, one's life would be changed.[31] Accounts of the moral life, in other words, cannot do without the theme of formation or transformation. But perhaps this way of putting it is still misleading in that it suggests something mechanical—first believe, then observe the consequences. Instead, let us say that to see the truth as a tradition presents it is to begin a process of being transformed by it.[32] My greatest hesitation about *Democracy and Tradition*, as I suggested at the outset, is that it has not changed my life.[33]

---

31. I intuit that when Stout turns to talking about universal kinds of practical inference, what he is striving toward indirectly is "true inferences." Yet, in contrast to what I am describing here, he describes this truth more in terms of the ways such truths are justified.

32. This way of putting it was inspired by Hauerwas's discussion of Reinhold Niebuhr's theology in the book based on his Gifford Lectures. Hauerwas identifies the god of Niebuhr's theology by noting that it is not the kind of god believing in whom would require transformation of one's life. See Hauerwas, *With the Grain of the Universe*, 138.

33. Having said that, I feel the need to recount an anecdote about Stout told me by one of his fellow residents of Princeton, New Jersey. Stout once came to a neighborhood book group in which they were studying *Democracy and Tradition* to field questions and participate in their discussion. One participant asked Stout, "Why exactly do you call yourself a pragmatist?" "I don't 'call myself a pragmatist'" Stout is rumored to have responded. "My friends tell me that's what I am." This response of Stout's suggests to me that his pragmatism as lived contains something that does not arise in the written account of practical reason in the book under discussion.

Conclusion

I have argued at length in this book that practical reason has a political character by displaying the connections between accounts of human agency, practical reason, and politics. I first pursued these connections in Anscombe, and then used her example as a test for other thinkers. Taylor was found wanting in some respects, whereas Hauerwas was found to display the politics of practical reason in an exemplary way.

How does recognizing the political character of practical reason matter in moral philosophy and especially in theological ethics? In the introduction I also stated that the form of practical reason has been threatened in our times by a predilection for abstraction. Anscombe implies that such abstraction is behind the moral theories she calls "consequentialist." Such theories are unable to distinguish between "foreseen" consequences of one's action and the intentions that give them their shape. They have lost sight of practical reason in favor of the "observer's point of view."

My emphasis on the political character of practical reason has been meant to provide a way to guard against such distortion.

I want to suggest and briefly comment on three temptations of theological ethics today related to the failure to recognize the political character of practical reason. They stem from the discussions in my previous chapters.

First, a temptation of this sort occurs when a spirit of individualism/universalism inhabits theological ethics. "Ethics for anybody" ultimately means that communities do not matter. As a result, we are *per force* left with the solitary individual. Universalism and individualism are corollaries of one another. The problems with this approach show up in its treatment of communication across communities or traditions. It tends to have an unrealistically facile (and sometimes violent) stance regarding the possibility of diverse communities coming to a common moral understanding. Not that inter-communal dialogue isn't possible and desirable. Only it is harder than this approach would have us believe. We must simply recall that it cannot be carried out easily or without attention to the communally embodied habits of those whom we are trying to understand.

A second temptation that flows from the failure to recognize that practical reasoning is political in nature is to imagine the "ethics" in theological ethics as having its source outside Christian doctrine and practices. Thus, to do theological ethics involves "adding on" extrinsic moral principles or theories to the discourses and embodied practices of Christians. Oftentimes this means that what is particularly Christian in theological ethics will be the "motivation for" or "subjective side" of morality. The objective ground of ethics is said to be known in some other, typically non-historical, manner. We saw, for example, how Albrecht derived her conception of justice from feminism and "women's experience," later to apply it to practices and self-conceptions of the church. Not only was the church seen as corrupted by patriarchy, but more importantly it is so vitiated as to have no resources within for confronting this corruption. As this last shows, the extrinsic model will be tempted to consider the "outside" source as itself essentially pure of corruption. Whether because of suspected thorough corruption as in Albrecht, or for some other reason, the extrinsic model neglects the embodied practices of tradition as means to correct injustices. Recognizing the political character of practical reason points us in the direction of such practices by recalling that ethics begins in practices ordered toward achieving common goods.

A third temptation expresses itself in an orientation toward the theoretical rather than the practical and material. One version is found in a preference for looking at our social life as "culture" rather than politics. Culture here is understood as a kind of speculative vision, visible to some degree in our practices, that encompasses our imagination of the world and ourselves in it. It therefore accounts for a mostly pre-conscious orientation to the world and the objects of experience, coloring the meaning of such objects for us and thus shaping our agency in relation to them. In the terms of hermeneutics, which is itself related to this approach, this might be called our "self-understanding."

A close cousin to culture so understood is "ontology," taken as the configuration or package of what is real. Ontology here means the shape of reality as it can on occasion be brought into reflection, including our understanding of ourselves and our orientation as agents within that "space."

Taylor provides a sophisticated rendition of culture in this sense in his concept of a "social imaginary."[1] A social imaginary is a combination of a conception of the human agent and a social order within which its actions are intelligible. The ground of this concept is Taylor's subtle understanding of the relation between practices and the self-understandings that make them what they are. All such practices carry with them an implicit self-understanding shared among the participants. That this is the case means that a theory intending to explain a given practice—a "social theory"—cannot remain aloof, but insofar as it takes hold contributes to changing the practice it meant to explain. Such explanations, he argues, cannot neglect either, and the attempt to name one side *the* efficient cause ultimately unravels.[2]

Elsewhere, while tracing the transformation of social practices in his histories of modernity and of the secular, Taylor develops his notion of a social imaginary by attempting to display the interdependence of ideals or speculative orders and material practices in the explanation of historical changes such as from hierarchical states to egalitarian ones.[3]

The problem with the culture or ontology approach to human social life is its tendency to distort social life by generating an unhealthy closure toward others. This problem comes to light in the engagement to which I referred in chapter 2 between Taylor and Clifford Geertz on the relationship between "natural sciences" and "human sciences."[4] Geertz's challenge to Taylor stems from the fact that Taylor has developed his own ontology of human social life through a contrast with the "neutral" ontology of natural science. But, Geertz asks, what if the

1. See Taylor, *A Secular Age*, 159–76.
2. See my earlier discussion, 68–75.
3. For his use of the concept of a social imaginary to illumine historical changes in social practices, see his comparison of the move toward representative government in England, the United States and France in, Taylor, *A Secular Age*, 196–207. With respect to the relation of ideals and practices in explanation, see chapter 5, "The Spectre of Idealism."
4. Geertz, "Strange Estrangement," 83–95.

ontology he supposes to be that of natural science is a fiction, or simply not what scientists in fact presuppose about reality? And if this is so, then what might be the resulting distortions in Taylor's ontology of human social life?

Geertz's challenge shows that Taylor's method can lead to a distorted account of the interrelations of these communities of inquiry. He argues that Taylor's method indirectly facilitates an inadequate understanding of natural science itself as a monolith defined by a single rational technique. This results partly from the very polarization it creates.

The supposed self-understanding of natural science as issuing from a "God's eye point of view" whose representations of reality will "hold the mirror up to nature," is largely the product of nineteenth-century positivists. It is also in part the creation of hermeneutics itself. Geertz emphasizes, however, that the positivists represent a reification thrust upon natural science, rather than its inherent conception of itself. His thesis in part is to warn us against such reifications, for he believes that such interpretive overlays will continue to prevent us from seeing what natural scientists actually do and how they think.

He therefore behooves us to move from a metaphor of two unbridgeable continents to that of an "archipelago" of distinct disciplines of investigation.[5] Taylor's dichotomizing framework for the understanding of human and natural sciences fosters a *dialectical* relationship between two kinds of science, where Geertz argues in contrast for a *dialogue* among several sciences. As he has implied, dialogue is supe-

---

5. The alternative map provided by this new metaphor would promote the travel of methodological questions from one theoretic island to another, making questions of the relationship between the disciplines live ones. Geertz believes that only keeping the waterways open for such exchange will prevent the loss of new discoveries resulting from the too narrow and reified self-understandings to which each of these communities of inquiry is tempted to fall prey. For without the challenges with which the self-understandings of other theoretic communities bring to them, the self-understanding of each individual community is bound for distortion. Geertz writes, "The outcome of this artificial and unnecessary estrangement [i.e. between human and natural sciences] is, at once, the perpetuation within the various natural sciences of outmoded self-conceptions, global stories that falsify their actual practice, the 'sterile', 'half-baked' and 'implausible' imitations that those outmoded conceptions and false stories induce in human scientists ignorant of what in fact, physics, chemistry, physiology and the like come to as meaningful action , and, perhaps worst of all, the production of various sorts of New Age irrationalisms supposed to unify everything and anything at some higher, or deeper or wider level" (Geertz, "Strange Estrangement," 95).

rior to dialectic in that it promotes seeing all forms of human inquiry as bounded by space and time. All are contingent, and thus only hubris and/or idol-worship could cause us to see the rules of one as possessing a logical (metaphysical) necessity that all are bound to accept a priori. Thus, dialogue between scientific communities prevents both the reification of any community's self-understanding and a false hegemony of one community's practices.

What conclusion can we draw from Geertz's challenge of Taylor? The ontological impulse itself, here, seems partly responsible for a distorted understanding of disciplines of inquiry and the terrain of their interrelations. It tends, we might say, toward closure and reified boundaries that hinder rather than help our understanding of what goes on both within them and outside of them.

In theological ethics, the tendency of the culture or ontology approach toward closure, or "singularity,"[6] may aid and abet the second temptation of universalizing. I believe it is in some part responsible for a tendency to mistake some positions as "sectarian" because of their refusal to engage in translation projects that marginalize concrete practice and first order discourse. Hauerwas perhaps has born the brunt of this effect. Further, and a challenge closer to the heart of Hauerwas as I have presented him in this book, the ontology approach can push theological ethicists toward a distorted understanding of their own practical reasoning and its political ground.

One context for this problem is the way one copes politically with otherness. Scott Bader-Saye has recently wondered whether Hauerwas's focus on the pair "Church-world" distorts his account of the church's politics by making it insufficiently vulnerable to the "haunting" of others who are neither "church" nor "world."[7] He believes that Hauerwas's work is not as "disrupted" by the Jews as it ought to be, though his awareness that for Christians "salvation comes from the Jews" means that this could be remedied. By contrast, Bader-Saye argues, Milbank's commitment to ontology, what Romand Coles has called the "compulsive singularity" of his narrative, makes him unable to be haunted

6. The term is borrowed from Romand Coles, who refers to the "compulsive singularity" of the logic of John Milbanks's narrative in *Theology and Social Theory*. See Coles, "Storied Others and Possibilities of Caritas," 331–51. Cited in Bader-Saye, "Haunted by the Jews," 191–209.

7. Bader-Saye, "Haunted by the Jews," 191–209.

by the Jews, and thus leaves him with a distorted understanding of Christian politics.

In conclusion, recognizing the politics of practical reason will be important for us. Not only in clarifying crucial aspects of human agency where ethics is concerned, but also in avoiding several temptations that impoverish our work. Learning to read Hauerwas well, though not uncritically, offers a skill for making us politically discerning.

Bibliography

Albrecht, Gloria. *The Character of Our Communities: Toward an Ethics of Liberation for the Church*. Nashville: Abingdon, 1995.

———. "In Good Company: The Church As Polis." *Scottish Journal of Theology* 50 (1997) 219–27.

Anscombe, Elizabeth. *Intention*. 2nd ed. Cambridge: Harvard University Press, 2000.

———. "On Brute Facts." In *Ethics, Religion and Politics: Collected Philosophical Papers III*, 22–25. Minneapolis: University of Minnesota Press, 1981.

Aristotle. *Nichomachean Ethics*. Translated by Martin Oswald. Indianapolis: Liberal Arts, 1962.

Bader-Saye, Scott. "Haunted by the Jews: Hauerwas, Milbank and the Decentered Diaspora Church." In *Unsettling Arguments: A Festschrift on the Occasion of Stanley Hauerwas' 70th Birthday*, edited by Charles R. Pinches et al., 191–209. Eugene, OR: Cascade, 2010.

Baxter, Michael. "The Church as Polis? Second Thoughts on Theological Politics." In *Unsettling Arguments: A Festschrift on the Occasion of Stanley Hauerwas' 70th Birthday*, edited by Charles R. Pinches et al., 132–50. Eugene, OR: Cascade, 2010.

Beauchamp, Tom L., and James F. Childress. *The Principles of Biomedical Ethics*. 5th ed. New York: Oxford University Press, 2001.

Bell, Daniel. "Deliberating: Justice and Liberation." In *The Blackwell Companion to Christian Ethics*, edited by Stanley Hauerwas and Samuel Wells, 182–95. Malden, MA: Blackwell, 2006.

Bellah, Robert. "The Rules of Engagement: Communion in a Scientific Age." *Commonweal* 135 (2008) 15–21.

Coles, Romand. "Storied Others and Possibilities of Caritas." *Modern Theology* 8 (1992) 331–51.

Colorado, Carlos. "Transcendent Sources and the Dispossession of the Self." Paper presented at the Society of Christian Ethics, Chicago, IL, January 2009.

Edelman, Gerald M. *Bright Air, Brilliant Fire: On the Matter of the Mind*. New York: Basic, 1992.

Emerson, Ralph Waldo. *Emerson: Essays and Lectures*. New York: Literary Classics, 1983.

Flanagan, Owen. "Identity and Strong and Weak Evaluation." In *Identity, Character and Morality: Essays in Moral Psychology*, edited by Amélie Rorty and Owen Flanagan, 37–66. Cambridge: MIT Press, 1990.

Fletcher, Joseph. *Situation Ethics*. Philadelphia: Westminster, 1966.

Foley, Richard. "Justification, Epistemic." In *The Routledge Encyclopedia of Philosophy*, edited by Edward Craig et al., 1:157–65. New York: Routledge, 1998.
Frankfurt, Harry. "Freedom of the Will and the Concept of a Person." *Journal of Philosophy* 67 (1971) 5–20.
Geertz, Clifford. "The Strange Estrangement: Taylor and the Natural Sciences." In, *Philosophy in an Age of Pluralism: The Philosophy of Charles Taylor in Question*, edited by James Tully and Daniel Weinstock, 83–95. Cambridge: Cambridge University Press, 1994.
Gilligan, Carol. *In a Different Voice: Psychological Theory and Women's Development*. Cambridge: Harvard University Press, 1982.
Gustafson, James. "The Sectarian Temptation: Reflections on Theology, the Church and the University." *Proceedings of the Catholic Theological Society* 40 (1985) 83–94.
Hauerwas, Stanley. "Casuistry in Context: The Need for Tradition." In *In Good Company: The Church as Polis*, 169–84. Notre Dame, IN: University of Notre Dame Press, 1995.
———. *Christian Existence Today: Essays on Church, World, and Living In Between*. Durham: Labyrinth, 1988.
———. *A Community of Character: Toward a Constructive Christian Social Ethic*. Notre Dame, IN: University of Notre Dame Press, 1981.
———. "The Demands of a Truthful Story: Ethics and the Pastoral Task." *Chicago Studies* 21 (1982) 59–62.
———. *The Peaceable Kingdom: A Primer in Christian Ethics*. Notre Dame, IN: University of Notre Dame Press, 1983.
———. *Performing the Faith: Bonhoeffer and the Practice of Non-Violence*. Grand Rapids: Brazos, 2004.
———. "The Significance of Vision: Toward and Aesthetic Ethic." In *Vision and Virtue*, 28–47. Notre Dame, IN: University of Notre Dame Press, 1981.
———. "Situation Ethics, Moral Notions and Moral Theology." In *Vision and Virtue*, 11–29. Notre Dame, IN: University of Notre Dame Press, 1981.
———. "The Virtues of Alasdair MacIntyre." *First Things* (September 2007).
———. "Why Justice is a Bad Idea for Christians." In *After Christendom?: How the Church Is to Behave If Freedom, Justice, and a Christian Nation Are Bad Ideas*, 45–68. Nashville: Abingdon, 1991.
———. *With the Grain of the Universe: The Church's Witness and Natural Theology*. Grand Rapids: Brazos, 2002.
Hauerwas, Stanley, and Charles R. Pinches. *Christians Among the Virtues*. Notre Dame, IN: University of Notre Dame Press, 1997.
Hauerwas, Stanley, and David Burrell. "From System to Story: An Alternative Pattern for Rationality in Ethics." In *Truthfulness and Tragedy: Further Investigations in Christian Ethics*, 15–39. Notre Dame, IN: University of Notre Dame Press, 1997.
Hauerwas, Stanley, and L. Gregory Jones. "Introduction: Why Narrative?" In *Why Narrative? Readings in Narrative Theology*, edited by Stanley Hauerwas and L. Gregory Jones, 1–20. Grand Rapids: Eerdmans, 1989.
Hauerwas, Stanley, and David Matzko. "The Sources of Charles Taylor." *Religious Studies Review* 18 (1992) 286–89.
Hunter, James Davison. *To Change the World: The Irony, Tragedy and Possibility of Christianity in the Late Modern World*. New York: Oxford University Press, 2010.

Kallenberg, Brad J. *Ethics as Grammar: Changing the Postmodern Subject.* Notre Dame, IN: University of Notre Dame Press, 2001.
Kant, Immanuel. *Religion within the Limits of Reason Alone.* Translated by Greene and Hudson. New York: Harper & Row, 1960.
Kovesi, Julius. *Moral Notions.* London: Routledge, 1967.
Lints, Richard. *The Fabric of Theology: A Prolegomenon to Evangelical Theology.* Grand Rapids: Eerdmans, 1993.
Long, D. Stephen. *The Divine Economy: Theology and the Market.* New York: Routledge, 2006.
———. "How to Read Charles Taylor." *Pro Ecclesia* 18 (2009) 93–107.
Lovibond, Sabina. "Absolute Prohibitions without Divine Promises." In *Modern Moral Philosophy*, edited by Anthony O'Hear, 141–58. Cambridge: Cambridge University Press, 2004.
———. *Realism and Imagination in Ethics.* Oxford: Blackwell, 1983.
———. "Religion and Modernity: Living in the Hypercontext." *Journal of Religious Ethics* 33 (2005) 617–31.
Lyons, John D. *Exemplum: The Rhetoric of Example in Early Modern France and Italy.* Princeton: Princeton University Press, 1989.
MacIntyre, Alasdair. "Critical Remarks on *The Sources of the Self* by Charles Taylor." *Philosophy and Phenomenological Research* LIV (1994) 187–90.
———. "Epistemological Crises, Dramatic Narrative, and the Philosophy of Science." *The Monist* 60 (1977) 453–72.
———. Review of *Philosophical Arguments*, by Charles Taylor. *The Philosophical Quarterly* 47 (1997) 94–96.
McCormick, Richard. "Does Faith Add to Ethical Perception." In *Readings in Moral Theology*, No 2: *The Distinctiveness of Christian Ethics*, edited by Charles Curran and Richard McCormick, 157. New York: Paulist, 1980.
McDowell, John. *Mind and World.* Cambridge: Harvard University Press, 1994.
Mulhall, Stephen. "Sources of the Self's Sense of Itself: A Theistic Reading of Modernity." In *Can Religion be Explained Away*, edited by D. Z. Phillips. New York: St. Martin's, 1996.
Murdoch, Iris. *The Sovereignty of Good.* New York: Schocken, 1970.
Murphy, Debra Dean. "Community, Character, and Gender: Women and the Work of Stanley Hauerwas." *Scottish Journal of Theology* 55 (2002) 338–55.
Musil, Robert. *The Man Without Qualities.* Translated by Sophie Wilkins. New York: Knopf, 1995.
Outka, Gene. "Character, Vision and Narrative." *Religious Studies Review* 6 (1980) 110–18.
Pakaluk, Michael. *Aristotle's Nicomachean Ethics: An Introduction.* New York: Cambridge University Press, 2005.
Pinches, Charles R. "Democracy, America and the Church: Inviting Wendell Berry into the Discussion." In *Wendell Berry and Religion: Heaven's Earthly Life*, edited by Joel James Shuman, 239–60. Lexington: The University Press of Kentucky, 2009.
———. *A Gathering of Memories: Family, Nation and Church in a Forgetful World.* Grand Rapids: Brazos, 2006.
———. "Hauerwas and Political Theology: The Next Generation." *Journal of Religious Ethics* 36 (2008) 513–42.
———. "Stout, Hauerwas and the Body of America." *Political Theology* 8 (2007) 9–31.

———. *Theology and Action: After Theory in Christian Ethics.* Grand Rapids: Eerdmans, 2002.
Pincoffs, Edmund. *Quandaries and Virtues: Against Reductivism in Ethics.* Lawrence: University Press of Kansas, 1986.
Porter, Jean. *The Recovery of Virtue: The Relevance of Aquinas for Christian Ethics.* Louisville: Westminster John Knox, 1990.
Rasmusson, Arne. *The Church as Polis : From Political Theology to Theological Politics as Exemplified by Jürgen Moltmann and Stanley Hauerwas.* Lund: Lund University Press, 1994.
Raz, Joseph. *Practical Reasoning.* New York: Oxford University Press, 1978.
Rorty Amélie, and Owen Flanagan, editors. *Identity, Character and Morality: Essays in Moral Psychology.* Cambridge: MIT Press, 1990.
Rorty, Amélie, and David Wong. "Aspects of Identity and Agency." In *Identity, Character and Morality: Essays in Moral Psychology,* edited by Amélie Rorty and Owen Flanagan, 19–36. Cambridge: MIT Press, 1990.
Ryan, Mark. "Agency and Theological Ethics." PhD diss., University of Virginia, 2006.
Shahid, Irfan. *The Martyrs of Najran: New Documents.* Brussels: Societe des Bollandistes, 1971.
Shuman, Joel James. "Discipleship as Craft: Crafting the Christian Body." In *Unsettling Arguments: A Festschrift on the Occasion of Stanley Hauerwas' 70th Birthday,* edited by Charles R. Pinches et al., 315–31. Eugene, OR: Cascade, 2010.
Smith, Nicholas H. *Charles Taylor: Meaning, Morals, and Modernity.* Malden, MA: Blackwell, 2002.
Steinfels, Peter. "Modernity & Belief." *Commonweal* 135 (2008) 14–21.
Stout, Jeffrey. "Comments on Six Responses to *Democracy and Tradition*." *Journal of Religious Ethics* 33 (2005) 710–16.
———. *Democracy and Tradition.* Princeton: Princeton University Press, 2004.
———. "The Spirit of Democracy and the Rhetoric of Excess." *Journal of Religious Ethics* 35 (2007) 3–21.
Taylor, Charles. *The Ethics of Authenticity.* Cambridge: Harvard University Press, 1991.
———. *The Explanation of Behavior.* London: Routledge, 1964.
———. "Explanation and Practical Reason." In *Philosophical Arguments,* 43–60. Cambridge: Harvard University Press, 1997.
———. "The Motivation behind a Procedural Ethics." In *Kant and Political Philosophy: The Contemporary Legacy,* edited by Ronald Beiner and William James Booth, 337–60. New Haven: Yale University Press,1993.
———. *A Secular Age.* Cambridge: Harvard University Press, 2007.
———. "Self-Interpreting Animals." In *Philosophical Papers 1: Human Agency and Language,* 45–76. Cambridge: Cambridge University Press, 1985.
———. "Social Theory as Practice." In *Philosophical Papers 2: Philosophy and the Human Sciences,* 91–115. Cambridge: Cambridge University Press, 1985.
———. *Sources of the Self: The Making of the Modern Identity.* Cambridge: Harvard University Press, 1992.
———. "Understanding and Ethnocentricity." In *Philosophical Papers 2: Philosophy and the Human Sciences,* 116–33. Cambridge: Cambridge University Press, 1985.
———. "What is Human Agency?" In *Philosophical Papers 1: Human Agency and Language,* 15–44. Cambridge: Cambridge University Press, 1985.
Tinsley, E. J. *The Imitation of God in Christ.* London: SCM, 1960.

Tully, James, and Daniel M. Weinstock. *Philosophy in an Age of Pluralism: The Philosophy of Charles Taylor in Question.* Cambridge: Cambridge University Press, 1994.
Welch, Sharon. *A Feminist Ethic of Risk.* Minneapolis: Augsburg Fortress, 1990.
Wells, Samuel. *Transforming Fate into Destiny: The Theological Ethics of Stanley Hauerwas.* Eugene, OR: Cascade, 1998.
White, Stephen K. *Sustaining Affirmation: The Strengths of Weak Ontology in Political Theory.* Princeton: Princeton University Press, 2000.
Winch, Peter. "Understanding a Primitive Society." *American Philosophical Quarterly* I (1964) 307–24.
Yoder, John Howard. *The Original Revolution.* Scottsdale, PA: Herald, 1971.
———. "What Would You Do If . . . ?" *Journal of Religious Ethics* 2 (1974) 82–83.

www.ingramcontent.com/pod-product-compliance
Lightning Source LLC
Chambersburg PA
CBHW022010220426
43663CB00007B/1036